Database Archiving

Morgan Kaufmann OMG Press

Morgan Kaufmann Publishers and the Object Management Group™ (OMG) have joined forces to publish a line of books addressing business and technical topics related to OMG's large suite of software standards.

OMG is an international, open membership, not-for-profit computer industry consortium that was founded in 1989. The OMG creates standards for software used in government and corporate environments to enable interoperability and to forge common development environments that encourage the adoption and evolution of new technology. OMG members and its board of directors consist of representatives from a majority of the organizations that shape enterprise and Internet computing today.

OMG's modeling standards, including the Unified Modeling Language™ (UML®) and Model Driven Architecture® (MDA), enable powerful visual design, execution and maintenance of software, and other processes—for example, IT Systems Modeling and Business Process Management. The middleware standards and profiles of the Object Management Group are based on the Common Object Request Broker Architecture® (CORBA) and support a wide variety of industries.

More information about OMG can be found at http://www.omg.org/.

Morgan Kaufmann OMG Press Titles

Database Archiving: How to Keep Lots of Data for a Very Long Time
Jack E. Olson

Master Data Management
David Loshin

Building the Agile Enterprise: With SOA, BPM and MBM
Fred Cummins

Business Modeling: A Practical Guide to Realizing Business Value
David M. Bridgeland and Ron Zahavi

A Practical Guide SysML: The Systems Model Language
Sanford Friedenthal, Alan Moore, Rick Steiner

Systems Engineering with SysML/UML: Modeling, Analysis, Design
Tim Weilkiens

UML 2 Certification Guide: Fundamental and Intermediate Exams
Tim Weilkiens and Bernd Oestereich

Real-Life MDA: Solving Business Problems with Model Driven Architecture
Michael Guttman and John Parodi

Database Archiving
How to Keep Lots of Data
for a Very Long Time

Jack E. Olson

WITHDRAWN

AMSTERDAM • BOSTON • HEIDELBERG • LONDON
NEW YORK • OXFORD • PARIS • SAN DIEGO
SAN FRANCISCO • SINGAPORE • SYDNEY • TOKYO

Morgan Kaufmann Publishers is an imprint of Elsevier

ELSEVIER

Morgan Kaufmann Publishers is an imprint of Elsevier
30 Corporate Drive, Suite 400, Burlington, MA 01803, USA

Library of Congress Cataloging-in-Publication Data
Application submitted.

ISBN: 978-0-12-374720-4

For information on all Morgan Kaufmann publications,
visit our Web site at: *www.mkp.com* or *www.books.elsevier.com*

Printed in the United States of America.

08   09   10   11   12   5   4   3   2   1

I dedicate this book to my grandchildren:
Gavin, Harper, and Dru—and grand they are!

Contents

PART 3   Designing Database Archiving Applications

PART 4   Database Archiving Application Software

PART 5   Administration of the Database Archive

Preface

This book is about archiving database data. It is not a general purpose book about archiving. It is also not a book about archiving any or all kinds of data. It is about archiving data in traditional IT databases (e.g., relational databases, hierarchical databases, and structured data in computer files). Examples of source data for archiving are data in DB2 DBMS systems on IBM mainframe systems, data stored in VSAM KSDS databases on IBM mainframes, and data stored in Oracle DBMS systems on Unix servers. It does not include data in spreadsheets or smaller relational systems such as Microsoft Access databases on desktop computers.

This perspective might seem narrow; however, this is a critically important emerging topic in IT departments worldwide. Actually I should say that the topic *has* emerged. The need to archive database data is showing up everywhere, although the database tools industry has been slow to provide tools, methodologies, and services to effectively accomplish it. Most IT departments know that they need to have an effective database archiving practice and are trying to figure out how to build one.

The data that needs to be archived from databases is generally the most important business data enterprises keep. It must be retained under very strict rules as specified by laws and common sense. These are not small amounts of data. The archival stores will eventually reach data volumes unheard of even by today's standards.

Archiving is becoming a much more important topic because it is a part of a major shift in thinking about data that is occurring throughout the United States and most of the rest of the world. This shift demands that enterprises manage their data better than they have in the past and manage it in a way that serves constituents other than the operating departments of an enterprise. The constituents I am talking about include auditors (both internal and external), government investigators, customers, suppliers, citizens' groups, and plaintiff lawyers for lawsuits filed against corporations. Data is becoming more *public* in that it reflects a company's activities and performance. As such, it must stand up to rigid scrutiny and be defended as accurate and authentic.

The constituent base also includes businesspeople within the enterprise who are not trying to assert a wrongdoing or to defend against one but rather who legitimately want to look at historical data to achieve some business goal. Although some will say that this is the role of a data warehouse and business intelligence, the reality is that data warehouse data stores generally do not go back more than two or three years. Sometimes you need to reach back farther, and thus the database archive becomes the logical source.

Archiving data is one facet of this massive change in thinking about managing data. Other parts are database security, database access auditing, data privacy protection, data quality, and data clarity.

The principles of archiving database data are not particularly different from archiving anything else, viewed from the highest level. However, viewed from a low level, the details of database archiving are very different from archiving other types of data. This book drills down into the topics that a database archivist needs to know and master to be effective.

Since there has been no need or attempt to archive database data until recently, there's no large body of experts who can guide an IT department through the process of building an effective database archiving practice. In fact, for most IT departments, there are *no* experts sitting around and little or no organized practice. Everyone is starting on a new venture that will mature into a standard practice in a few years. For now, on your journey you will undoubtedly encounter many stumbling blocks and learning experiences.

In addition to a lack of experts, there is a lack of educational material that can be used to understand how to become a database archivist. Hopefully this book will reduce that shortcoming.

HOW THIS BOOK IS ORGANIZED

Before getting too deep into database archiving, it is helpful to begin by looking at the generic process of archiving to determine some basic principles that apply to archiving just about anything. Understanding these concepts will be helpful in later grasping the details of database archiving.

From the basics, the book moves on to discussing how a database archiving project comes into existence, gets organized, and acquires basic goals and policies. This is an area that is poorly understood and yet crucial to the success of database archiving projects.

This discussion is followed by a detailed treatment of designing a solution for a specific application. All the factors that need to come into play are discussed, as are criteria for selecting one path versus another.

A description of software required to execute a database archiving application follows the discussion of database archiving design. The strengths and weaknesses of various approaches and the features that you should look for are all analyzed.

Administration of the application from day to day over many years is then discussed, followed by some additional topics on the fringe of database archiving. Topics include archiving data that is not business critical, the role of the archive in e-discovery, and other ways to view the execution environment.

ORGANIZATIONS THAT ARE LIKELY TO NEED DATABASE ARCHIVING

This book is about database archiving for large database applications. The types of organizations that would benefit from building a database archiving practice are any that have long-term retention requirements and lots of data. This includes most public companies and those that are private but that work in industries that require retention of data (such as medical, insurance, or banking fields). It also includes educational and government organizations. The book refers to all organizations as *enterprises*.

WHO THIS BOOK IS FOR

This book is intended for the archive practitioner, referred to here as a *database archive analyst* or simply *archive analyst*. The book assumes that a person has adopted this position as a full-time job and possibly as a new career path. I say *new* because this topic is not taught in universities, nor have many IT departments been practicing it until recently. Database archiving will become a standard business activity in the next few years, and all IT departments will need experts on the topic to be effective. This generates the need for a new profession, just as data modeling, data warehousing, data quality, and data security have spawned specialist data management positions in the last decade. Those who enter into this field will find it a challenging, complex, and rewarding experience. If you become an expert in database archiving, you will find a large demand for your services.

After reading this book, the database archivist will be armed with a complete understanding of archiving concepts and will be conversant with the major issues that need to be addressed. This knowledge should enable the archivist to establish a database archiving practice, evaluate or develop tools and methodologies, and execute the planning and operational steps for archiving applications.

Other data professionals such as database administrators (DBA), data modelers, application developers, and system analysts will also benefit from the concepts presented here. The requirements for archiving data from databases should be considered when implementing data design, application design, application deployment, and change control. The data archivist is not the only person who will be involved in the process. For example, the database administrator staff will need to understand the impact of the archiving process on their operational systems and the impact that their actions could have on the archiving process. Likewise, data modelers will need to understand the impacts of their design decisions on archived data, particularly when they are changing existing data structures.

IT management will also benefit from reading this book. It will help them understand the principles involved in database archiving and help them in creating and managing an effective organization to control database archiving. An effective organization archives only what is needed to be retained for long periods of time, does not archive too early or too late, and uses storage devices wisely to minimize cost while preserving the integrity and safety of the archived data. If done correctly, archiving can benefit an enterprise and return more value than it costs, thus not becoming simply another expense.

So let's get started.

Acknowledgments

It took a lot of conversations to accumulate the thoughts and ideas that went into this book. There is little literature on the topic of data archiving and no place to go to get education. I started this journey three years ago with the belief that archiving was going to emerge as an important new component of the future data management—and I was right.

I visited a number of IT departments on the way to discuss their needs and understanding of the topic. In the course of doing so, I talked to dozens of IT professionals. I found a strong understanding of the concept and general problems with database archiving. I found little in the way of implemented practices. Those that did exist were primitive and lacking in many ways. Here I want to acknowledge the strong impact of these meetings on my understanding and development of this subject. I cannot list the companies due to confidentiality agreements, but many of you will remember my visits.

I also want to thank the Data Management Association (DAMA) organization for its support of my work. I visited a large number of DAMA regional chapters and gave presentations on the problems involved in managing long-term data retention. *All* of these meetings added new information and insights into my knowledge of the topic. In particular I want to thank John Schlei and Peter Aiken for aiding me in getting on calendars and in supporting my quest for knowledge. They are both giants in the data management space. I also want to thank all the DAMA regional chapters I visited for adding me to their agendas and for the lively discussions that took place. I visited so many chapters regarding this topic that DAMA International gave me a Community Service Award in 2007.

The company I work for, NEON Enterprise Software, launched a development project to produce software to be used for database archiving. At the time of launch I was not part of the development organization. In the past three years many people in that company have spent many hours with me discussing detailed points regarding this subject. You learn so much more about a technology when you have to produce a comprehensive solution for it. Those in the company who I want to single out for their help and education are John Wright, Ken Kornblum, Kevin Pintar, Dave Moore, Whitney Williams, Bill Craig, Rod Brick, Bill Chapin, Bruce Nye, Andrey Suhanov, Robin Reddick, Barbara Green, Jim Middleton, Don Pate, John Lipinski, Don Odom, Bill Baker, and Craig Mullins. Many others also were involved in the project and were helpful. I must also add Barbara Green, Carla Pleggi, and Sam Armstrong, who helped in getting the draft copies ready for the publisher. As technical as I am, I am a cripple when it comes to using technical writing tools. I needed their help.

I especially want to thank John Moores for his encouragement and support on this project.

Finally I want to acknowledge the patience and understanding of my family in putting up with me while I worked on this book. Without their support this book could not have existed.

PART

Archiving Basics

1

These introductory chapters will introduce you to the basic concepts of database archiving. They will teach you to think like an archivist. You will be shown various forms of data archiving and where database archiving fits within the broader category. You will get a precise definition of database archiving. You will be shown the basic components of a database archiving solution.

Database Archiving Overview

1

Archiving is the process of preserving and protecting artifacts for future use. These artifacts have lived beyond their useful life and are being kept solely for the purpose of satisfying future historical investigations or curiosities that might or might not occur. An *archive* is a place where these artifacts are stored for long periods of time. They are retained in case someone will want or need them in the future. They are also kept in a manner so that they can be used in the future.

Archiving has existed in many forms for centuries. For example, the United States government employs a national archivist. The Presidential libraries are archives. Newspapers retain archives of all stories printed, since papers began to be published. Museums are archives of interesting objects from the past. Your local police department has an evidence archive. When a collection of items is placed in the cornerstone of a building during construction in anticipation that someone 100 or more years in the future will uncover it (a time capsule), an archive is being created and the creators are acting as archivists.

An archive is created for a specific purpose: to hold specific objects for future reference in the event that someone needs to look at them. The focus is on the objects that are to be included in the archive. Each archive has a specific purpose and stores a specific object type.

The process of archiving follows a common methodology. No matter what you archive, you should go through the same steps. If you leave out one of the steps, you will probably run into problems later on. This generic methodology is discussed in Chapter 3. However, before we go there, it is important to set the scope of this book.

The discussion that follows segregates data archiving into categories that are useful in understanding where this book fits into the broader archiving requirements. It also establishes some basic definitions and concepts that will be used later as we get deeper into the process.

1.1 **A DEFINITION OF DATABASE ARCHIVING**

Database archiving is the act of removing from an operational database selected data objects that are not expected to be referenced again and placing them in an archive data store where they can be accessed if needed. This is a powerful statement for which each part needs to be completely understood.

Data objects   A *data object* is the unit of information that someone in the future will seek from the archive. It represents a business event or object; it is the actual "thing" you are archiving. An example is banking transactions, such as deposits and withdrawals from customer accounts. The basic unit of an archive is a single transaction. Each transaction is a discrete object that reaches a point in time when it is ready to be archived. The data stored for a transaction would include all the particulars of the event, such as the account number, date, time, and place the transaction occurred; the dollar amount; and possibly more. This information might be wrapped with additional information, such as the account holder's name and address from the account master record, to make it a more complete record.

Another example of a data object might include an entire collection of data, such as production records for an airplane. The goal might be to archive the records for each individual airplane after it has been built and is ready to be sold. You might move this information into the archive one year after the airplane enters service. Although the archive object may have many different types of data, it still represents data for only a single airplane.

Selected data objects   You will have thousands of similar data objects in an operational database at any given point in time. These objects have unique characteristics in regard to their role in your information-processing systems and business. One characteristic is how long the data objects have been in the database. Some might have been there for months; others were created just a second ago. Some might be waiting for some other event to occur that would update them; some might not. Some might have a special status, others not.

In archiving, not all data objects are ready to be moved to the archive at the same time. The user must develop a policy expressed as selection criteria for determining when items are ready to be moved. Sometimes this policy is as simple as "All transactions for which 90 days have passed since the create event occurred." Other times it is more complicated, such as "Archive all account information for accounts that have been closed for more than 60 days and do not have any outstanding issues such as uncollected amounts."

The key point is that the database contains a large collection of like data objects. Archiving occurs on a periodic basis—say, once every week. At the time that a specific archive sweep of the database is done, only some of the objects will be ready to be archived. The policy used to select those objects that are ready needs to be defined in data value terms using information contained within or about the objects. The selected objects will probably be scattered all over the database and not contained in a single contiguous storage area or partition.

Removing data objects   The point of archiving is to take objects out of the active, operational environment and place them in a safe place for long-term maintenance. For database data this means that data is written to the archive data store and then *deleted* from the operational database. The whole point of archiving is to take data out of the operational database and store it safely for future use and reference.

In some instances, covered in later chapters, data that is moved to the archive is also left behind in the operational database and then deleted later. These are special circumstances; however, even here the archived data is frozen in the archive for long-term storage and considered archived. The copy left behind in the operational database is no longer the "official" record of the object.

Not expected to be referenced again   This is an important point for database archives. You do not want to move data from the operational database too early. The correct time to move it is when the data has a very low probability of being needed again. If there are normal business processes that will need to use this data, the data is probably not ready to be moved. Any subsequent need for the data should be unexpected and a clear exception.

Later chapters will discuss special circumstances in which this rule may be relaxed.

Placing them in an archive data store   The *archive data store* is a distinctly different data store than the one used for the operational database. The operational databases are designed and tuned to handle high volumes of data; incur high create, update, and delete activity levels; and process many random query transactions over the data. The data design, storage methods, and tuning requirements for the archive data store are dramatically different from those for operational databases. The archive data store will house much larger volumes of data, have *no* update activity, and infrequent query access.

In addition, other demands for managing the archive data store influence how and where it is to be stored. For example, the need to use low-cost storage and the need to have backup copies in geographically distributed locations are important considerations. Many of these requirements also dictate different storage design decisions as to how and where to store archived data.

The point is that the archive data store is a separate data store from the operational database and has uniquely different design and data management requirements.

Can be referenced again if needed   Even though the archive contains data that is *not expected* to be accessed again, it is there precisely so that it *can* be accessed again if needed. It makes no sense to bother archiving data if it cannot be accessed. Archives exist for legal and business requirements to keep data just in case a need arises.

The process of accessing data from archives is generally very different from accessing data for business processes. The reasons for access are different. The type of access is different. The user doing the accessing is also different. Queries against the archive are generally very simple but may involve large amounts of output data.

It is important that the archive query capabilities be strong enough to satisfy all future requirements and not require the user to restore data to the original systems for access through the original applications.

It is critical to understand the likely uses that could arise in the future and the shape of the queries that result. Anticipating these factors will impact decisions you make regarding how and where to keep the archive data store.

1.2 FORMS OF DATA ARCHIVING

It is important to understand the difference between data archiving and database archiving. *Data archiving* refers to a broad category of archiving that includes many subtypes. *Database archiving* is one of those subtypes.

Data archiving is a term that applies to keeping inactive information collected by an enterprise. Data is collected in many forms: paper documents, emails, computer files, and so on. Most data today is collected and stored electronically by computers. Only some of it is stored in databases using structured database management systems.

Figure 1.1 lists several categories of enterprise data. Almost every enterprise uses all these categories. The list demonstrates that data archiving applies to many diverse types of data. As we shall see, the requirements for storing different types of data and the problems that need to be solved vary from one category to another.

Physical documents Not all data originates as or is maintained in electronic form. Years ago, all data was nonelectronic. Today there are still many examples of important physical documents that must be retained for long

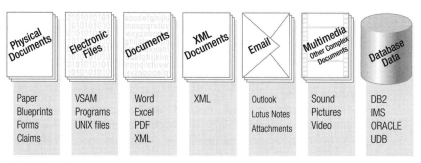

FIGURE 1.1

Categories of enterprise data.

periods of time, including blueprints, order forms, photographs, and application forms. For example, if an enterprise receives written orders, the original order containing an authorizing signature might need to be maintained for legal reasons even though the information may be entered into a computer system. A medical prescription written by a physician is a perfect example.

In some cases the documents may be scanned into computer files and maintained in that form. In other cases the law requires that the actual original piece of paper be retained.

Of course, maintaining physical documents has a whole set of unique problems. For example, receipts attached to an expense report may contain information printed on photostatic paper. The printing ink used to create these receipts will fade with time. In fact, these receipts will be legible for only a few years. If they need to be maintained for longer periods of time, special precautions against clarity decay might need to be taken. It might also be necessary to keep a copy of the documents made on a standard copier whereby the printing will have a longer storage life.

Moving data to electronic form when allowed by the rules governing retention is always the best strategy.

Electronic files   The most basic form of electronic archiving is *file archiving*. File archiving has been around for many years, and many software products on the market do a superb job of satisfying requirements. File archiving basically refers to making a copy of an entire file as known to the operating system file system and storing it somewhere else. The goal of file archiving is to move data to storage devices that are cheaper than those used for operational systems. Often this means pushing it to tape instead of keeping it on disk.

Sophisticated storage subsystems that provide extensive data management functions can be very useful for file archive stores.

In file-level archiving, you move data away from the frontline disk storage attachable to operational systems. You move clutter from the active systems.

File-archiving systems know nothing about the content of the files. It simply copies bytes, with no understanding of the content. The criteria for deciding when a file is ready to be moved to the file archive are generally based entirely on the time that has elapsed since the file was either created or last accessed.

To access a file from a file archive, a user must have an appropriate application program that understands the data content of the file. The archiving system can only return the data, not selectively search or return portions of a file. The archive system generally does not provide application programs that can make sense of the data.

Since database systems store data in operating system files managed by the file system, file-level archiving is not appropriate for these files. This is because any specific file will contain a mixture of data that is old and inactive and data that is new and active. Data to be archived is not separated into files containing only archivable data. Additionally, because database files are accessed all the time due to applications that scan them or perform utilities on them, no time period exists when they are not "accessed." This means that file-level archiving will never consider them candidates for archiving.

Text documents Companies accumulate a large number of text documents that generally take the form of Microsoft Word files, Acrobat PDFs, spreadsheets, PowerPoint documents, and similar file types. Some of these are required to be kept for long periods. One such archive could include résumés submitted to the company personnel department. Another might be legal briefs created and used by a law firm.

This type of archiving looks at these objects as more than mere files. Along with each file goes a collection of identifying information that can be stored in the archive to help locate specific documents or categories of documents. This identifying information is often referred to as *metadata,* although the term means something different when it's used for databases. For example, each legal document may have associated with it a case identifier, the author of the document, date last changed, type of brief, date created, date submitted to a court, and more. It's necessary to capture this document metadata for proving chain-of-custody issues in legal proceedings involving the archived documents. These information tidbits can be stored in indexes that can be used in searching for documents. In fact, indexes often maintain additional keywords extracted from the text of the documents that aid in finding documents based on content.

Document archiving generally also requires the ability to maintain versions of a single document. This is not uncommon in legal issue archives. Thus the archiving facility must know which documents are merely versions of the same document and know their time order.

In addition to the search capability, document archiving is sensitive to file type. It knows the difference between files of type .doc, .pdf, .xls, and .ppt. It has the ability to open, read, and display information from the documents using the file type.

This requires that the archiving facility maintain programs that do the processing of the document types for as long as the documents are in the archive. If newer versions of these programs become available from the software companies and they are not compatible with older versions of data, the older versions of the application programs must be maintained, or the documents stored under them must be converted to the newer format. This needs to be a function of the archiving system.

XML documents An archive of XML documents is considered self-defining because each data element has identifier tags in its text body, describing what the element means. However, it is self-defining only to the extent that a future reader can understand what the identifier means. Often the identifiers convey little useful information.

The difference between these and the previous category of documents is that you shouldn't require special programs to understand XML documents; they are self-documenting. If the identifiers are clear enough to the user, this will be true. However, if you have ever looked at XML documents you know that this is not always the case.

To create an effective archive, the XML archiving function needs XML search functions and a catalog of identifiers used in documents, with expanded explanations for what they mean to a future reader. It should also have other XML tools beyond search to aid in the presentation of information contained in the documents.

External indexes can be built and maintained that include the content of specific identifiers or keywords used in text components of XML documents. Implementing external indexes can significantly improve performance in finding desired documents over a large body of XML documents. In fact, when the volume of documents gets large enough, the XML search engines working from the internal content will become dysfunctional, so searching by way of external indexes will be necessary.

Like other file type archives, XML is an evolving standard, which means that the archiving tools need to be updated from time to time and possibly old versions of tools maintained to handle XML documents created under older, possibly incompatible standards.

Emails This form of electronic archiving is the most known and the most discussed. There have been numerous high-profile cases involving enterprises' inability to satisfy legal discovery requests for emails. There have also been many high-profile cases in which emails provided from an archive for a legal case have sent executives to the slammer or have cost the company millions of dollars in judgments.

The process of archiving emails has a very special set of requirements. On the surface it looks relatively simple: Save the date, time, sender, receiver, and text of each email. In addition, there is much more to be done. You also need to save the attachments. You not only need to save them, you need to have available programs that can OPEN, READ, and PRESENT their content. This process is very much like document archiving. This may require multiple versions of the programs if the emails cover a large span of time in which the programs changed their way of recording information.

A common error of email systems is to fail to provide attachment programs and to assume that the archive reader's systems have the appropriate programs. This could be a disaster waiting to happen years later when someone who needs to see an attachment cannot find a program that can process it.

There are other problems to be solved in email archiving. One is to get rid of the junk emails that do not need to be in the archive. Junk emails and internal emails for broadcasting Joe's birthday or "Donuts are available in the company kitchen" and the like need to be culled from the emails and excluded from the archive. These are obvious examples; in reality there is a very large fuzzy line between what obviously *must* be included and what obviously *must not* be included.

An additional problem comes in eliminating duplicate emails. For example, say that Sam sends an email to 10 people. All 11 emails (Sam's original email and the other 10 received emails) do not need to be kept; only one copy is needed. Another form of duplicate elimination is to recognize the common email chain. A chain begins by one person sending an email, a receiver sending a reply, the original sender sending a reply to the reply, and so on. These chains can go on and on. A good archive system will identify and eliminate all but the last email in the chain, which should include the text of all the preceding messages.

In addition to addressing these concerns, the email archiving system should keep an index detailing to whom the email addresses really belong. Without this index, an email reader in the distant future might have no idea who was the real person who sent or received an email.

Multimedia and other complex documents   *Multimedia data* refers to pictures, videos, and images scanned into a computer. It is not unusual for an organization to have a requirement that these documents be kept for long periods of time. For example, a casualty insurance company could require that field agents photograph automobile accidents or storm damage to houses and keep the images in archives for many years. Most likely, the requirement would involve using digital cameras, with the resulting computer files typed to the representation format. Many such formats for pictures, scanned images, and videos can exist in the universe of possible input sources.

Other examples of complex documents are digitized X-rays or output of magnetic resonance imaging (MRI) devices. Specialized presentation programs are needed to display the archived documents. This technology and the programs that manipulate the electronic representation of these documents are evolving as well, requiring that the archivist understand the latest and the oldest processing programs needed and to make sure that they are available.

These types of objects may also have special search algorithms that can locate elements of images by reading the content of documents. Such search algorithms can become unusable if the number of documents to be searched becomes too large. An archiving solution may consider pre-searching objects as they are placed in the archive and building external indexes of common characteristics.

Databases   Data stored in relational, hierarchical, or network databases falls under the heading of databases. This category also includes flat files that have records that conform to a specific record layout known to the user.

Data from these sources is highly structured into data fields that are grouped into records, rows, or segments, which are then grouped into files, tables, or databases. Structural relationships between tables or between hierarchical database segments may also be known and important to the user of the data.

Database data has a unique problem in that archiving needs to pull some data out of the database while leaving other data behind. You don't archive an entire database at one time, at least not typically. You normally select data items from within the database to be archived while leaving unselected items behind.

Special problems are attached to this form of archiving. The archive must capture and maintain the metadata for each application as well as the data itself. The metadata must explain the structure of the data as well as the semantic meaning of each data element.

Another problem in database archiving is that for any specific application, the metadata and its corresponding data objects will change over time because applications never remain the same. This means that data for a specific application may have one structure for part of the data in the archive and a different but most likely a very similar structure for another part of the data. Tracking the metadata evolution for an application is a unique problem.

Another obstacle can be the enormous amount of data that accumulates in a single database. Envision the number of data records needed to record the credit card transactions of any of the large credit card providers for just one year. Now imagine the amount of data for that same company with a 25-year retention requirement.

Physical versus virtual database archiving There are two variations on database archiving. In the case of *physical database archiving*, the data removed and sent to the archive is taken from the physical database storage and definitions. For example, in a relational database, the objects to be removed and stored are defined in terms of the tables and columns of the physical database. There is no consideration or concern about the application programs that were used to generate the data in the relational tables.

In some database applications the table representation of data is so complex or intertwined that the actual business objects cannot be discerned by looking at table and column definitions. This situation is generally the result of poor database design. Unfortunately this situation is very common with commercially available packaged applications.

The archivist needs a source of reliable data objects and their representation to define what the archive will look like. This definition is generally possible through the application programs. The application programs have interfaces to extract data for specific data objects in a meaningful structure, to search for objects, and to delete objects. When the archivist uses these application interfaces instead of the underlying tables, this is referred to as *virtual database archiving*.

You should now be convinced that data archiving is not a single topic or technology. Each category of data archiving has its own set of problems and challenges. An archiving system built to satisfy one category will not work for another category. This is reflected in the commercial archiving systems available in today's market. Each product targets a specific category of data. Some products are further tailored to a specific industry. In the case of database archiving, there are archiving products that target only a single packaged application using virtual database archiving methods.

All these archiving categories require highly complex products and methodologies to support them and to keep them current over the long term.

1.3 **THE DATA LIFELINE**

To fully comprehend the concept of database archiving, it is critical to understand the phases data passes through in its lifetime. These are phases of expected uses. Figure 1.2 shows the phase components.

Create   Data is created at a specific point in time. The event or object the data records might have existed prior to being recorded, but the electronic record of it might not be created until sometime later. For example, years ago when I was in the Navy, paper forms were collected and mailed from "ship-to-shore" installations where data was then keypunched. After the keypunch and key-verify stages, the data was processed to create an official record within the information systems. The time difference between the event and the actual appearance of the electronic record could be several days or even weeks.

This demonstrates that there is a difference between the date on which the event that needs to be recorded occurred and the time at which an electronic record is created to put the data into a database. Today this difference is generally not important. The database record will generally contain a CREATE DATE or TRANSACTION DATE or some other field that documents the data event. It generally does not keep a data element showing the date it was entered into the database.

The fact of putting the record into the database is important. It establishes the record as an official record of the enterprise. From that time on, the record must be managed, must not be lost, and must maintain its accuracy.

Operational   Once created, the data object has the characteristic of being in an operational state. This means that it is expected to be used in executing other business transactions for the enterprise.

One scenario is that the data is used to create other data objects, as in an invoice created from a purchase order. If there is anticipation that the object will be used for creating additional business objects, then the object remains in the operational state. It must be in the operational database to be able to play its continuing part in the business process. If it is removed too early, it cannot trigger subsequent transactions.

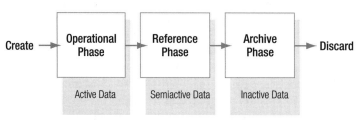

FIGURE 1.2

Data expected-use phases.

Another possibility is that the data object is updated over time. The initial creation might not complete the business process. For example, a loan application can be created, but over a period of time, the object can turn into either an accepted or rejected application. There may be multiple intermediate states for the data object, such as submission to the loan committee, waiting for credit checks, and so on. The business object has other operational events that change its content.

Sometimes applications do not allow updates to a data object. For example, in credit card transactions, the initial recording is never changed. If an error is discovered in the initial recording, a new data object is created to adjust for the amount of the error. The two data objects may be linked through data object identifiers, but they are separate data objects.

A data object may remain in an operational state for a micro-second or for years. The shorter time applies to data that is not expected or allowed to be changed once it's created. The longer time span may refer to a data object that records an object that will persist for years. An example is the loan header data for approved loans. It will exist and possibly be updated until the loan is paid off. Another example is a customer record. Since a customer can change his or her address, phone number, or even name, the object is susceptible to updates at any time in its life and therefore remains in the operational state as long as the customer remains a real or potential customer.

Reference A data object enters the reference phase when it has no potential to participate in other transactions that either create new data objects or cause updates to it but for which there continues to exist a reasonable expectation that the data will be used in queries. This expectation requires that it be available on a timely basis.

The query or "look" at the data can also involve looking at operational data along with it. For example, if a report showing received orders is generated every month, an order data object must be included in the report, even though it may no longer have the characteristic of operational data. Some of the orders in the report may still be operational, and others are reference.

Remember, our present discussion refers to the characteristic of the data, not its location. Location will be discussed later.

If we go back to the credit card transaction application example, the data for a transaction is operational for possibly a month (long enough to generate a bill to the cardholder and payments to the vendor). After these other data objects are created, this becomes reference information. The length of time it remains in the reference phase depends on the probability of access. The company may choose to keep it in reference for six months to accommodate the possibility of a cardholder asking for information from a previous billing cycle.

This same data item may be needed to generate those end-of-year reports credit card companies send to cardholders, itemizing every transaction for the entire year. If so, the reference phase of the data item is the time from the creation date until the end-of-year report is run. When you combine all the expected reference requirements, some transactions will have a six-month reference state and others a one-year period; others still will have a time period between six months and a year.

The reference state of a data object can also be extended because of particular events. For example, data recording an automobile accident may normally be considered in a reference state for six months, but the time may be extended for individual accident objects due to the severity of the accident (an accident-related fatality or high-value property loss) or because of litigation initiated as a result of the accident.

Archive The archive phase of a data object's life begins when the data object is not expected to participate in operational transactions and is also not expected to be referenced again. *Not expected* is a fuzzy phrase. Although it might not be possible for a data object to be a participant in an operational event, it is always possible for it to be referenced. In fact, the very act of keeping it in an archive implies some expectation of access, even if very small. The line between the reference phase and the archive phase needs to be drawn using common sense.

Most companies with high volumes of transactions know where to place the line and what conditions govern establishing the line. After processing a few billion credit card transactions a year, an organization gets a pretty solid understanding as to when data is no longer expected to be used again. It is purely historical data used to make these decisions.

Discard *Discard* is an event that refers to the removal of the data object from the electronic systems. It is deleted, shredded, and destroyed. Sometimes the term *forensic discard* is used to imply that, for a specific application, the data is removed from the computer systems so thoroughly that forensic software cannot revive it. The bottom line is that the data is no longer in the systems and can never be accessed again.

Data languishes in the archive phase until discard. The length of time it remains is determined by the enterprise. The default time is indefinite. *Indefinite* is a valid discard point for some data. For example, universities have no discard time for student records. They stay in the systems forever, no matter how much some of us would like to see them destroyed.

In practice, enterprises generally want to destroy data objects whenever they are allowed to do so after they have served all expected business purposes. Data retention periods mandated by law have stretched out to very long periods, so much so that you might expect them to be set to indefinite. Still, most enterprises set policies to discard data whenever these periods end for specific data objects. I cannot tell you the number of times that I have heard the phrase, "If I have to keep it 25 years, I want it out of my systems in 25 years and one day."

The result of long retention periods is that many data objects remain in the archive phase for years, waiting for a point in time when they can be legally and safely discarded.

Database administrators frequently have trouble with the concept of discard. They have been trained to always keep data or be able to revive it if lost. When given a requirement to execute a discard function, they instinctively want to log the content before discard or back up the data source first. This only defeats the purpose of discarding.

The timeline for a data object is generally a straight line from create to discard, although there are cases where data for specific data objects backtrack on the line due to some intervening event. For example, an unexpected lawsuit on data may cause claims data in the archive phase to revert to the reference phase.

1.4 **TYPES OF DATA OBJECTS**

There is one more definitional component about data that we need to address: the type of data object in relation to change activities. Data either records the occurrence of an event or describes the existence of an object.

The fundamental characteristic of event-recording data objects is that the data elements can have only one value for the lifeline of the data object. It does not change. The only reason to change the data would be to correct the invalid recording of the data in the first place. Examples of event data are sales transactions, loan payments, flights flown, and stock trades.

Conversely, data may also describe long-surviving objects—for example, an employee, a building, an airplane, a customer, or a storage bin. Data objects for these types of objects may contain information that cannot change (such as your birthday) and information that can change (such as your address, your name, the assessed value of a building, or the weight of an airplane).

Data objects that describe events and data objects that have only nonupdateable data elements within them are easy to deal with for archiving. They reach nonupdate status very early, either instantaneously or after a period of time when auditing processes may correct invalid recording. Thus they move quite logically down the path of operational to reference to archive to discard.

On the other hand, data objects that have data legitimately updated during their lives present unique problems. Take, for example, customer records. Customer record information such as names, addresses, phone numbers, and contact names can change at any time. If this information does change, the data doesn't leave the operational phase until the client is no longer a client. The question that the archivist must ask is whether there is a need to archive intermediate versions of the data objects and not just the most recent version.

Two implementations that involve the intersection of these ideas must be understood. In one implementation the user stores transaction data objects whenever a change is made, showing the before and after values for changed data elements. In this case, any version can be reconstructed from an archive of the initial version and all change transactions.

In another implementation, a separate snapshot of the data object is saved whenever an event transaction occurs that references the object. For example, the customer information is replicated every time the customer submits a new purchase order to show the values for the customer data object that existed at the time of the transaction event.

As you can see, updatable data objects present special problems. The ability to archive properly may depend on how the application systems are implemented.

1.5 DATA RETENTION REQUIREMENTS VERSUS DATA ARCHIVES

People often say that they need to archive data for regulatory reasons. This is never a correct statement. The laws never specifically say that you need to archive data. Laws only stipulate that you must retain data for a specified period of time and produce it on demand. The way you retain the information is solely up to you.

This means that if you do intend to move data to an archive data store for part of the retention period, you are free to decide when it moves. The laws say nothing about this decision.

Laws also are not always the governing factor in determining the retention period for data. Each enterprise has other competing interests in keeping data; some are business reasons known only to the enterprise. For example, the enterprise might want to improve customer confidence by retaining data for longer periods and providing it when customers request it. The enterprise might want to keep data around to conduct market analysis until after an entire model year has been sold and serviced for a number of years.

The retention requirement is the longest line of all individual requirements. In the past this was usually set because of internal business interests, not legal requirements. In recent years this relationship has changed. The business lines have not gotten shorter; the legal lines have gotten longer. Recent laws have caused legal lines to be much longer than business lines for many types of data.

In addition, some data falls under multiple laws, each of which has different retention requirements. For example, banking transaction data could be subject to different retention lines in different countries, significantly impacting an international banking enterprise.

An enterprise looks at all requirements for retention of specific data objects and sets a policy based on the longest line. Figure 1.3 shows how these relationships have changed over the years.

1.5.1 Database Configuration Choices

The user can keep all data in its basic form in one database for all retention period requirements, or the user can move data from one database to another for different periods of the data's lifeline. The time spent across all the databases

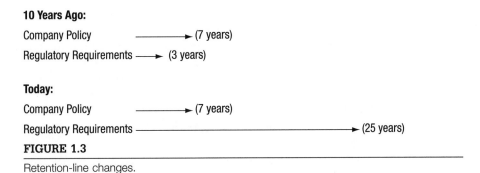

10 Years Ago:

Company Policy   ⟶ (7 years)

Regulatory Requirements ⟶ (3 years)

Today:

Company Policy   ⟶ (7 years)

Regulatory Requirements ————————————————⟶ (25 years)

FIGURE 1.3

Retention-line changes.

should satisfy the data retention requirements. Figure 1.4 shows the most common configuration choices.

Operational only   The user can maintain a single database, the operational database, and keep all the data there for its entire retention period.

Operational and reference database   The user can move data from the operational database when the data enters the reference phase of its lifeline and keep it there for the remainder of the retention period.

Note that the difference between a reference database and a database archive store is that the reference database has an identical structure to the operational database and can be accessed directly from the operational applications.

Operational database and archive data store   In this model, the user waits until the data has entered the archive phase of its life and then moves it

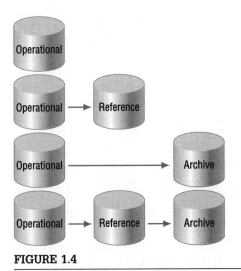

FIGURE 1.4

Database configurations for satisfying retention requirements.

out of the operational database and into the archive data store, where it will remain until it exhausts the longest retention period.

A database archive store changes the data deliberately to make it independent of the original structure and applications that created it.

All three   The data sits in the operational store until it enters the reference phase of its life and is moved to the reference database. It sits there until it enters the archive phase of its life and is restructured and moved to the archive store for the remaining period of time, to satisfy the longer retention period.

1.5.2 Why Not Keep Data in One Database?

There are three compelling reasons that keeping all the data in one database for its life becomes less viable for many applications:

- There's too much data
- Extreme retention requirements
- Need to protect the authenticity of data

Too much data   Data volumes have been expanding at double-digit rates for years. Databases have gotten so large that keeping all the data in one place is becoming impractical or even impossible for some applications—impractical when the existence of archive data increases the time and cost of transactions, of utility functions such as backup and recover, or of extraction runs for finding data for business intelligence (BI) data stores beyond time frames that are acceptable, and impossible in cases where the database management system (DBMS) cannot physically support the volumes. In many IT operations, data clutter is becoming data blight.

Extreme retention periods   Retention periods that span decades rather than just a few years cause inactive data to be subject to many, many alterations to keep up with application changes to the structure and semantics of data elements. The retention periods many applications are facing are likely to outlive any reasonable expectation of continuing the application in its present form.

Need to protect the authenticity of data   Data in an operational database is vulnerable to unwelcome changes. It can always be altered by IT staff with special privileges typically granted to database administrators (DBAs). Data can usually be updated by a host of other staff members who have legitimate (or not-so-legitimate) reasons to change the data. Or employees could change the data by mistake. Data in operational environments is more exposed to mischief by people not expected to update data. These people can be either internal or external hackers, employees out to get back at the enterprise for some grievance, or other unsavory individuals.

Maintaining data in the forward, exposed operational environment increases the likelihood that it will become corrupted. The longer it is kept there, the more difficult it is to defend its original authenticity.

1.5.3 **Reasons for Using a Reference Database**

A reference database isn't necessary if data moves to the archive phase quickly enough. If it doesn't and the volume of data in the operational and reference phases is too much for efficient operational performance and management, a reference database should be used. Moving data to an archive data store before it enters the archive phase of life can be disastrous if operational application programs cannot access it or if alternate forms of access directly from the archive are too frequent to support efficient performance.

Remember, the archive data store is optimized for long-term storage, not for fast query performance nor for having a large number of queries executed against it in any given period of time.

1.6 **THE DATABASE ARCHIVES AND OTHER DATABASE TYPES**

Data may move from operational databases to other databases besides reference databases and archive data stores. For example, data can be moved to operational replicates, disaster recovery copies, a data warehouse, or a business intelligence analytical database. You normally would not archive data from these other databases since they do not represent the enterprise's official version of the data. They are intended as throwaway versions.

Sometimes people mistakenly think that since a data warehouse keeps data for a long period of time, it can be used as an archive data store. It is highly unlikely that any data warehouse is sufficient for this purpose, for the following reasons:

- Data warehouses generally do not keep data long enough. They normally keep three to five years' worth of data, not decades' worth.
- Data warehouses generally do not keep detail on data. They summarize, integrate, enhance, and normalize data.
- Data warehouses are stored in DBMS systems, which fail to provide the ability to store the volumes required or to protect the authenticity of data.

In very rare cases it is possible to let a data warehouse double as an archive. However, it would have to be carefully engineered to satisfy all requirements of both. This is rarely possible and should not be considered a viable option.

SUMMARY

After reading this chapter, you should have learned the following:

- Database archiving is a slice of the larger topic of data archiving.
- Data archiving is a slice of the larger topic of archiving.
- Archiving is a complex topic.

- There is a difference between data retention and data archiving.
- The data archivist makes many decisions regarding an application in terms of the way data is to be managed for its life. The decisions are different for different applications.
- Databases and data stores can be employed for different phases of the data's life to effectively manage the needs of many diverse users.

You will learn a lot more detail as we move through this book and hopefully be able to make the right decisions for each application.

The Business Case for Database Archiving | 2

Enterprises are trying to reduce IT costs, not increase them. They are trying to reduce the number of data-related administrators, not increase them. Why does a company want to hire a data archivist, invest in database archiving software, build a complex array of data stores for holding archived data, and have to manage this construct for decades to come? The cost over doing nothing appears to be quite large. At first glance there appears to be no valid business reason for embarking on this journey. IT management has many other problems they would rather be spending their time and money on.

When you look at the various business issues, it becomes perfectly clear that having a mature database archiving practice is essential for protecting the enterprise from potentially disastrous harm. Regulatory requirements are being imposed at an ever-increasing rate and failure to comply with them can be very costly, embarrassing, or both.

In addition, database archiving can have economic value for many applications due to beneficial side effects, many of which can easily justify the cost of archiving. But if archiving is so helpful, why has it not been considered earlier? Why is it only now emerging as a "must-have" data management function?

2.1 WHY DATABASE ARCHIVING IS A PROBLEM TODAY

There are three reasons that database archiving (and other forms of data archiving) has become a hot ticket. These reasons are regulatory changes, data volume increases, and data aging.

2.1.1 Regulatory Changes

Over the last 10 years governments have been actively passing regulations that affect corporate governance and, more specifically, data governance. These rules affect all sorts of corporate entities: business enterprises, both big and small; government organizations, local through national; educational institutions; charitable institutions; and others.

Many people believe that these regulations are overburdening and are imposing an unnecessary and high cost on doing business, but they are here now and are likely to stay.

It seems that enterprises are being required to assume a new attitude of responsibility and accountability. The laws recognize that every enterprise has many stakeholders who are entitled to know what is happening and require assurances that the employees are acting professionally and responsibly.

Stakeholders in a business enterprise consist of investors, officers, and managers of the company; other employees; customers; and sometimes even the public. For example, in a small manufacturing company, investors are entitled to accurate and timely information on business activity and financial condition to allow them to make reasonable decisions regarding their investments. The employees are entitled to work for a company that protects their health, their pensions, and their personal information. If employees have a stock plan, they have the same interests as an investor. The customers are entitled to know whether the company is financially capable of meeting its responsibilities to them and whether they are disclosing all the risks of using their products. The public at large is entitled to know whether the company is satisfying all environmental rules, paying their fair share of taxes, and serving as a good corporate citizen in other respects.

In a business that is more sensitive to the public, the interests of stakeholders get even higher. In health care enterprises, issues of data privacy become much more important. In banking and financial management, the internal practice of handling commissions and trades becomes a topic of full disclosure. In pharmaceutical companies, accurate public reporting of clinical trial results and disclosure of potential side effects are essential for customers to evaluate whether or not to use the company's products.

Implicit in all these interests is the right to investigate and file suit against the company if it is not operating in a responsible way and if its behavior has possibly caused harm. To protect the right of stakeholders to investigate and file suit for redress, data regarding the corporate activities must be retained for a sufficient period of time. The government, city, or state in which the corporation does business; customer groups; investor groups; employees; or concerned citizen groups may launch investigations at any given time. Each entity has a right to demand that the enterprise do business properly and each is entitled to enterprise information to help determine if the enterprise has not.

This wave of demanding responsible business management is not restricted to the United States. Many other countries have gotten caught up in governance and have passed regulatory requirements that are equally demanding and, in some cases, more demanding than those passed in the United States.

The requirements of record keeping and record retention have become extensive. Some examples include:

- Keeping detailed banking transactions for 50 years
- Keeping aircraft manufacturing records until planes are no longer flyable (this could be 70 or more years)
- Keeping medical records for the lifetime of the patient plus one year
- Keeping records collected on citizens by a government entity for 70 years

Retention requirements have increased from just a few years to decades. The vast majority of regulations in this area have been passed in only the last 10 years, with many only in the last five years. *The single most important reason database archiving has reached the level of interest found today is that increased regulations have extended the length of time records must be retained.*

In the past, when business potential was the determining factor in how long data was kept, regulations were either nonexistent or only mildly demanding. Companies might have kept financial information for seven years to satisfy potential Internal Revenue Service (IRS) review of tax records; otherwise, this information might have been disposed of much earlier.

Today regulatory requirements are the dominant factor in determining how long to keep data.

2.1.2 **Data Volume Increases**

The relentless increases in the volume of data collected by enterprises of all sorts are another reason for the current surge in interest in database archiving. Increases in the range of 40–60 percent per year are commonplace. Some enterprises experience data volume increases of greater than 100 percent per year. This is a well-documented trend, with increases commonly in the range of 40 percent or more per year.

One reason for an increase is globalization of enterprises. As corporations expand their business to sell in more countries, their business volume naturally increases. Today all companies aspire to be global, and to be global requires that a company be large.

Another factor is the Internet. Not only does the Internet make it easier to be global, it makes it easier to do business in any country. The Internet permits many more transactions than a customer might otherwise conduct. When customers can buy things easily over the Internet, they tend to do more transactions. They don't have to get in their cars to go to the mall to make the transactions. For example, because of the Internet I have purchased far more books per year than I ever bought before.

To become larger, companies often acquire competitive companies. Merger and acquisition events result in bigger companies with more transactions and more data. When the IT application systems consolidate as a result of an enterprise acquisition, the data in a single database balloons to a much larger amount.

Industries such as banking, insurance, online book buying, online auction sites, and brokerage firms are examples in which companies have grown extremely large and data volumes have exploded to unheard-of levels.

There appears to be no end in sight to this trend. As countries in Eastern Europe and Asia grow their economies to be like Western economies, these same companies will flock to them and will increase the number of transactions even more.

Data volumes have reached the point at which keeping all the data in one database is no longer the wisest strategy. In fact, in an increasing number of cases it is no longer possible.

When you combine the business activity-induced increases in data with significantly increased retention requirements, you end up with a projected data housing problem of enormous proportions. Since the laws are not retro-active, the data pileup is just beginning. By this I mean that if you have a new regulation for 30 years' retention, you don't have to worry about data discarded prior to the law. You probably do not have the last 30 years' worth of data in your databases; therefore, the accumulation is starting from the oldest retention period used at the time the law was passed. If you project the data volumes that will result, you get off the charts pretty quick. This projection is shown in Figure 2.1. Data volume is not the only issue. Data aging is another concern.

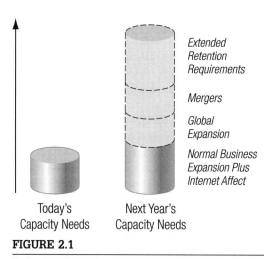

Today's Capacity Needs   Next Year's Capacity Needs

FIGURE 2.1

Projecting data volume explosions.

2.1.3 **Data Aging**

Aging of the IT function in enterprises is another factor related to the increased interest in data archiving. Today's retention requirements are often longer than many IT departments have been in existence. IT dates only from the 1950s, with many applications first hitting computers in the 1960s and '70s. IT departments have not been around long enough to worry about what to do with all the data they have been collecting. Consider your home as an analogy. You stuff away things like a pack rat into closets, the attic, and basement for years and years. Suddenly, when all the space has been filled up, you realize that you need a plan to dispose of old stuff you don't need.

Similarly, many corporate IT departments are just now reaching the point at which they must do something about all the data collected and squirreled away in databases.

2.2 **IMPLICATIONS OF NOT KEEPING DATA**

So, if the primary reason for keeping data longer is to let other people investigate us and, based on *our* data, to fine us, litigate us or otherwise cause some other unfortunate circumstance, why don't we simply dispose of the information earlier? The answer lies in what happens when you get caught not having the data when one of these dreaded events arises.

This is how it works: When someone needs some of your data to build a case against you, they have to convince a government official (usually a judge) to grant *discovery rights*. This means that they can demand data from you and expect to get it. The judge listens to their plea for why they want the data and sets the definition of the data that is allowed. You get to argue your side with the judge to narrow the scope of discovery by arguing that the data the complainant asks for is not relevant, too broad in scope, or too expensive to gather and produce. The judge ultimately decides what data the complainant gets.

When you have reached this point, you are given a specific period of time in which to deliver the data. This too can be negotiated, but it is generally 30 days.

If you fail to deliver the data, you are in default and subject to penalties. In a lawsuit the penalty is that you lose the case. The court assumes that the lack of delivering discovery data means that the plaintiff's suspicions are true and you lose. You are not given an opportunity to argue the merits of the case for your side. You simply lose.

In addition to the presumption of guilt levied on you as a result of not delivering the data, you may be fined for not following a law that mandated that you keep the data. So you get a double penalty.

This scenario has happened multiple times. Companies have had judgments and/or fines levied in the range of hundreds of millions of dollars for merely failing to satisfy a legitimate data discovery request.

So, what is going through the judge's mind when she grants a discovery request? The rule is to be fair to both parties. If the plaintiff is asking for data that is unreasonable to produce, the judge may narrow or eliminate the discovery request. If there are no laws saying how long you should keep data, the judge has wide latitude in narrowing the discovery request. A common argument used in the past was that the business destroyed the data as a normal part of its business process after a reasonable period of time.

That said, if a law exists that requires you to keep data for 25 years; no judge on the planet will feel it unreasonable for you to produce it if in fact the request falls within this 25-year period. It is a guaranteed slam dunk that you will be required to produce it and will suffer severe penalties if you do not.

There are a number of components that the court will expect of data delivered as a result of discovery. Figure 2.2 shows the components that the courts will expect of any data you deliver as a result of discovery.

The first component is the data itself. It should be complete, with no information missing. It should be the exact data requested.

The second component is an explanation of the data. The courts are very clear that you must explain the meaning of your data. A column name of DEP35COL1 does not convey any information to the reader of the data. This means that effective metadata, complete with semantic information, is a required part of the discovery output for database data.

The third component is reasonable presentation of the data. The courts require that you provide data in a presentation format that is comparable to

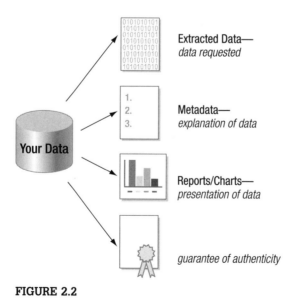

Extracted Data—
data requested

Metadata—
explanation of data

Reports/Charts—
presentation of data

guarantee of authenticity

Your Data

FIGURE 2.2

Discovery requirements.

what your own employees would be expected to see and use. You cannot simply print the raw data and expect the user to make sense of it. This requirement is often satisfied through negotiation with the plaintiff (possibly in a court hearing with the judge as referee).

The fourth component is a reasonable guarantee that the data is authentic. This means two things: (1) that the data is accurate and (2) that it has not been tampered with since it was created. Time to ratchet up the interest level in data quality as well as in data archiving. Plaintiff lawyers will have a field day if they can substantiate that the data delivered is flawed or suspect in any way.

The "good citizen" argument   Another reason enterprises want to be good keepers of data is to protect their reputations. Respected status in the public eye can be tarnished if press reports hammer an organization for either not keeping data it was supposed to or for not being able to defend the authenticity of its data. In many corporations, the public goodwill lost due to bad publicity is worth more than the impact of paying a fine or losing a local judgment.

The flip side   The outcome of recent lawsuits and investigations has shown how powerful data can be in making or breaking a case. More and more, data is becoming a powerful tool in creating or pursuing complaints against enterprises.

Enterprises have been lax in not only in keeping data but also equally lax in destroying data. There has been a new awareness of the importance of discarding data when it is not required to be kept any longer.

The laws are very clear that if you have the data, it can be used against you. If the law mandates that you keep data 15 years and you have data that is older than 15 years, all of it can be the target of discovery and used against you. If you keep it, it can be brought into the proceedings.

Just as the laws that mandate data retention automatically define what is reasonable to request, these same laws establish what is not reasonable. If the law says that you must keep data 15 years and you have a policy to destroy that data when it is 15 years and one day old, you are above reproach.

These days most enterprises are establishing both data retention and data discard policies because doing so makes good business sense.

2.3 DATA VOLUME ISSUES

The high data volumes that are being seen in IT departments present an array of very different problems that have nothing to do with regulations. In some cases reducing data volumes in operational systems will justify archiving data solely on its own.

The problem is simply that databases are getting bloated from all the data being put into them. Although disk storage has become cheap and will continue to decline in cost, the problem does not lie in disk capacity; the problem is in the impact of the high volume of data on operations.

DBMS systems are optimized to handle high transaction rates over large volumes of data. However, they have boundaries too. They are *not* designed to handle arbitrarily large volumes. When the volumes get too high, the operational characteristics start falling apart, specifically in these areas:

- Transaction processing slows.
- Physical file limits are reached.
- Operation of data management utilities takes longer.
- Operation of data loads and extracts takes longer.
- Time to recover from system failures grows longer.
- Time to recover from data center disasters grows longer.
- Cost of hardware (disk storage and systems) increases.

Let's examine these issues in greater detail.

Effect on transaction processing Having inactive data intermixed with active data will adversely impact transaction processing. More data pages must be read from the file system to locate the desired data. Operating system buffer page reuse becomes a lower percentage of pages processed. Additional data may cause indexes to have more levels. Free space cannot be as effective since inactive data takes up lots of valuable space. If you have a bunch of inactive data occupying adjacent space, you are wasting free space after reorganization of a database is completed. High- and low-value computations can also be wrong since they consider all rows of the database to have an equal probability of being used.

It is simply harder to tune a database that contains a great deal of inactive data. The DBMSs we use do not know how to selectively treat inactive data separately from active data when they do optimization.

The result is that our systems are not crisp. They are not performing at optimum levels.

How much inactive data does it take to impact performance of transaction programs? Certainly a number above 50 percent would have a large impact. Most analysts estimate that operational databases that have not shed inactive data have anywhere from 60–80 percent inactive data. The math gives us a compelling reason to address the topic of database archiving.

Hitting physical file limits The volume of data in some systems is actually hitting the DBMS limits in terms of the amount of space available to store a single table, IMS database, or the like. This is a situation that several years ago no one ever thought would occur, but it is happening today in many IT departments.

The impact on database administrators (DBAs) is to find solutions. They can spend an increasing amount of their time dealing with technical short-term solutions such as partitioning data in ever more partitions, reallocating space, redesigning data structures, and other approaches that work but which all have a disruptive cost and carry a risk of an unwanted outage.

An alternative is for the application manager to implement a sound database archiving solution that will almost always clean out enough data to make the current physical architecture of the application's operational database sufficient for years to come.

Operation of data management utilities   DBAs spend a lot of time and energy planning for and executing data management utilities. These include database reorganization, backing up data files, updating statistics, building or rebuilding indexes, checking constraints, and rebinding plans.

Keeping a large amount of inactive data in operational databases will obviously increase the execution time for these functions by a proportionately linear amount. The presence of this data may trigger the need for execution of these utilities more often, since the DBMS cannot manage file allocations, free space management, or perform other functions as effectively.

Operation of data loads and extracts   Enterprises today execute a lot of bulk data loading into large databases as well as data extracts for myriad uses. This activity has increased in recent years. In one shop I visited they claimed to be doing over 1500 data extracts every week from their primary databases used for populating data warehouses, data marts, special BI databases, and who knows what else.

A *data feed* is a stream of data records coming in all at once that need to be added to an existing database. The reasons for increased data feed activity include the integration of data across departments, across divisions, and in many cases across enterprises. Many business ventures have emerged that work exclusively from data feeds, such as reinsurance companies, mortgage buyers, and credit rating companies.

When a database contains a large amount of inactive data, data extract and load processes take much longer to run. To do most extracts, the process requires a scan (reading of the entire database). It just takes longer the larger the database. Although load functions might not need to touch every data page, the process is slowed by having to find free space. In addition, you often want to create an image copy of a database after each load execution. This will cost more time, space, and money if the database has significant amounts of inactive data.

Recovery from system failures   System failures that require restoring an image copy and then playing the log forward from that point to get a consistent state will certainly take a larger database more time to recover from than a smaller one. This means that the applications are locked out for longer periods of time, waiting for the recovery to complete.

It can be argued that bloated databases can cause more recovery situations. For example, they could result in more space allocation problems that cause a system failure when they try to dynamically allocate space for the ever-growing database.

Recovery from data center disasters   Just as routine recoveries take longer, disaster recoveries do as well. Disaster recoveries result when the system is lost or compromised and a recovery needs to be done on another system, often at another data center location. Disaster recoveries generally involve much more than one table or index; they usually require the recovery of several tables and/or indexes.

It only stands to reason that it will take longer to complete a disaster recovery of large databases than of smaller ones. The image copies will be proportionately larger and the amount of disk storage to be written will be larger as well. Steps for building indexes or, in the case of IMS, logical relationships will take significantly longer with inactive data present.

This can be a huge issue for an enterprise when the time to execute a disaster recovery is of critical importance to the enterprise. Each minute can cost thousands or, in some cases, millions of dollars.

When things fall apart, keeping operational databases lean can be largely beneficial.

Increased cost of hardware   Larger databases require more disk storage for data, indexes, and image copies. Although disk storage is getting cheaper, the disk storage that is on the front line supporting operational databases is still a large expense. Pushing data to archive data stores where it can be stored on less expensive storage devices can result in significant disk storage cost savings.

Archiving data should not result in the need for more total disk storage. The data is either in the database or in the archive; it is still the same amount of data. Archiving inactive data has two beneficial results. One is that it can compact the data, thus using less space than if it were retained in the operational databases. The other is that it can use less expensive disk storage. So you have less overall disk storage and a higher percentage of what you have is lower cost.

Not only will companies see lower disk storage expense if they archive inactive data, they will also see less demand on operational systems that could well result in lower system costs. Since the databases are leaner, query steps, scans, utilities, and extracts will all run in less CPU time. This also includes transaction programs that require looking at a lot of data (complex queries). All these factors can reduce the demand on CPU cycles as well as main memory usage. The result can be that operational applications can be run on less expensive, smaller systems or that system upgrades will occur less frequently.

2.4 **CHANGE MANAGEMENT**

Implementing database archiving practices can also impact the way you do application changes. Application changes come in two "flavors": minor upgrades and major reengineering efforts.

Minor upgrades often require modifications to database definitions and, as a result, to data stored under the previous data structure definitions. When this happens, a process of unloading and loading data occurs that "adjusts" old data to the new definition. Obviously this takes longer if there is more data.

Reengineering an application normally involves a massive amount of data readjustment to match the new application definitions. Again, obviously, if you have less data, the time to execute this task decreases.

There is also the possibility of not changing old data but instead letting the database archive retain data under the old definition and have the new application only accept new data. With this approach, all old data continues to be processed by the old version of the application until it all ends up in the archive data store. At that time, the old application can be removed, and sometimes the system itself can be removed if the old application was the last application on the system. In essence, the old and new applications run in parallel until all old data ends up in the archive.

This can be particularly useful when you're merging enterprises or departments. Instead of combining both the applications and the databases, the application that will be shut down as a result of the merger is merely run in parallel until all its data ends up in the archive data store and under management of the archive system. In that case there's no need to convert data.

2.5 **CURRENT DATABASE ARCHIVING PRACTICES**

Many IT departments have invented their own database archiving processes due to a lack of standard tools. Many of these practices are not well thought out and can result in a practice that will get the enterprise in trouble some day.

Let's explore some of these undesirable practices.

Keep data in operational databases   This is the old standby: Do nothing and let inactive data accumulate in operational databases. As we have seen, this strategy becomes costly to the IT budget as the databases reach unmanageable size.

This strategy also fails to preserve the original content of data, since modifications to data structures will sometimes require that older data be modified to conform.

Put in UNLOAD files   Many IT departments copy data from operational databases to UNLOAD files that are stored for the long haul. They are placed in file archiving systems for movement to cheaper storage.

This practice is loaded with problems. The UNLOADS are dependent on the application data structure at the time of the UNLOAD. When the data is called on to answer a query, there might not be a place into which to LOAD the data that has a matching data structure, matching application program, or matching system environment. The only way to guard against this problem is to continually modify the UNLOAD files to match any data structure changes. This becomes an unmanageable process after the number of UNLOAD files becomes too large.

Store data in parallel databases   Storing data in parallel databases that have the same structure as the operational databases is another common practice. This too is fraught with dangers. The parallel databases must be upgraded to reflect data structure changes every time the operational database has such changes. This means that the data must change. This strategy carries the same expanding time requirement problem seen in the UNLOAD case.

Parallel databases also require up-front, expensive disk storage. This will bring a huge cost as the parallel database expands.

Most ad hoc solutions carry with them a higher risk and a higher cost than what you can achieve by doing things correctly.

SUMMARY

There are two cost factors involved in the decision to build a database archiving practice:

- Cost avoidance, which means avoiding the huge cost in dollars and reputation that can result from not complying with requirements to retain data and produce it on demand
- Savings from operational systems that come from employing an effective database archiving practice for large databases

Either of these factors alone can generally justify spending the time and money to build an effect practice. In fact, the return on investment can generally justify the cost of a new practice within just a few years.

Cost factors are not the entire story, however. The legal issues of managing data correctly can reduce risk of embarrassing and/or debilitating legal encounters. This is surely worth something.

Practicing database archiving the right way is a must. A poorly thought out practice can negate any business case savings that you might have expected from archiving.

Generic Archiving Methodology

3

This is a special chapter. It isn't a mandatory read and doesn't give you specific guidelines on database archiving. What it does is convey the message that all archiving activities involve essentially the same steps, and each archivist must answer the same questions. The answers to the questions drive the design of the resulting archive store and practice.

If you want to skip this chapter, go right ahead. But if you are interested in being an archive practitioner, it will help you build a solid conceptual base that will directly relate to your future responsibilities.

The term *archive analyst* refers to someone who builds the design of an archive and sets the rules for operating it. An *archive* is a system that consists of policies, practices, places, and objects. Once activated, the system has certain activities and responsibilities that continue as long as the archive exists.

An archive analyst takes the objectives for an archive and designs an archiving system that accomplishes the objectives. Another term is *archivist*. This is someone who executes the operational steps and is responsible for the integrity, completeness, and availability of the archive on a daily basis. An archive does not run by itself; it requires a designer, an operator, and an administrator.

3.1 THE METHODOLOGY

Let's imagine that you are an archive analyst given the task of building and managing an archive for something—anything.

To begin, you need a methodology, or a series of steps that will get you where you want to go. Such a methodology is show in Figure 3.1. These are planning steps that will result in a complete design of an archiving system for a specific archiving application. In the abstract you would do these steps only once. Then you would put the plans into motion: Archiving and archive administration would begin.

✓ Define motivation for archiving

✓ Identify objects to archive

✓ Determine when to move to archive

✓ Determine how long to keep

✓ Determine when objects will not be needed

✓ Determine how to dispose of objects

✓ Determine who has access to archive

✓ Determine form of archive objects

✓ Determine place for archive

✓ Determine operational processes

✓ Determine administrative processes

✓ Determine change process

FIGURE 3.1

Steps in the archive-planning process.

In reality, we all know that every plan needs the ability to change. You need to plan for change or at least think through the implications of changing the design and/or policies after implementation has begun and has been in motion for some time. Many of the decisions you make cannot be changed without creating an incomplete or inconsistent archive.

It is a good idea to document all the planning decisions so that in the future others who become part of the process will understand your intentions. For a casual archive such as mom's recipes, this might not be necessary. For more serious archives such as a database archive or a Presidential library, this is an extremely important document or collection of documents. A checklist for documentation and planning is included in Appendix A. Use this to get started and modify it accordingly to fit your own specific needs.

Examples will help illustrate the steps described. Some examples will pertain to electronic archiving and some to nonelectronic archiving.

It might be helpful for you to consider your own example of something that might need to be archived to help you think through the steps. Archiving family photographs or family documents are two suggestions.

Although these steps should be followed no matter what you archive, the execution of the overall plan varies significantly depending on what is being archived. The questions are the same, but the answers take you to different places. Though the planning process is identical for all archiving applications, the resulting design can be significantly different.

3.2 DEFINE MOTIVATION FOR ARCHIVING

You decided to design an archiving system for a reason. You need to thoroughly understand the reason for archiving since it can result in an expensive proposition for yourself or your company. Be sure to specifically define and document that reason.

When the planning process is complete, you could decide that you don't need an archiving system to satisfy the requirement.

In reality you are not defining the requirement for archiving; you are defining the requirement to keep something for an extended period of time. Archiving is a *solution* to the requirement, not the requirement itself. If you fully define the requirement for retention, you can better judge the needed level of archiving. Not having an archiving system might be okay; having an archiving system that falls short of satisfying the requirement could be disastrous. On the flip side, having an archiving system that overkills vis-à-vis the requirement can be wasteful of people and dollar resources.

An archiving application can be driven by multiple motivations. Each should be documented and independently understood. Often only one of them is dominant and ends up determining all the design parameters of the resulting system. That's okay; however, changes to motivations over time could end up causing one of the others to take the dominant position. This has occurred in many instances for enterprise database data where legal considerations have moved ahead of company policy to dominate the retention decision-making process.

Often the motivators are given to you as either vague or overly general mandates. "Save all emails," "let's preserve the essence of this event," "it would sure be nice to capture mom's recipes for the next generation," and "Congress says we must keep medical information for a hundred years," are examples. Try to investigate sufficiently to determine exactly where the mandates are coming from and, in the case of legal requirements, understand the specific laws and sections that apply to what you are doing.

3.2.1 Motivators

Figure 3.2 shows some of the common motivation categories that could initiate an archiving project.

Legal requirements Sometimes the decision for retaining data is not a choice: It is mandated by a law or an enterprise's constitution or bylaws. This is certainly a major factor in database archiving.

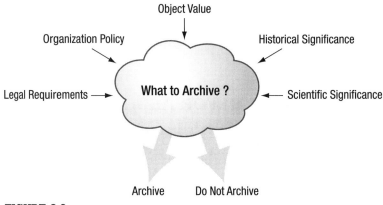

FIGURE 3.2

Motivation categories used in determining what to archive.

When laws mandate long retention periods, the definition of archiving is frequently vague. For example, a law might say that you must keep all banking transaction information for 25 years, but it generally does not spell out what data fields of the banking information you need to keep. Certainly the date, time, banking location, transaction type, dollar amount, and account number would be needed. But suppose that the bank also captured a field in the transaction to show whether it was raining out at the time and place in which the transaction was done. This could be done to correlate the transaction rates per hour to weather conditions. Should this data be included in the archive? Probably not, since it has no long-term value. It certainly would not be a violation of any law to leave it out.

In other words, even when a law specifically identifies data objects that need to be retained, there could still be commonsense decisions to be made at the data element level in terms of what satisfies the legal requirement and what does not.

Legal requirements also apply to your personal life. The government dictates that you need to keep information that backs up your income tax returns for seven years. If you get into a dispute with the IRS and do not have the data, you are at a distinct disadvantage. Another example is that you might need to keep records on the purchase of your home should you decide to sell it years later. Likewise, any asset you own that could be considered an investment requires retention of purchase information to establish the basis for determining capital gains.

Organizational policy In addition to legal requirements, there could exist policies in the enterprise that dictate what gets saved beyond its operational life. The organizational policy might require a retention period for more than or less than the legal requirements.

An example is your credit card company that tells you that you can expect to get detailed transaction information for up to six months after the transaction occurs.

After that, you are out of luck. How long does a bank promise you access to detailed information? How long can you expect an insurance company to keep records on your claims? These questions are answered through policies established by the company and available to you on request.

Consider educational institutions. How long do they keep data on students, courses taken, and grades received? The policy of most schools is to retain this data forever, even though no law says they must. Forever is a long time. This is an example of a retention period that I call *indefinite*, which has special implications on the rest of the archiving decisions that will be made later.

Value   Value should always be considered in determining your retention period.

Some objects have value that remains a long time. Some objects depreciate slowly, some increase in value over time. They could be capable of being sold for significant amounts of money in the future.

When you think of paintings from masters like van Gogh or Picasso, there could certainly be a day when nobody would want them, but that day is a long way away, so retaining the paintings for their resale value is clearly a valid motivation.

Another function of value is that proper maintenance of the objects while in the archive during the retention period might be necessary to maintain or increase the objects' value.

Vintage cars in mint condition, gold coins, and Elvis Presley memorabilia are some examples of objects for which value is likely to increase over time and should be retained.

Value is not only attributed to items that have value if sold but also value internal to the enterprise. For example, database data is generally not of value in the market after a short time, but it could be valuable to the enterprise internally for doing future business intelligence analysis. This could cause a company to set a policy to save for several years data that the company might not otherwise save.

Historical significance   Historical significance is another motivator for which to keep something. This applies to the Declaration of Independence, Presidential tapes, dinosaur fossils, photographs of buildings, and much more. Virtually all museums and galleries are archives. The process of deciding what gets into these archives and how these archives are managed falls completely within the methodology described here.

Sporting organizations have a passion for historically significant data retention. The Olympic organization considers the identification of every participant and the result of every event as data to be retained forever. Baseball has retained unbelievably detailed data for more than a century, but even there decisions need to be made. Certainly the scores and the play-by-play line scores of every game are of historical significance, but is the radar-gun recording of the speed of every pitch important? Some baseball buffs think so.

Most items that have historical significance will set a retention period of *indefinite*. This will determine the way this data is preserved and protected.

For enterprises, detailed data is generally not of much historical value. Such things as annual reports, minutes of board meetings, pictures of CEOs, and the like could be of historical value. At many sites IBM has mini-museums that display early versions of computers and other technology. It's always fun for me to visit them, since I worked on many of these computers in my past. Similarly, Boeing has a museum of airplanes it produced in the past.

Still, historical significance is in the mind of the beholder. For one person an object might be of historical significance, whereas for another person it is not. It can sometimes be tricky to decide on behalf of an enterprise what is and what is not historically significant.

Database data is generally not of much historical significance, although it can be. For example, repair data on airplanes or automobiles might be historically significant for someone who is trying to plot progress of the evolution of technology over time.

Corporate data can also be useful in recording information about historical events. For example, data on Hurricane Katrina will be documented in great detail and kept well into the future. Some of the interesting historical information for future researchers will come from insurance claim information contained in corporate databases.

Scientific significance   Data of scientific significance includes a host of things. It differs from historically significant data in that *historical significance* refers to saving objects about an event that future generations will be interested in learning about, whereas *scientific significance* means that the objects or data could have value in future scientific studies or to support conclusions made by future scientists. Clearly, some objects have both characteristics.

Some examples of scientifically significant objects are:

- Results of experiments
- Telemetry data from space missions
- Photographs of cosmic activity
- Weather recordings
- Moon rocks
- Crash data on airplane disasters
- Disease incidence data

It is hard to predict when this data will stop having potential for scientific use, hence its *indefinite* retention time.

3.2.2 **Motivation Initiation**

So, how do these projects get started? Pursuing an archiving project requires strong organizational skills and perseverance, not just the pack-rat syndrome. Pack rats often simply save indiscriminately and ignore many of the steps involved in proper archiving. Organization and diligence is needed for optimum results.

Determining what to keep is important. Organizations collect a lot of things in the normal course of business. Some of this data is important to keep, some is not, and some is in a gray area.

Every enterprise should have an enterprise archivist who looks at the entire organization and makes decisions about archiving. The National Archivist does exactly that for the Federal government. So do some other organizations, although most organizations do not have an enterprise-level archivist.

Instead most enterprises start archiving projects when a new rule is imposed by the government or following a bad experience in a lawsuit. In other words, the initiation of an archiving project is typically reactive, not proactive. This is unfortunate because some valuable information is lost that might otherwise have been maintained.

3.2.3 Documentation

Every archiving project should begin with a thorough investigation of the reasons for archiving. This process should involve executives, line managers, lawyers, auditors, and any other stakeholders in the subject area. Specific documents should be generated and signed off on to establish the findings and decisions made during the investigation.

You probably don't need to do this for home archiving projects unless you are truly an over-the-edge control freak.

3.3 IDENTIFY OBJECTS TO ARCHIVE

The next step is to identify the objects that you want to keep in accordance with the mandates established in step 1.

For example, a newspaper must decide what to keep in long-term storage. Will it keep all published articles or articles written only by its staff (excluding wire stories)? Will it keep pictures? The actual images of pages? The classified sections? What about special sections like "Food" or "Homes"? Advertising inserts and comic strips? If a newspaper prints multiple editions each day, does it keep all editions or just the final editions?

So you see, just a simple thing like your morning newspaper involves many archiving choices. Now that newspapers offer Websites with abbreviated articles, how much of this information is kept in an archive after it is removed from the Website? Things like the weather report can change several times during the day. Is each version kept, or just one version for each day?

Using the example of the home archive of documents and pictures, you certainly do not want to keep all pictures that you take. You will need some criteria to determine which ones go in the archive and which ones do not. When you set these criteria, it might motivate you to take pictures that you might not otherwise take. For example, you might want a picture of each of your children on their birthdays to show how their appearance changed over time. This could motivate you to capture specific poses (such as standing up) at each birthday party.

The emergence of digital photos makes it easier to sort, select, and pick the picture you want to save.

For family documents, you should list the document types you want to keep. The obvious choices are birth certificates, diplomas, marriage certificates, and death certificates. But what about tax filings or your children's report cards? You could get into some conflicting arguments over the list.

Just as an art museum must determine which artists and which of their paintings to include in its collection, you need to create a process with guidelines so that those responsible for the operation of the archive can execute their assigned tasks consistently and objectively over time.

3.3.1 **Classification Process**

You can use a formal process called *classification* to help determine what to archive. You first take the object types that are relevant to the project mandate as described in step 1. You then analyze them to determine which you keep and which you do not. Classification also records other factors, as described in this section.

For database data there exist complete consulting practices for this very purpose. These consultants will come to your offices, inventory your data, and classify it according to the relevant laws and policies and will record mandatory retention periods.

Think of classification as a big spreadsheet. The rows contain various objects that have been identified. As shown in Figure 3.3, the columns are the characteristics described in this section (legal, corporate policy, value, historical, scientific). Additional cells can be added that pertain to the specific topic. The cells contain the determination of the characteristics important to the object.

Object	Legal Retention Period	Applicable Law or Regulation	Policy Retention Period	Source of Policy	Object Value Retention	Object Value Indicator	Data Privacy Requirements

FIGURE 3.3

Example of a classification spreadsheet.

Classification of database data can be done at the record/segment/row level, or you can drill down to specific data elements. We will address this idea in greater detail in a later chapter.

Whether or not to use an archive Classifying objects does not mean that you will archive them, even if the retention periods are quite long. Remember that archiving means removing objects from their operational context and putting them in a separate place where they are managed under special long-term retention rules established by the archivist.

If objects are classified that have low volumes of data and/or relatively short retention periods, moving them to an archive might not be necessary. For example, if you want to keep your tax records for only the seven required years, you can simply keep them in your drawer at home and throw away the oldest return after a new return is filed. This does not qualify as an archive, although you are retaining the data for seven years.

On the other hand, if, at the time of filing, you make copies of your tax returns and store them outside your home, possibly in a safe deposit box, then you are archiving.

The question that needs to be answered is whether leaving the objects in the operational environment will satisfy all the long-term retention requirements. To determine this, you must complete the planning steps.

Recurring versus nonrecurring archiving Before gong further it is important to explain the difference between a recurring and a nonrecurring archive. A *recurring archive* saves instances of a specific object type that are generated over time (sometimes a new one every millisecond). Thus the archive has objects flowing in and out of it on a regular basis, as with automated teller machine (ATM) transactions, bank deposits, insurance claims, stock trades, and the like. Most database archiving falls into this category.

A *nonrecurring archive* records information about a single event, such as data about a hurricane, a chemical plant explosion, an airplane crash, or astronauts landing on the moon or something like the evidence box for a crime. In this case, data flows in over a very short period of time and the archive then becomes "locked" for the duration of the retention period. Nonrecurring archives can last for decades or even have a retention requirement of "indefinite."

Nonrecurring archives usually contain many different object types. They may contain photographs, measurement information, personnel information, expert witness testimony, and much more. Recurring archives generally have only one object type.

For an enterprise that is likely to encounter events that require long-term nonrecurring archiving, it is a good practice to anticipate the events and data you will want to retain and for how long. Then, when the event occurs, you can go about efficiently gathering and protecting the data. Not anticipating an event can lead to chaos when the event occurs, which can result in missing information that could be important later and possibly cannot be retrieved retroactively.

You would use this same methodology to develop the archiving plan for both recurring and nonrecurring archive designs.

3.4 DETERMINE WHEN TO PUT OBJECTS IN THE ARCHIVE

If you decide you need an archive to store the objects for the balance of their retention period, you are implying that at some point you remove them from the operational environment and insert them into the archive store.

Before you make this critical decision of whether or not to use an archive store, it is strongly recommended that you carefully consider all of the following steps. Even if you end up keeping the data in the operational environment, your management of the objects in that context might very well be influenced by consideration of the issues we are about to discuss.

The best approach is to start by assuming that you will be creating an archive, complete the entire planning process, and then decide if an archive is necessary.

Deciding when to move objects to the archive is a policy step. You are establishing a policy that will be executed over and over again as objects meet the policy conditions for movement. The key in setting the policy is to not move objects too early or too late. The policy should be crisp and clear so that anyone can understand it.

Let's consider the case of a Presidential library. A Presidential library moves items to the library only after the President leaves office and the library is built and is ready to receive all the materials. If the President is still in office, the materials are not in the archive. If the President is out of office, the materials are either in the archive or being sent to it. This is a nice precise policy statement.

Don't move too early or too late   This is an important aspect of the policy. The general rule is to not move an object to the archive until it is no longer expected to be needed in the operational environment. In other words, the object should not be moved until it is complete, meaning that it will not be updated or changed again.

These guidelines are only that—guidelines. Of course, there is always the potential that you'll need to access the object or you wouldn't need the archive in the first place. The guideline is an estimate of the probability of the data being needed back in the operational environment. The probability should be low—very low.

My tax returns are a great example. I keep the "archive" in a file cabinet buried in a closet under a stairwell. Getting to the old data is like digging up lost treasure. I generally go back to the returns multiple times in the year or two after filing. My policy is to move the previous year's pile to my cabinet upstairs (operational place) and move the one from two years ago to the cavern under the stairs (archive place). I learned this the hard way. I was moving too early and had to crawl into the cave too often.

Another factor to consider is that some archives are actually more exposed to access than they would be in the operational environment. This fact can influence your decision either way. In the case of a Presidential library, you don't want wide exposure too early. The President might get impeached. So it would be best to wait until that possibility has passed. This rule applies to lots of government information that needs to remain classified and out of the public eye until it ages to the point it becomes of only historical interest. The factor to consider here is how accessible is the archive and is that a good thing or a bad thing?

The converse is to not move too late. One consideration here is whether the objects are exposed to damage or tampering in the operational setting. If the archive environment is more secure than the operational environment, moving objects to it should be done as early as possible.

Accessibility is also a factor here. Sometimes the archive is more publicly accessible and that is desired. For example, moving technical papers into a publicly accessible Internet repository would be a good thing to do.

Sometimes the desire to archive early is so important that the objects are kept in both environments for some period of time. This is possible for objects that can be copied, and it certainly applies to database data. In a later chapter we will explore how this decision gets made explicitly for database applications.

Timing generally does not need to be precise. If you move items based on a policy that says they must be 90 days old, moving them in 91 days or 93 days generally presents no problem. An item becomes eligible for movement based on the policy and gets moved at the next archiving event that looks for such objects. The policy establishes *eligibility*, meaning that it should not be moved before that time.

There are those cases in which timing is a critical factor. For example, if protection of the content of the data from inadvertent or malicious tampering is a consideration, the policy should be to move things as soon as they are created.

Will someone know where to find it? Your policy should be precise enough that people looking for data will know that the data can always be expected to be in the operational environment or always in the archive, or maybe in either. They should not be confused about where to look. This implies that any stakeholders in the objects will know that an archive exists and know the policy for moving objects to it.

This also implies that you should not make frequent changes to the policy. This point reinforces the concept that the policy should clearly indicate how quickly something is expected to be moved after meeting eligibility criteria.

Scope of criteria   Establishing the criteria for when an object becomes eligible for movement to an archive can be simple or complex. My tax return example presents very simple criteria. So does the example of the Presidential library. However, sometimes the criteria can have many conditions.

For example, the criteria for moving an insurance company's claim information could read "90 days from receipt of the claim request unless the incident involves a loss of life, in which case it is two years, or involves damages over $2,000, in which case it is one year. If there is an outstanding dispute over the claim amount or a pending legal action, then the claim is not moved until the dispute or litigation is completed." In this example many conditions are used to qualify each independent claim for movement.

Much as with other steps in the process, you sometimes need to answer questions from other steps before finalizing the criteria. Note that many of the questions are interdependent on each other.

Some IT departments want to use archives to push data out of overloaded operational databases and so to speed up performance. Once you have decided to archive, this should not be the criterion. The criteria for deciding when to put something in the archive should be based on an *enterprise* policy. An item should not be archived until it is no longer likely to be used in another business transaction, including reports. Once the data has satisfied all expected business uses, it should be archived as soon as possible. After all, this is the reason you are establishing the archive.

3.5 DETERMINE HOW LONG TO KEEP OBJECTS IN THE ARCHIVE

This step is vitally important because it could determine whether or not you use an archive at all. It will also determine how you will answer many of the remaining questions regarding the way objects in the archive are managed.

Earlier in this chapter we described the motivators for setting retention periods. The spreadsheet that was produced shows the motivators that influence retention periods and the intended retention periods for each. Clearly, you want to set a retention period as the longest period required of all the motivators. You might want to consider padding it with some additional amount of time to provide some protection against cutting it too close.

Figure 3.4 shows the key elements to consider in determining how long to keep objects in the archive. These are discussed in detail below.

Indefinite retention length   A common retention length is "indefinite": You don't plan to ever throw objects away. This is certainly the case for paintings at the Louvre, for Presidential library content, for gold coins, for academic

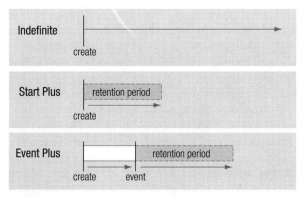

FIGURE 3.4

Determining how long to keep objects.

records at universities, and many more archives. If you adopt this policy, you need to pay serious attention to issues discussed in later steps regarding protection and preservation.

You should always think twice before you set "indefinite" as the objective, since doing so can have undesired consequences. Take time to consider the issues important to your enterprise and set a realistic retention length.

Event stop times   A second category of retention times is expressed in terms of a stopping event—for example, if you are saving documentation on a purchase of a home and subsequent home improvements made and paid for, in the event you sell your home. The retention period may be expressed as seven years after the sale of the home. This gives you time to file any tax forms for the capital gain (or loss) plus the period up to the IRS "doesn't care anymore" time. If you are in the business of buying and selling homes for profit, this would be a good statement of when you can destroy documentation.

Your death is an important event when it comes to your home archives. You have probably set an "indefinite" retention period for your personal archive. When you die, your survivors will either adopt the archive and continue keeping things or reset the retention period to one nanosecond after your demise and begin backing up the dumpster to your front door. I suspect that much of my stuff will end up in that giant trash bin.

What is the start time?   If your retention length is not indefinite nor based on a future event, you need to understand what the start time is for counting against the retention period. This is not always obvious. For example, if you are saving purchase order information, is the start time for counting when the purchase order is dated, when it is entered into your system, when the last product is shipped to satisfy it, or when the customer pays for it?

Most of the time you use the point in time at which the object was created, although that time could have different meanings to different people. For example, for an auto accident insurance claim, some people might consider the create time as the date and time of the auto accident, whereas others might consider it the date the claim was filed.

Note that the end of archive time is not a function of when data is moved to the archive; it is a function of the time it spends in the operational environment plus time spent in the archive plus time spent in any intermediate places. The time of the move event to the archive is irrelevant to determining the retention length.

Establishing a specific discard policy The discard policy is an established rule that can be applied to objects to determine whether they have reached the end of their retention period. These rules can be simple (seven years from the date I file my tax return) or complex.

The discard policy is a reenactment of the rules set to determine how long you need to keep things. In other words, you are selecting the rule that defines the longest retention line of the various factors you established earlier as requirements.

Failing to set a discard policy is the same as setting one to "indefinite." If you manage the archive with an indefinite retention policy, you can set a more specific discard policy later with no harm. If you set a policy that is too short and want to extend it later on, it might be too late to apply to objects that were already discarded through the earlier policy.

When in doubt, leave things in the archive longer than you need to.

The effect of old data is often overlooked in designing an archive. I hear people say that the required retention period is 25 years and therefore they don't have to worry about the discard policy for a couple of decades. What they are overlooking is that some of the data that will flow into the archive when it is first implemented could already be several years old and have been sitting in the operational databases for all that time. In fact, it is possible that your discard policy will trigger discard activity the first month after archiving begins.

If it is a factor, it is a good idea to determine in advance what the shortest archive life will be for old data. The whole point of setting a cap on the length of time things are stored in an archive is to avoid negative consequences that could occur. Otherwise we would just set all lengths to indefinite.

Some negative consequences of keeping data in the archive too long are:

- Exposure to legal action
- Cost of storage
- Cost of administering the ever-growing archive
- Running out of room in your house

3.6 **DETERMINE WHAT TO DO WITH DISCARDED OBJECTS**

If you have determined that you are not going to keep things in the archive forever, you not only need a policy to determine when an object is no longer welcome in the archive; you need to have a plan on how to remove it. Tossing it into the dumpster is certainly a viable plan for some things but not others. The issue of how to dispose of something is determined by the consequences of not disposing of it properly as well as the cost of disposal.

If you are trying to avoid the possibility of your data being used in legal actions, you need to remove the data using zero-out or electronic shredding technology. In other words you might need to use techniques that will foil legal data forensics software. This is not illegal. If you are not required to keep data anymore, it is perfectly legal for you to dispose of it in such a way that no other software can reinstate it. For paper documents, burning or comprehensive shredding might be appropriate.

When disposing of objects, you must be sure to dispose of any copies you made to protect the archive. A common mistake is to toss the primary copy and then forget to toss any copies you made. If you do not discard the copies, the data still exists.

Keeping records   Sometimes you may want to keep records indicating that objects have been removed from the archive and destroyed. The records could indicate only the date of a destruction event and the number of objects. The records might go further and provide a list of object identifiers that were destroyed.

The point of a record is to establish for the purpose of potential litigation that you have a firm policy on when to discard data, a firm and consistent approach to destruction, and proof that these policies are executed consistently. It doesn't look good if you only destroy information five days after receiving discovery orders from a judge. Your policy on *how* to get rid of things should be documented and followed.

3.7 **DETERMINE WHO NEEDS ACCESS TO ARCHIVES AND HOW**

In designing any archive, the potential users must be taken into consideration, even though the expectation of use may be very low.

The people who will be looking at things in the archive will generally be different people from those working with it in the operational environment. For home archives it might be future generations not yet born. For database data it could be lawyers, auditors, or customers who would never normally look at it.

Make a list of people you expect or want to have access to the archive and what that access will be like. Can they touch it, alter it, take it out with the expectation of returning it?

If the archived objects are super-sensitive, you might require a surrogate to access the objects. In this case a person is assigned to search the archive on behalf of the actual person who wants the data. This is to ensure that the requestor does not see more than he is entitled to.

Sometimes accessing objects in the archive is not the same as accessing the same objects in the operational environment. For example, database data in an archive is heavily searched. Results are generally listed. A powerful search capability is needed that might not be necessary in the operational environment. This could require that you restructure data to make it more accessible through search capabilities.

Sometimes you are looking for just one small piece of information from the archive; other times you are looking for a lot of data. For example, in a lawsuit, you might want to see all data for auto accidents in Chicago between 2003 and 2005, but you might never make this type of request in the operational phase.

You might also have to provide data from both the operational database and the archive to satisfy a single request. The request can encompass some data that has been archived and other data that has not aged enough to be moved to the archive.

Plan for facilities for authorized people to get the access they need. This can involve assigning specific rooms, special equipment such as microfiche readers, or the like. You might have to provide computers to help in the viewing, as well as trained staff to assist in the search.

It might be more convenient for you to make copies of items in the archive for the people who need access instead of letting them "have at it" in the actual archive. Sometimes this is precisely what the requestor wants. For example, you might search the archive databases and extract data into another working database for the requestor to use.

The "who" and "how" might suggest that you add descriptive information to the objects to make future access easier for people who might not be familiar with the original application.

3.8 DETERMINE THE FORM OF ARCHIVE OBJECTS

At first glance determining the form of archive objects might appear to be a small step; however, for some archives it is a major factor, and for most determining the form of archive objects requires some careful consideration before archive design is complete.

The form of the object in the archive sometimes will be the same as it was in the operational environment. Still, many times the object should be transformed from one form into another form to preserve its existence, capture its context, or make it more accessible.

Preserving existence If the object will be subject to decay, special measures should be taken when putting objects in the archive. This is true for most physical objects that will have a long retention period, such as paintings (which can fade) as well as most physical paper documents used for commerce.

Consideration must be given to either changing the form of the object at the time of entry to the archive or establishing a management process for items in the archive to retain the essence of the object. This could involve putting an object in airtight sealed containers (stamps), making copies on paper that is more durable through time (receipts or other paper documents), or spraying the object with a protectorate (display forms of machinery).

The second part of this step is to establish a procedure for management of the object while it is in the archive. For example, paintings in art museums that are expected to last for thousands of years will require periodic restoration activities; otherwise they will eventually deteriorate to the point at which they no longer convey their greatness.

An electronic example of this is long-term data storage. There currently exists no computer data storage devices that you can put data on and expect it to be readable in 50 years. This doesn't mean that you cannot keep data for 50 years; it means that you must periodically recopy the data to new media. This step could be required every four years, for example. Failure to do this will result in loss of data before the required retention period ends for applications with retention periods measured in decades.

You need to determine whether making the change will invalidate the purpose of the object being in the archive in the first place. If the change in any way invalidates the authenticity of the object, it should not be done. Note that, for example, painting restoration does not diminish authenticity but rather reestablishes it.

Preserving context Context is important. It tells someone in the future what the object is and why it is there.

For example, if you have a moon rock collected by an astronaut rover, you would not just put the rock in a box and store it in a room. Years from now, someone might look at it and say, "This looks like a rock; I wonder where it came from." You need a document that says it is a moon rock and that it was collected on a specific date by a specific device. You might also want to include a history of tests performed on the rock and any scientific findings that have been developed in the period between collection and storage in the archive. This process is preserving context.

Although it is extremely important, most people dealing with data systems fail to properly appreciate this step in the design process. This step states that all stored data should have contextual data stored with it; for database data, this means rock-solid metadata. Who has rock-solid metadata?

A trivial story on context illustrates the pitfalls of omitting this step. My wife saved pictures of our two daughters as they were growing up by merely throwing them in boxes. Although our daughters are four years apart in age, when we looked at pictures of them many years later, we could not identify who was who in many of the pictures. Although we could always say it was Susan or Aimee at the time the pictures were taken (when the differences in their looks were obvious due to the difference in age), we never realized that they were essentially identical twins when each of them was age 1, age 2, age 3, and so on. A simple recording of name, date, and place on the back of the pictures would have preserved the context.

Another example of the importance of preserving context is a recent story about telemetry data collected from a space mission that was maintained diligently for years. When current scientists had a need for it, they retrieved the data with no problems, but they had no idea what the data elements holding the data stood for. The data was fine, but without the metadata it was unusable.

Making the object more accessible Another action you might take to change the form of an object in the archive is a change to make the object more accessible in the archive.

An obvious example is database data where data may be coming from a source created from a legacy application that is clearly on its last legs. It may encode data in a tricky way that might not be understandable to someone in the future.

The archive process may change the storage form of the data to a more durable structure, reencoding data values to make them more obvious to a future user, implement a more elaborate indexing scheme, and change all character data to Unicode. No change is made to the content of the data, just to the form of the data. The changes are done to make the data more accessible and understandable to future users. It does not diminish the authenticity of the data in any way.

3.9 DETERMINE WHERE THE ARCHIVE WILL BE KEPT

This is probably the most important step. There are many factors to consider in deciding where to physically keep the archive. The answers to questions in earlier steps weigh heavily on the decisions you make here.

Deciding where to put an archive centers on the two requirements of protecting the archive objects for the duration of their retention periods while making them available to people entitled to see or use them.

Remember, an archive is a storage place. It can consist of computer files, as in database archiving, or it may be a physical place, as in a Presidential library. Wherever it is, it needs to provide a level of protection commensurate with the importance of the objects.

3.9.1 Determining the Consequences of Losing Archive Objects

The first consideration in determining the archive place is to assess the impact of loss of archive objects. The loss can have little or no material impact, or it could have a devastating impact.

For example, what would happen if the Louvre were to burn to the ground and take all the paintings with it? The loss to future generations would be unfortunate, although everything in the Louvre is well documented in books with pictures, commentary on the painters and their techniques, and more. Future generations would still benefit from the archive, even though it would not be as great as having the real thing.

A little-known fact: The Soviet Union under Stalin wanted its citizens to have access to much of the world's art without actually allowing them to travel to places outside the Soviet Union to study and appreciate them. To mitigate this, Stalin commissioned the best artists in the country to produce replicas of the great art of the world: paintings, sculptures, and so on. These replicas can be seen in a museum in Moscow today. They're not the real deal, but they're pretty close.

The consequences of losing enterprise data can include such things as federal government fines, lawsuits from customers or investors, loss of customer confidence, and inability to look back in performing business intelligence analysis. Such a loss could cost an enterprise millions or even billions of dollars.

In assessing the consequences of archive loss (besides losing your job), you need to consider not only what the tab will be if the objects are lost but also whether they can be recreated from other sources. Can copies suffice, can pictures suffice, or can data be reconstructed from other data sources? This information can help determine what you do when you put something in the archive and how you manage it during its life.

3.9.2 **Determining What to Protect Against**

Many things can cause a loss of objects in the archive. Figure 3.5 shows some of the more common ones. It also shows the generic source of the villains. This is quite a list, but you might find more factors than these depending on the type of object being archived.

For any archive, you need to list the specific potential threats to that archive considering the length of the retention period, which is an important factor in determining how you provide some of the protections. That said, if you have a short retention period and decide later that you want or need to extend it, you might have already mishandled some of the objects in the archive. The implication is to err on the side of overprotection whenever possible.

People-related risk factors

Theft, damage, corruption, and war are four categories of people-related risks discussed in this section. No doubt there are other categories.

Theft   Theft is a deliberate act on the part of an unauthorized person to steal the content of the archive. Theft can be real in that the actual archive object is stolen, or it can be virtual in that the archive object remains but the content is copied.

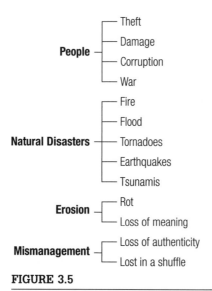

FIGURE 3.5

Common causes of archive object loss.

Physical theft brings up images of paintings being stolen from art museums. The thief gains entry as an authorized viewer (a member of the general public), gains proximity to the target object, and cuts it out of the frame. Data can also be stolen by taking laptops, servers, tapes, hard drives, or diskettes.

It is important to understand the risk of someone physically walking off with your archive. That person might or might not be someone with legitimate physical access to the archive objects or storage media. You might need to guard against even the authorized person walking off with your stuff. Consider locking down, gluing down, using special storage cases, or, in the case of data, storing on media or machines too large to haul off.

Sometimes things "go missing" because someone removes something from the archive and forgets to return it. The individual might not have bad intentions, but if the object is not returned, the result is the same as if it had been deliberately stolen. If people are authorized and expected to remove items from the archive place and return them later, there must be a system of check-out and check-in. You also must monitor items that are out too long and take steps to retrieve them.

The second form of theft involves making a copy of the archive. Sometimes making a copy of the archive is fine, even encouraged, but usually it is unacceptable. Corporate data usually falls in the latter category. Proper protection for a corporate data archive includes hacker protection, authorized security management for access, and complete access audit trails.

Damage Damage to the archive caused by people can take many forms, such as hacking into computer systems and changing or deleting file contents. Another is physical vandalism, such as physically destroying objects or defacing paintings. This could include deliberate setting of fires or flooding of a space.

Corruption   Archive corruption includes attempts by people to alter the content of an archive to gain some personal advantage. We see this in corporate employees trying to destroy documents or alter data in advance of a lawsuit or federal investigation. Another example is the removal of documents from the national archives by a leading political figure in advance of an investigation.

The gist of this is that sometimes you need to protect the content of an archive from your own staff—even your boss.

War   When wars develop, indiscriminate destruction occurs all over the place, affecting people and property. Thus an archive can be exposed to destruction or the loss of people necessary to understand and manage it due to military events. The implication is that you need to consider where you put your archive and have a plan for what to do if threatened with such an unfortunate event.

In this day of global enterprises and offshore outsourcing, it might be tempting to put the archive function and the physical archive in another country. Consideration should be given to how vulnerable that country is to political instability and potentially war.

Natural disaster-related risk factors

Fires, floods, tornadoes, hurricanes, earthquakes, tsunamis, and sink holes occur all too often. If your archive needs to survive for decades, you must consider even the potential occurrence of the worst flood experienced in the last 100 years.

The location of an important archive needs to be in a safe building that can withstand any expected natural event without risk. This could mean putting the archive in a different site than the one where the objects originate.

Another technique is to duplicate (or triplicate, or more) the archive. This is easy for data and not so easy for physical objects. However, physical objects (paintings, sculptures, and the like) can be photographed to allow at least some aspects to be remembered in case the original is lost.

Erosion-related risk factors

An archivist needs to consider the possibility of erosion of the archived objects during the life of the retention period.

Physical erosion can include exposure to air, sunlight, humidity, radiation, or even sound waves. For example, air might expose an object to rusting.

If you're planning to keep your archive in outer space (such as a time box sent from Earth), you need to consider the exposure to your archive of various forms of radiation, meteorites, or just plain space junk.

Like anything else, media has shelf life, too. Tapes are generally considered good for seven years; CDs for 20. Many retention requirements are much longer than this, so a policy of recopying the data to new media on a periodic basis must be implemented. For safety, the period that it is allowed to rest on one surface should not be more than half of the manufacturer's stated shelf life. Some enterprises want archives recopied every year, just to be safe. Don't forget that backup copies need to be recopied as well. Since these might exist on a different media type (for example, disk for archive, tape for backup), the policy can differ for the backups.

The termite story   Okay, here I have to tell my termite story—a true story. As a young U.S. Navy officer in the late 1960s, I was in charge of the data processing department of a large naval air station in Hawaii. We did business applications: payroll, accounting, inventory control, and so on. All the data was stored on punched cards.

When a fiscal year ended (always June 30 for the government), we boxed up the cards we wanted to keep for the previous year, piled them on a pallet or two, and put them in a warehouse without air conditioning. This was our database archive.

One day I got a request from HQ to produce a report comparing costs by department for the prior five years. I grabbed a sailor and went to the warehouse to retrieve the punched cards I needed to complete the request. When I pulled the first box from one of the piles, the entire pile imploded inward into a cloud of dust. Upon examination, the entire interior of the pile of cards had been consumed by termites. No data, no report. Not good for Jack.

There are a lot of lessons in this story about how *not* to build an archive.

Loss of meaning   Another form of erosion has to do with understanding the content of the data. We tend to store data in the form in which it exists at the time of archiving. This presumes that all interpretation of the bits of data will be supportable in the future, but this is not always true.

Data is stored using encoding schemes described in code pages. We are all familiar with EBCDIC and ASCII coding—still the most popular forms around. Yet as we speak, these are being replaced by Unicode. In the near future, the use of EBCDIC and ASCII will stop and generic data-viewing programs won't know what they are. This can have the effect of rendering archived data unintelligible. This has already happened with some of the old 7-bit encoding schemes used on computers retired from use only a few years ago.

The same is true of encodings of images or soundtracks. Encoding standards change from time to time and older ones eventually get retired from use. Archives that retain data in older formats are at risk.

This implies one of two remedies: (1) maintaining reader application programs for all formats stored in the archive as long as needed or (2) transforming data to newer formats when standards change. The first approach is dangerous because often these programs depend on operating system versions to execute, which in turn might depend on particular hardware to run. You could end up having your archive become the national museum of computing platforms. Since data-encoding standard upgrades are always totally inclusive of older standards, the second approach is the more reasonable. However, the trick is knowing when you need to employ it.

If you think about erosion of the ability to understand archive objects, think about sand scripts and stone carvings from ancient Egyptians or Mayans. These ancients were recording facts for future generations (archiving) in a language that they understood. These languages, often encoded in pictorial form, became lost in time, leading archeologists to speculate as to what was originally meant.

Archive mismanagement

Another thing to protect against is loss of information due to archive mismanagement, and two of them are singled out here: lost in the shuffle and loss of authenticity.

Lost in the shuffle   You can have a robust archive program clicking along for several years and then, because of organizational changes, the whole thing gets lost or at least out of control. The types of organizational changes I refer to are reorganizations, acquisitions, data center consolidation, and outsourcing. Whenever the business organization responsible for an archive changes in any way, careful steps must be mapped out and followed to ensure continuity of its archives.

Loss of authenticity   Loss of authenticity refers to a failure to maintain audit trails on actions against objects in the archive, failure to set up the archive to ensure that it is managed by only authorized staff, or practices that alter the content of data to facilitate processing.

This last point is a common failing. Whenever a standard DBMS is used for the archive, a tendency to modify data in the archive to account for changes in data structures in the operational environment basically diminishes the authenticity of the original data. This is done because the DBMS being used is not capable of holding and processing data with multiple data structure definition versions.

A loss of authenticity protection of data erodes its usefulness in defending your enterprise in investigations and lawsuits.

3.9.3 Determining Requirements for Making Archive Objects Accessible

Determining where the archive will be located has to do with the potential users of the archive and how they will use it.

Make a list of all potential user types. This could be a small group of very trusted users or a large group consisting of everyone in the world. For example, public archives are open to anyone. You would want these archives located in major cities with easy access. On the other hand, corporate archives are very private and access will be very limited and controlled.

Once you know the archive's potential users, you need to indicate how they will view the archived objects. Will they be able to pick them up and handle them, move them to another room, move them offsite? Or will they be required to view them only from a distance and in a controlled way? The answer has a large impact on the design of the archive place.

You also need to determine what equipment you will need for users to gain access to the archive data. Do you need microfiche readers, PCs with viewing applications installed, copiers, or printers? Do you need special security, such as controlled access rooms with room monitors?

Lawsuit discovery processes today often want data delivered to them in electronic form. This implies that the archive should have the ability to copy data to other databases or build load input files to allow the external law firm employees access to the archive data through only this indirect form. Thus the user is an external law firm but the access method is to provide electronic media with data of interest copied to it. This implies that the archive have an assigned staff person who can generate such extracts.

3.9.4 **Requirements for the Archive Location**

After you have thought about these things and have a pretty good idea of what you need, you then design the archive location in detail. You need to determine the capacity needed as well as other factors described in this section.

Capacity needed For physical objects such as machines, paintings, old PCs, or paper documents, you need to estimate the physical size needed for holding all the archive objects. I worked in a building shared by a mortgage company once and I could not believe the amount of physical paper documents they saved on a regular basis. They were trucking out piles every week. I don't know how much room they needed in their archive, but it certainly must have been large.

For electronic data you need to determine how it will be stored. Will you use disk devices, storage subsystems (SANs), magnetic tape, or something else? How much of each will you need? How many machines will you need that are dedicated to storing and managing the archive?

Location types Location types can be listed by form and by geographical location. Form choices can include such things as a building, a bunker, a drawer at home, a safe deposit box, computer disks, salt mines, or a time capsule. Give careful consideration to capacity, security, and access.

Finally, you need to figure out where to put the archive. Should it be at the corporate HQ, an offsite location, in another country?

Cost of options Once you have settled on lists for the form and place, you need to consider the cost of each option. Construction costs, rental costs, air conditioning, light control, security services, and any other factors need to be considered. Make sure that an attempt to limit cost does not compromise the requirements of your archive.

One place or multiple places For electronic archives, you need to consider adopting multiple locations where copies of the data will be stored. For electronic data this is a possibility that should not be ignored since it adds valuable layers of protection. Be sure that the locations are geographically disbursed enough to achieve total safety from the physical risks outlined earlier.

A multiple-location archive solution should not depend on one location to function. For example, don't simply duplicate the data, also duplicate the control information, the metadata—everything. This way if a physical disaster occurs, your backup sites can operate as a primary site automatically. If you are unable to access or interpret the stored data, your backup site could become worthless.

A physical object archive can be set up in multiple locations and the objects divided among them. That way a disaster in one location would not cause all the objects to be lost. The common practice of museums loaning artifacts out for exhibit to other places accomplishes this goal in a different but effective way.

3.10 **DETERMINE OPERATIONAL PROCESSES NEEDED**

After you have determined what you are going to keep, how long, where, and how you are going to protect it, you need to design the operational steps. This is an important part of the archive design process. The other parts are useless if you or your organization are not going to execute in accordance with the rules defined previously.

So, what process definitions do you need?

- Process for identifying objects ready to be moved
- Process for removing objects from the operational environment
- Process for preparing objects for storage in the archive
- Process for putting objects into the archive
- Process for making objects available for access
- Process for identifying objects to be discarded from the archive
- Process for discarding the objects from the archive

Identifying objects ready to be moved to the archive   You defined the policy for identifying ready-to-move objects in an earlier step. For the process definition, you need to specify who is going to execute this task and how often. Will it be done once a year, once a day, or once every minute? Will it be done through a computer program, by a person, by a committee?

For archiving electronic data, this can be a batch job that is managed by a job scheduler. If this is the case, there must be a process of ensuring that the job executes when it is supposed to and, if it does not run successfully, to diagnose the reason for the failure and take corrective actions.

Removing objects from the operational environment   I distinguish the process for identifying objects ready to be moved from the process of actually moving them, since they are distinctly separate acts. In many cases these processes are executed simultaneously, as in computer programs that do archiving. However, for physical objects the steps may be done at different times and by different people. For example, a museum might have a committee meet twice a year to review candidates for items to be placed in the museum. Once they have done this, the museum staff then goes about acquiring ownership of the objects.

For databases this step must take into consideration integrity controls to ensure that system failures do not cause data to be lost (removed from the operational environment but not placed in the archive) or the inverse of data getting duplicated (put into the archive but not deleted from the operational databases).

Preparing objects for archive storage   You need to define a process for preparing objects for the long time they will be spending in the archive. Such functions as data transformation, making copies, applying protective coating, or other means of preparation must be documented. Who is going to do this, materials they will need, how soon after extraction this will be done, and what records should be created and kept to document the event should all be put in writing.

Putting objects into the archive   Putting objects into the archive might require transport to another location, possibly making space for the new objects, or other activities. The process definition should include the integrity and security protections needed to execute this step. Certainly for valuable physical objects, special care should be taken to provide adequate security en route.

For electronic data this is also true. There have been reported instances of data being lost in transit where the data was transported by physical tapes and just "fell off the truck." This excuse does not fly in court.

A computer-to-computer exchange should also be protected, if needed, through such means as encryption on the wire or backups and restart capability in case something goes wrong in the process of sending the data. This step also includes making backups and updating inventories of what is in the archive.

Making objects available for access   The process or processes that will be instituted whereby authorized people can gain access to the archive must be very carefully drafted and approved. This can entail setting access hours, doing background checks of candidate viewers, establishing sign-in/sign-out procedures, and whatever else might be appropriate.

Identifying objects to be discarded   A process needs to be drafted for determining which objects in the archive are ready to be discarded. The frequency of execution, who will execute, and how to monitor and document whether it happens or not should all be included.

Discarding objects   After objects have been identified for discard, a separate process needs to be in place for executing the discard actions. This can consist of throwing things in a dumpster as they are being identified. It can include selling at auction physical items that you are no longer interested in keeping but that still have value. For data, the process should include electronic shredding of primary and backup copies of the data for the discarded objects.

3.11 DETERMINE NECESSARY ADMINISTRATIVE PROCESSES

At this point you have most of the archive designed. One other step is to design the administration that needs to go along with it. Although this may seem unimportant, it can in fact become a critical factor in defending your actions in an investigation or adding legitimacy to the archive.

Security administration Over time a large number of people may be involved in the design and operational steps. You need a clear definition of how people get into and out of the process. How do you select people for committees? What do you do when an archive analyst leaves the organization? How do people get access authority to computers used in the process?

All your work can be compromised if you do not have strong security control. This is true not only when you execute processes but also in how you assign and revoke authorizations to individuals or organizations.

Usually you think of only the people who will be accessing the archive and overlook those who are involved in archive planning, archive design, archive operation, and archive administration. They should have specific security requirements defined as appropriate for their roles.

Activity logs and inventories All the archive operational steps that are executed should have activity records of when, where, and by whom, as well as results. This information should be logged and maintained as long as the archive exists.

You might need to maintain detailed inventories of what you have in the archive. This information should be used for periodic checks to make sure you are not missing something. Inventories should be separate from the content description. They are used to quickly assess what is in the archive. Inventories for electronic data are just as important as those for physical objects. Having an external list of the applications, the data content, and archive storage files as well as backup files constitutes an electronic archive inventory.

Process audits You might want to have an outside organization audit your procedures and activities on an annual basis and recommend ways to improve the operation of the archive. This is truly a must for highly sensitive archives.

You might also need to develop training programs for individuals to undergo before they can work with the archive. Reading this book would be a great place to begin.

3.12 DETERMINE REQUIRED CHANGE PROCESSES

As in all aspects of life, changes occur and we must adapt to them. Archiving systems are no exception.

Requirement changes The archiving system design started with identifying requirements. Requirements can and will change. New laws will be passed;

corporations will change their policies. These changes can result in dropping the archive entirely or most likely extending the retention period. Changes in privacy laws can alter the way you manage security or even change the form of data in an archive.

When a change is implemented, some objects might fall through the cracks. For example, if you had a policy of discarding objects after five years and the government changes the requirement to 10 years, you will have a gap of data that was discarded under the old policy but would still be retained under the new policy. This data cannot be retrieved; it is gone forever. Most law changes are not retroactive, so this is generally not a problem. However, it is *very* important to document that this gap exists in the data, and why.

Object changes   In the database world, the data models for an object change all the time. Value domains expand, new data columns are created, wholesale redesigning of an application's data structures can happen. The organization's business units are not going to freeze data structure definitions just so the archive can have consistent data objects.

When you archive data for changing applications, data from one period will be different from data from a different period. These differences must be acknowledged and documented. It could be invaluable later to explain why differences in data structures exist.

To create an archive that contains everything needed to explain the data saved, it is imperative that you completely integrate application database change control procedures with archive change control procedures. Please read that sentence again—it is vitally important.

Operational changes   You might need to make adjustments to the operational aspects of the archive based on experience. You could need more capacity. You could need to strengthen security based on attempts to compromise or steal objects. The archiving system should be monitored all the time to find ways to make it more efficient and more secure.

Any changes to the archive system design need to be documented and preserved to justify differences in the archive objects when they are viewed in future years.

SUMMARY

After reading this chapter you should be able to think like an archivist. Armed with this methodology you should be able to design all sorts of archives. It is important for you to follow the steps. Do not omit any one of them. Failure to archive properly can result in lost or damaged objects. You generally cannot recover from the damage caused by mistakes. The archivist must be diligent in operational control as well as in planning.

From the discussion in this chapter you should realize that an archive is not a place but rather the opposite. For some the term *archive* might suggest things placed at rest and forgotten. However, an archive is a system requiring diligent execution of steps over and over again to collect, preserve, protect, and make data available for use.

If you read no further in this book, you would be a better archivist for having read this chapter. You would be sensitized to many issues you must face as you practice the art of archiving. The remaining chapters concentrate exclusively on the topic of database archiving. Along the way we'll apply the basic principles and considerations described in this chapter.

Components of a Database Archiving System

Now that we have covered the general concepts of archiving as it applies to the physical as well as the electronic world, we are ready to shift our focus to database archiving. Some of the concepts presented from here on could well apply to other forms of archiving, but again, our concentration will be on database archiving.

Figure 4.1 presents the basic parts of a fully designed and ready-to-use database archiving solution. Any of the components can be implemented as a procedure, a set of executable scripts, or a computer program. This chapter emphasizes that each component is necessary and the form it takes can vary depending on a particular implementation approach (or budget).

Understanding this component structure will be important in reading the rest of this book, so let's get started and introduce you to the components you need to create a database archiving system.

4.1 THE DATABASE ARCHIVING ORGANIZATION

The archiving organization is the starting point and obviously the most important component. Database archiving is a complex topic and requires an intense focus on the problem over the course of many years. It cannot become the part-time job of a database administrator or the province of junior staff. It requires a robust charter, clear mandate, qualified staff, and support of management.

The building block of the organization is the *mandate*. I like mandates. If management tells me to start a new project, I always want to establish a mandate that spells out precisely what the problem is that I am asked to tackle, the constraints I have to work with, the relationships I am allowed to create with other organizations, and the desired outcome.

After you have established the mission through a clearly defined and agreed-on mandate, you need to assemble *people*. Initially you can assign a team to study the problem to determine what people skills are needed for the long term. Pay careful attention to this topic, since the data archivist serves many

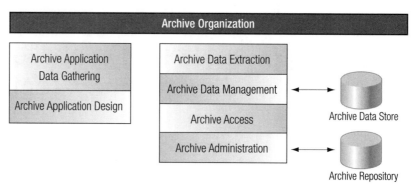

FIGURE 4.1

Components of a database archiving solution.

masters and will require many diverse skills. The archivist must have solid technical skills, organizational skills, and people skills.

You need to determine where in your enterprise's organization the archiving function belongs. This is a key component because it can make or break the project. You need organizational focus (meaning that you and your boss will be dedicated to these tasks) and support (meaning that you need the staff, funding, and organizational clout to get your job done). It is imperative to have organizational focus so that other priorities will not trump the importance of this function from time to time. Support is of equal importance. You will have to work with many other departments, get chunks of their time, and get their willingness to do their parts in the process.

After you have all these things in place, you need to set some *objectives*. For example, you need to decide what the separate database archiving application projects are, prioritize them, and establish what you need to satisfy each of them. Some objectives might include things like minimum disruption of operational system performance, use cheap storage for inactive data, become independent of IMS, and so on.

Obviously you will need a *budget*. In Chapter 2 we touched on the likelihood that you will probably get all your costs back at some point through more efficient operational systems and savings in hardware. No one will believe this unless you document the relevant metrics to prove it. In the meantime you will need funding to get started and to get to the point where the archiving system is paying for itself.

4.2 ARCHIVE APPLICATION DATA GATHERING

After you are sufficiently staffed and have some money to spend, you need to pick your first database archiving application and get started. You will need to take time to gather data about the application for which you are building an archiving solution. This is a time-consuming and often frustrating task. You need a lot of structure to accomplish this goal.

You might have several database archiving applications to address, especially if archiving is a new function for your enterprise. The applications you identify should be prioritized to determine which one or ones to proceed with first.

You need a formal way of identifying information, gathering that information, validating it, enhancing it, and storing it for later use. You also need mechanisms to ensure that you are informed when this information changes. The information on which your design is based is critical to the success of this endeavor.

The information you need to gather includes requirement sources, database topologies, database structure diagrams, metadata of database entities, information on data quality, and more. This topic will be covered in greater detail in later chapters.

4.3 ARCHIVE APPLICATION DESIGN

After you have gathered everything about the archiving application, you need to build an archiving application design. The design has two components: data design and policy design.

Data design encompasses topics such as deciding what specific rows, records, and segments you will have to move to the archive and possibly what fields within them. It also includes strategies on how related data is handled when a unit of data is moved. It covers how data might be transformed—both transformation of individual data value representations and transformation of data object structure definitions.

Policy design involves establishing rules for when data objects get moved as well as addressing what happens to the data in the operational systems and what happens when data objects are discarded from the archive. It can also include rules for managing data in the archive, such as backup requirements, storage cost objectives, and test requirements for ensuring that everything is working.

The design process probably commands a formal design tool. You can decide for yourself what computer support you will need for this tool when you do your first application. After you have completed reading later chapters of this book, you will be in a better position to evaluate design tools. Some of these tools will be generic data management tools that were not built with database archiving in mind. Others will be more specific to database archiving. There are not yet many of those around.

4.4 ARCHIVE DATA EXTRACTION

Archiving application data gathering and archiving application design are design components, whereas data extraction is an action component. *Data extraction* refers to the computer programs that will search the operational databases, find data ready to be archived based on the archive extract policy, send the data to the archive data store component, and either delete data from the operational system or mark it as having been archived.

In addition to the actual extract process, this component deals with operational issues such as scheduling runs, the impact on normal operations of running archive extract processes, data integrity, and recovery from failure conditions. Archive extract executions can have an enormous impact on operational environments. They must be designed and implemented with care.

4.5 ARCHIVE DATA MANAGEMENT

Another action component, archive data management, will receive data from the archive data extract component. It will reformat the data to match the archive data design and keep it in the data store that is being used for the archive. It should also provide callable API routines to retrieve data from the archive store.

Topics applicable to this component are structure of the archive store as a data repository, integrity and recovery management of the data, storage rules to achieve cost goals, and efficiency in retrieving data.

The issue of efficiency is critical to this component since it will handle extreme volumes of data. Efficiency covers many areas, including storage efficiency, load efficiency, and access efficiency.

Management of the archive store is just as much a continuing data management task as managing any of the operational databases.

4.6 ARCHIVE ACCESS

This component satisfies user requests for data from the archive store. It should have capabilities of retrieving data in multiple ways. It should support ad hoc queries, bulk data offloading from the archive, and presentation of metadata for the data.

A basic assumption of database archiving is that the data will outlive the applications that generated it, the database systems they were created in, and the operational systems on which the processes run. This means that the archiving system must be capable of satisfying all user requirements for data directly from the archive.

Archive access should not directly read the archive data store files but should use the API support provided by the archive data management component.

Archive access also involves security issues such as granting and revoking privileges for potential users of archive data and checking authorization rights on all attempts to use the data.

4.7 **ARCHIVE ADMINISTRATION**

Archive administrative functions can make or break an archiving project. In later chapters we'll cover several administrative topics that need to be planned and executed. These include security authorization management, application documentation, data inventories, access audit trails, execution logs, and archive audits.

Archive administration also includes maintaining the *archive repository*, a database that contains all the information about the archive. It does not contain the archive data that is put in the archive data store. Every archive project should have an archive repository. Storing the data without knowing where it came from, how it got there, and what it means negates the entire archiving process.

SUMMARY

All database archiving systems have the same components. They might be implemented in different ways and be identified by different names, but they are all necessary.

An archiving group requires a methodology for accomplishing tasks in a systematic and repeatable way that consistently yields successful results. The components described in this section are needed to support the methodology, making it imperative that they are clearly understood and implemented.

The foundation set by this chapter makes you ready to explore various factors that dictate the need for database archiving projects.

Establishing a Database Archiving Project

The following chapters explore how database archiving applications come about, how to collect and organize people and resources needed to tackle them, and the kinds of information necessary to design the archiving application. We'll also discuss how to set the strategy for a specific database archiving application. Realize that not all database archiving applications will have the same strategies nor use the same tools to accomplish them. The strategies must be tailored to the specific needs of the application and the tools must be chosen appropriately.

CHAPTER

Origins of a Database Archiving Application

5

Database archiving applications do not simply appear out of thin air. In reality a problem emerges for which database archiving is a solution. The problem comes first, followed by recognition of the problem; this then leads to a determination that database archiving is a solution to the problem. Finally, an effort to implement a database archiving solution emerges. This progression is shown in Figure 5.1.

Not all database applications have problems that lead to database archiving as a solution. The scope of those that do is usually restricted to a specific application or a specific unit of data within an application. An application usually belongs to a single business area. Database archiving is a business problem, and the responsibility usually belongs to the business unit.

Many of these problems, each with their own unique traits, may exist simultaneously and may result in multiple parallel efforts going on across IT at the same time.

You do not apply database archiving to *all* data in an enterprise. Nor do you craft a specific database archiving solution that would apply equally to all applications that need to be archived. Each archiving application determines its own requirements and builds an appropriate solution. They cannot all be the same because their requirements will be different.

An archiving organization A centralized database archiving organization may evolve in an enterprise from multiple parallel efforts. This means that the enterprise has established database archiving as a common function that deserves a common practice and is to be managed separately from the applications. We have seen this already with database administration, storage management, security management, and other functions.

This does not mean that the enterprise will use a common solution for all problems but rather that it will bring to bear a common set of experts, methodologies, and tools to each problem to create a consistent and professional response to all database archiving problems.

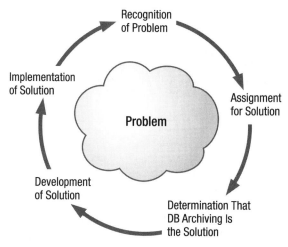

FIGURE 5.1

Origins of a database archiving application.

This topic will be considered in greater detail in Chapter 6. For now, we'll concentrate on the origins of an archiving application and explore the process of organizing your efforts to solve the application problem later on.

5.1 PROBLEMS THAT LEAD TO DATABASE ARCHIVING SOLUTIONS

Database archiving does not generate new operational applications nor does it generate new data; it solves problems that emerge with existing or prior operational applications. The applications are already in place before database archiving is or can be implemented.

All archiving applications are driven by one or more motivators. Chapter 3 covered motivators for archiving in general. The following list singles out and tailors the motivators that apply to database archiving:

- Operational databases have too much data, causing performance problems.
- Operational databases have too much data, causing administration problems.
- Operational databases have too much data, causing high disk storage costs.
- New requirements are levied that mandate longer retention periods.
- Applications are retired, leaving a problem with what to do with the old data.
- Applications are retired, leaving a problem with what to do with the old systems.
- New requirements are levied, mandating more security of data.
- New requirements are levied, mandating more protection of data authenticity.
- Lawsuits happen in which the enterprise is not able to meet e-discovery requests.

Motivators are always irritants to the operational folks. This is usually evident because the database administration group is complaining, the storage group is complaining, the data management group is complaining, the security group is demanding, or the compliance committee is demanding: Noise is being generated and it is getting louder. This can be new noise, or it could have been going on for some time.

5.2 RECOGNIZING PROBLEMS

What is noteworthy about the preceding list is that often none of the problems originate within the business group that owns the application or the data. They originate somewhere else. However, they won't be solved until the business group agrees that the problem exists and is willing to take it on to find a solution.

Some of the problems we've noted are purely internal IT. They have to do with managing operational system performance and cost. It is tempting to throw the problem to the database administration and storage management groups and let them fashion a solution. This is generally not a good idea. They are not aware of application issues that can influence a solution. For example, frequency of access to older data could dictate one solution over another.

This means that the database administration or storage management groups might recognize a problem but not have the authority, skills, budget, or application knowledge to fashion and implement a good solution.

The business group that will ultimately hold responsibility for the solution could be completely unaware of the problem. They need to be brought into the process early in order for a chance at a viable solution.

A second source of problems stems from new requirements coming from outside IT. This is a major source of new problems for business groups and includes requirements emerging from new laws and regulations and from the legal department dealing with the cost, efficiency, and legitimacy of satisfying e-discovery requests against older data.

The key to recognition is getting the right group involved as early in the process as possible. Even if the legal department knows about a data retention requirement, there is no guarantee that the group ultimately responsible for ensuring that the data is retained is aware of it.

It always amazes me how most enterprises lack sufficient communication to get problems to the right place so that they can be solved. IT departments are known for excessive compartmentalization of jobs and functions to achieve expert capabilities, which ends up creating barriers between groups.

Now more than ever, communication among IT groups, business units, and the legal department is absolutely essential.

Problems emerging from disasters Sometimes the need to archive data emerges from the consequences of not having archived in the past. For example, a lawsuit is filed against the enterprise, and staff are unable to find the data or they cannot defend the authenticity of the data. After losing the lawsuit, the enterprise could suddenly appreciate the importance of proper data management throughout the data life cycle. Too bad they didn't think of this before.

Problems emerging from compliance audits   A corporate audit of best practices in managing important data could certainly warrant the need for a database archiving application. These types of audits are already occurring in many companies.

For example, a company could initiate an audit of data security and discover that important data left in operational databases is dangerously susceptible to improper changes by employees. These employees might have other, legitimate reasons for update access to this data. If retaining the authenticity of data is important, data can be archived earlier in the life cycle to avoid unwanted updates.

The perfect storm   It is not unusual for multiple problems to arrive on your doorstep at the same time. For example, lengthening retention requirements could occur while bulging databases are affecting operational performance and at the same time that attempts to access previously saved data fail. One person aware of one problem might not be aware of the other problems. Though that person might be able to cope with the specific problem, a more global change needs to be made.

5.2.1 External Requirements

External requirements come about through changes to laws, regulations, or company policy. Making a connection between the change and a database application is not always obvious, but it is important to make.

An enterprise should have a process for making this connection. The department responsible for identifying and studying new laws and regulations should make it a regular practice to review new requirements with IT or business group staff because the legal expert alone might not be able to make the connection. Periodic meetings would allow the legal department to review what has been done to implement best practices around previously identified requirements.

The corporate compliance committee, corporate legal department, IT compliance officer, or data governance officer should lead such a process. In fact, a review of changes managed by these groups, the business groups, and IT staff should be included in a compliance checklist.

5.2.2 Trolling for Problems

An inverse approach is to have a person or team in either IT or the business groups look for problems. This is not likely to happen unless an archiving practice is already established at the company and one or more applications are already actively archiving. The senior data archivist would likely own this responsibility.

After a single database archiving application is complete and people see the dynamics in action, the motivators will be recognized more easily.

Trolling for archiving opportunities should not be done to artificially create work for the archive group. It should be done to make the enterprise more compliant or more efficient or to reduce operational costs.

5.3 ASSIGNMENT OF PROBLEMS FOR INITIAL STUDY

After a problem has been recognized, it is imperative that the right person be assigned to develop a solution. That individual will most likely be a data management expert within the business group that owns the data. At this point the data archivist is not necessarily the appropriate person, since at this stage database archiving might not be the appropriate solution to the problem.

It is probably worthwhile to have several people from multiple disciplines become trained in basic database archiving principles and archiving's potential to solve problems. Remember that it's a new technology, so they are probably not familiar with the concepts or archiving's value.

5.4 INITIAL PROBLEM STUDY COMPONENTS

A problem is earmarked for a database archiving solution after you have carefully explored the scope and parameters of the issues and considered the dynamic that a database archiving solution would have.

An exploratory effort should be the first step. A data management expert familiar with the business application should be assigned as the "owner" of the problem. This individual should request input from other appropriate staff.

5.4.1 Scoping the Problem

A problem statement should be crafted to begin the initial review. The statement should include the specific problem that originated the study, where it came from, and any other parameters involved. For example, a problem statement might look like this:

> *A new law, USXXXXX, stipulates that data collected on employees during interviews must be retained for five years after the interview or, in the case where the applicant is hired, for five years after their employment is terminated. The legal department contact for this law is Linda Salfisberg.*

This is a very precise statement about retention but very vague about what data to include. For example, should it include the applicant's formal application document? Would an electronic version of it suffice? Do you need both? What about correspondence from the applicant? Should it include data created during interviews? If the legal department has an opinion about what specific documents or elements of data should be included, this information should be added to the problem statement.

Scoping the problem also identifies the organizations that are affected, business processes that are involved, and databases that contain the targeted data. All departments that have a stake in the problem should be included.

5.4.2 Establishing Basic Requirements

The initial review should also include determining the goals of a solution. If operational performance is an issue, the scoping section should indicate what the target performance parameters might be. If protecting data is an issue, what level of protection is called for?

In addition to getting a rough indication of what constitutes a solution, it is also important to get agreement from the stakeholders on this point. You should identify in the documentation who agreed to the problem statement requirements in case there is a dispute later on.

You might need to collect some data for some of the studies. If the problem involves disk storage cost or excessive amounts of data, you'll need the amount of data in the database (in terms of byte footprint and/or number of logical records) plus the amount of new data created each month plus the amount of data retired each month. Disk storage cost numbers should also be acquired if that is an issue. The difference between disk storage costs for keeping data online versus archiving it to lower-cost storage devices could be important.

Another factor that is important to database archiving decisions is the length of time in the database that data is open to updates and the length of time after that during which there is a reasonable expectation of the information being used.

It is important to collect all the data, no matter what the reason for doing the study. This is because the final answer can incorporate more aspects than is implied by the triggering motivator for the study.

Another good question to ask in this phase of the process is the history of the application and any plans for significant future changes. For example, it makes a big difference if there is a plan to replace the application with another packaged application in the next six months.

Asking about history will help determine how some of the existing data may relate to stages in the data life cycle. Some good questions to ask include: What is the oldest data in the current database? When did you start using the current application? Is there data lying around somewhere from a previous version of the application? If so, how old is it? What format is it in? Are there applications available that can read that data?

It is important to determine whether a process already exists for archiving data for this application. If a process does exist, it should be described completely, since often a group thinks it is archiving although the process could have serious flaws, indicating that the old process should be disposed of and replaced with a more robust one. In fact, if there are no existing archiving practices using sound principles, it should always be assumed that flaws exist.

For example, if you are told that an archiving process is already in place and you discover that it consists of UNLOAD files dumped from databases and saved on tape, you can be assured that this system will not be able to return useful information when requested in future years. Some applications might be able to get by with ad hoc archiving practices if retention periods are short, but these so-called "solutions" collapse when retention times are extended to longer periods.

Remember to verify and document all the information you gather as you begin to establish a database archiving application.

5.4.3 **Establishing Archiving Application Goals**

The goals specific to each solution should be determined and documented as well. This can include goals such as reduction in operational database size, performance improvement targets, cost savings for disk storage, or preserving data while allowing applications or systems to be turned off.

Expectations should be verified with appropriate management. It might also be appropriate to get internal auditors to sign off on them if compliance factors are involved.

The expectations part is not a business case or return-on-investment statement. At this stage the solution is not available and therefore benefits cannot be quantified.

5.4.4 **Determining That Database Archiving Is Part of the Solution**

Do not assume that database archiving is always the solution to the problem you are trying to solve. The facts of each case should lead you to that conclusion. Archiving is an extra burden on the administration of an application and once started will consume time and money for years to come. If there are better solutions, use them.

For example, if the data volumes in the operational database are too large, thus seriously impeding effective application performance, moving data to a reference database might be the best answer, or if the data is simply no longer required it can be deleted.

In another example, where a data object is liable to be updated at any time in its life cycle, archiving is inappropriate. A better solution might be to split the operational database into multiple operational databases and have a means of federating them together when needed.

It might not be possible to determine absolutely whether database archiving is the right thing to do at this stage of the project. It also might be the case that the facts are not strong enough to support archiving and that more study is required.

5.5 DETERMINING THE BASIC STRATEGY FOR THE ARCHIVING APPLICATION

There are many strategy models to consider based on the way the application is employed within the enterprise. Strategies considered in this chapter are as follows:

- Simple, one-source strategy
- Distributed applications
- Parallel applications
- Retired applications

Let's explore each strategy in greater detail.

5.5.1 A Simple, One-Source Strategy

The simplest strategy and the one most assumed is to have all the data for the application in one operational database and then apply selection criteria against it on a periodic basis to find inactive data, remove it, and place it in the archive.

Figure 5.2 introduces a new term: *archiving stream*. Each time the archiving sweep is performed on the operational database, a unit of new data is created and placed in the archive. These archive units occur periodically; they are time ordered. An *archiving stream* is a sequence of archive units that contain data from the same selection criteria. This means that all the pieces of data in all the archive units are consistent in structure.

If the application consists of multiple business objects, it might have one archiving stream for all of them or multiple streams, each of which contain more business objects. For example, consider a banking loan application. There might be one archiving stream for loan payments and another for all other business objects. The loan payments can move to the archive in only a few months after the payment is made since they are simple transactions. The other objects

Application: Loan Archives

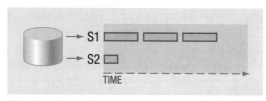

S1 = Loan Payments
S2 = Loan Documentation
FIGURE 5.2

Archiving view of a simple strategy.

remain in the operational database until the loan is closed and then all remaining objects are moved at once to the archive after some reasonable period of time. Hence, the application would have two archiving streams.

5.5.2 **Distributed Applications**

If your application has a distributed database structure in the operational world, you might need a more complex model. A *distributed database structure* means that the application is repeated within the enterprise for different business groups, with each instance having its own operational database. The application is the same but the data is not kept in one place. It is distributed over multiple operational databases.

This situation occurs frequently in large enterprises with multiple divisions or with operations in multiple countries. One example is the University of California system. It consists of nine campuses. The business applications are the same, but each campus operates separate data centers and has separate operational databases.

So, in this situation, the first question to ask is whether archiving is intended to cover all locations or just one. If the answer is just one, you use the simple strategy. If you are designing archiving for more than one of these locations, you need to decide whether each location has its own archive or whether the locations need to be merged into a single enterprise archive.

If each location maintains its own archive, you use the simple strategy approach but replicated x number of times. The administration of the archive function is more complex but the design is not. Two cases of distributed archiving strategy are presented in Figure 5.3.

5.5.3 **Parallel Applications**

Parallel applications present a case similar to distributed applications except that the different locations are using different data structures for the data. Most likely they are using different application programs for the same business function.

This situation occurs when different business units have the autonomy to develop their own applications, when business units are acquired through mergers and acquisitions, or when some units have moved to new applications and others have not (a timing issue).

In these cases you have to determine which locations you are archiving for: one, all, or just some of them. If you are archiving for more than one location and it involves more than one version of the application's data structures, you need to gather data and metadata separately for each location. Your archiving operations will produce multiple, parallel archive streams.

It is very difficult and generally unwise to try to combine the streams into a single archive store and format. Not only is it a complex data restructuring problem, it also takes the archive data too far from the original data values. This will

Application: Loan Archives

View #1

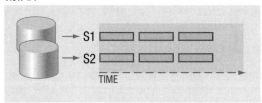

S1 = Loan Payments—North American Division
S2 = Loan Payments—Western Europe Division

View #1

S1 = Loan Payments—North American Division and Western Europe Division

FIGURE 5.3

Archiving view of a distributed application strategy.

diminish the authenticity of the archive in the sense that you might not be able to see what the original data looked like. In all probability you end up with multiple, parallel archive streams, as presented in Figure 5.4.

5.5.4 **Retired Applications**

It is not uncommon for data that was generated by an application no longer in use to be sitting around. The application might have undergone a major reengineering such as moving to another type of computer, operating system, or DBMS. It might have gone through a major data remodeling effort. It might have resulted from moving to a packaged application from an older application that was built in-house.

After the cutover to the new application, the question becomes what to do about the data being housed in the old database. In some cases the data is modified to fit the new application's data structures and loaded into the new operational database.

It is not uncommon to keep the old data in the old database instead of moving it to the new database. This may be necessitated by irresolvable differences in data structures. When this occurs, the solution for keeping the data is to keep it where it is and retain the older system and application in case the data is needed.

Application: Loan Archives

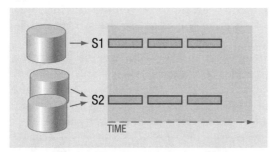

S1 = Loan Payments from North American SAP System
S2 = Loan Payments from Div X and Div Y Local Developed System

FIGURE 5.4

Archiving view of a parallel application strategy.

An alternative is to move all the old data into a database archive. Once in the archive, the data should become available to satisfy any need to access that data for the duration of its retention period.

When this is done, the archivist is most likely creating a new archive stream for the old data, since its data structure is most likely incompatible with any new data.

5.5.5 **Old Data in Active Databases**

We talked earlier about data sitting around in databases generated from retired applications; however, we often need to also consider old data for current applications.

A starting point   Is all data in the operational system eligible for archiving? Consider that there could be a point in time when data generated earlier is not needed and therefore can be deleted from the operational database without being moved to the archive. For example, if a retention period mandate has a stipulation that data generated from that point forward must comply with the new rule, you can ignore data generated earlier.

Data in UNLOAD files   The user might have removed data from the operational databases and placed it in UNLOAD files to lighten up operational systems while preserving inactive data. If this is done, that data should also be moved to the archive.

It is important to check the data format of each UNLOAD file to understand whether metadata changes were made that make the format of the unload files different from the operational data or different between successive UNLOAD files. This is often the case.

This data could be the starting point for the archive and might be the first archive unit in the archive stream to be continued with operational data, or it might be one or more independent archive streams based on structural differences.

Data in other archives Data might have been formally archived rather than moved to UNLOAD files. The archive could simply consist of a reference database in which the structure mirrors the operational database. The project leaders might want to capture this data in the archive as well, to give it more independence or more protection than it currently has.

If so, the strategy must include a plan to capture this data as well. This could involve moving data from one database archiving solution to another database archiving solution.

5.5.6 **Anticipation of Future Projects**

The strategy should also indicate the possibility of major changes to the application implementations, either known or anticipated in the future, and anticipate how they could affect the strategy.

Application changes Known plans to reengineer an application or to replace it with another application should be noted and studied to determine whether new archive streams will have to be engineered and how data created prior to the cut-over will be handled. This should become a part of planning all major application change introductions.

Application consolidation If a project exists that will consolidate either distributed or parallel application deployment into a single application using a single operational database, this fact needs to be noted and planned for.

When the consolidation occurs, one or more archive streams will be ended. Either one of them will continue to extend with data components coming from more sources, or a new archive stream will be started that reflects the consolidated implementation.

Merger and acquisition activities Mergers and acquisitions present special problems. Your enterprise is inheriting the database of other companies for the application in question. Most likely these will appear as parallel applications to the modeling done previously. If the previous company had retired applications or was archiving in some form, these things need to be accounted for as well. Eventually the inherited applications may be retired and operations consolidated into the mainstream application.

As you can see, all the strategy models can come into play when you pick up a new data center. The likelihood that both centers were using the same application solution with the same customization is nil.

Planning the archive response to a merger or acquisition should begin as soon as possible. Figure 5.5 shows how the strategy chart might look when you have many of these activities going on.

Application: Loan Archives

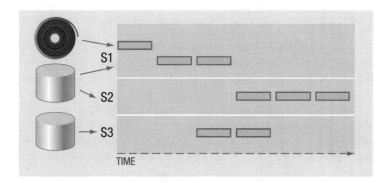

S1 = Loan Payments previously saved on tape backups: loaded into archive—6/15/07

S1 = Loan Payments begin archiving from operational system—6/16/07

S2 = Loan Payments begin archiving from new master system—01/01/08

S3 = Loan Payments from Div X Local System: replaced by Master System—3/15/08

FIGURE 5.5

Example of a complex application archive strategy.

5.6 **THE APPLICATION STRATEGY CHART**

An application archive strategy chart, similar to those shown in this chapter, should be generated and validated during the initial planning phase. It should be stored in the archive repository. It should be updated whenever any changes occur or are contemplated.

Archive users of the future will benefit from being able to tell how various archive streams came about and what business units contributed to the data stored in them.

SUMMARY

After reading this chapter, you should be aware that:

- Archiving is a response to a problem.
- Archiving is application specific; each solution can be different.
- Archiving applications can originate from many sources.
- The origin of a problem does not determine who gets to solve it.
- A study is necessary to gather important data for making decisions.
- Lots of people may participate in the study.

- The study needs to be documented.
- The decision to archive should occur late in the process.
- The decision should be based on facts that drive you there.

After a single database archiving application is completed successfully and placed in operation, people will see the dynamics in action. They will then be better able to recognize motivators, initiate a study, and make sound decisions.

Remember that building a strategy that identifies the scope of archiving for the application and the various archive streams will set the stage for the design work that follows. A good diagram of the archiving streams expected to be generated will be useful for anyone needing to understand the application's archive.

The archivist must consider all possible sources of data for the application and obtain approval as to which ones are to be archived and which ones are not. In the next chapter we will explore the resources required to put these plans into action.

CHAPTER

Resources Needed 6

After a careful study is completed and the decision is made to create a database archiving application, a team must be assembled and resources gathered to create the design and initiate implementation.

Not all the resources will be needed; in fact, some of them will be determined only as the project moves along. The resources typically required are:

- People
- Authority
- Education
- Archive server
- Software tools
- Disk storage

6.1 **PEOPLE**

Designing and implementing a database archiving application does not require an army of technical experts. However, it does require participation from a lot of people.

6.1.1 **In-House Participants**

To start with, you need a *department* to assume responsibility. This is typically an IT department charged with data management responsibilities, possibly dedicated to a single business area or application.

The project needs a *manager*. This is usually an individual responsible for many aspects of data management rather than someone dedicated solely to archiving.

The key person for any database archiving project is the lead archive expert. For our purposes we will refer to this individual as the *archive analyst*. This person is responsible for executing and overseeing all aspects of the project and should have legitimate credentials for working on this type of project. Education in database archiving, data management principles, data modeling, and related areas is a prerequisite. A description of a database archive analyst is presented in Appendix C.

The position of archive analyst should *not* be a part-time job. This job is too important; it involves a great deal of effort and dedication to get it right. When this responsibility is assigned to a person as a part-time job, there is the likelihood that there's another job that the person will recognize as his or her "real" job. This mistake has been made many times by assigning archiving responsibility to a database administrator or to a storage management staff member. This will never work. It could work if the person was a database administrator and was changing career paths and accepted a full-time assignment to database archiving.

A subject matter expert, referred to as an *application analyst*, is also required. This could be the same person as the archive analyst, or it could be a part-time assignment for someone else in the business unit who fully understands the data and business processes that are the target of the project. Note that the primary person is the archive analyst and *not* the application analyst. It is much more important that the archive analyst bring to the table expertise in designing and implementing archive applications. The application analyst will provide the application-specific guidance that will make the project work. If the application analyst is also the primary lead, the risk is too high that errors in design or implementation will be made.

A number of other roles provide incidental assistance in the prosecution of the project. These are all part-time contributors and need not be included in all day-to-day activities. These roles include the *database administrator,* who manages the operational system for the application, and a *storage analyst,* who handles the operational storage requirements as well as any new storage devices that will be needed to store the archive files. It is a good idea to include someone from the *application development* team responsible for the application. They can be very useful in interpreting metadata (or generating it) or in coordinating changes to archive design with changes in application data structures or content.

Other individuals responsible for aspects of data management of the application should clearly be involved as well. This would include a *data architect* for the application and a *data steward,* if one exists. Such folks are a source of good candidates to recruit as data archive analyst professionals. They have an ideal background to move into this role. Again, however, do not assume that you can simply assign archiving to their plate without making it a full-time endeavor. Depending on the application, involvement of someone from the *IT compliance office* or the *legal department* might also be appropriate.

It is a good idea to organize the players into a committee that will meet on a periodic basis—say, once a week. They can all become more knowledgeable about the process and technology if they're participating as a group. The makeup of the archive project committee is shown in Figure 6.1.

Archive Project Committee Members	
Full Time	**Part Time**
Archive Project Manager	Database Administrator
Archive Analyst	Storage Administrator
Application Analyst	Application Developer
	Data Architect
	Data Steward
	IT Compliance Officer
	Legal Department Representation

FIGURE 6.1

Archive project committee.

The committee could also be used to audit archiving activities after archiving operations begin.

Consulting services Some companies might choose to outsource the archiving project (specifically, the archive analyst function) to a consulting firm. This is not a bad idea if the company has no experience in database archiving and no one on staff who is schooled in the technology. If the consulting firm has a good track record working on such projects, using their experience could accelerate the project and improve the outcome at the same time.

You might already have been using consultants in the application business area, thus making them a logical choice for the application analyst role or other roles we've described. They might have worked on such projects as designing and building data warehouses, doing data quality assessments, reengineering applications, or migrating applications to new software or platforms. Such people would have a clear understanding of the application and the data, which would give them a head start on your archiving project.

6.2 AUTHORITY

Authority is a second resource required to do the job. This might seem obvious, but given the typical organizational complexity of most IT departments today, it is necessary to acquire the authority to proceed with your archiving project. I have seen projects in which an archive analyst is assigned but has no authority over people's time or money to acquire tools; as a result, nothing gets done.

The archive analyst must have the authority to *demand participation* of people. This might seem harsh, but too often we hear the phrase "I don't have time for that." This attitude should not be tolerated. Helping to complete the project requires prioritizing activities of all the players, full-time or part-time. Their managers must sign up to provide the help where and when needed.

The archive project needs a *budget*, since money is the ultimate authority. Financial resources are needed to fund full-time staff and tools as well as travel, education, disk space, and the like.

The archive analyst and possibly others will need *authorization access* to operational systems. They might also need to create and work with a test environment that includes a *snapshot* of the operational databases. This test database is probably not one to be shared with other application development activities. It should be dedicated to database archiving design and verification, since many of the functions will require specific data values to trigger events. Using someone else's test database would normally result in not having all the conditions needed in the data to exercise the archiving processes. The other group might object to creating data with dates that are 25 years old, for example.

6.3 EDUCATION

We list education as a resource because the practice of database archiving is so new. The archive analyst at a minimum must be formally trained on the principles of database archiving. Other members of the team might also benefit from some less formal training on database archiving principles.

In addition, the team, and particularly the archive analyst, might need schooling in the application itself. The application analyst can provide this education. The compliance or legal team members might also be used to educate the team on any laws or regulations that are driving the requirements.

6.4 REPOSITORY

You need a repository: an electronic place to store information about the project, information about the database you will be archiving from, and design information as well as to record activities involved in operating a database archive.

The database archive will last for years. It will have many design changes during its lifetime and will be managed by many different individuals.

Thorough documentation is even more important for the application archive. As you will see in subsequent chapters, the amount of data accumulated can be enormous. Someone needing to interpret 30-year-old data or to trace its genesis will appreciate any efforts you make now to make their jobs easier in the future.

The repository resource should consist of two things: a relational database and a document storage system. The relational database can be DB2 z/OS, Microsoft SQL Server, Oracle, or anything else comparable. Many tables will be implemented within this database, as you will see in subsequent chapters.

The document storage system will contain project documentation. This could include Microsoft Word documents, PDF files, spreadsheets, and more. It will contain such things as design documentation, legal documents that support retention periods, minutes of team meetings, and much more.

It would be an excellent idea to implement this system as a standard intranet Wiki site. It could serve as a central repository, with team members being able to access it from anywhere in the world.

6.5 ARCHIVE SERVER

The two repositories, both relational and document, should be kept together on an archive server. This server does not need to be on a dedicated machine, although that is not a bad idea. You need to consider how much the archive repository needs to be made secure. Certainly only a very few people should have access rights to the information on it, and it will be much easier to manage if it's maintained as a separate server.

6.6 SOFTWARE TOOLS

As in all IT projects, you will need to accumulate some software tools to assist in executing the archiving functions. These are tools that the archive analyst will use extensively.

Database archiving software   There are a number of database archiving software tools on the market today. Most of them are specific to a particular type of data source and operating platform—for example, Oracle archiving tools or DB2 z/OS archiving tools. Some archiving tools deal only with packaged applications, such as SAP, Oracle Financials, PeopleSoft, or Seibel; others work with the underlying physical tables.

These tools vary widely in their capabilities, strengths, and weaknesses relative to the specific archiving needs of an application. It is extremely important that you pick the one best suited for your needs.

After reading this book you will be a better judge of the usefulness of archiving software packages relative to your specific requirements.

Metadata management   When working with data management functions, we always seem to come back to this topic. Database archiving design and implementation steps make heavy use of metadata and require a high level of data accuracy and completeness. Most companies use homegrown solutions to manage metadata, whereas some use purchased software. No matter what you are using now, you need to do a thorough evaluation of available metadata software against the archiving project needs, not of the other application needs.

It is important for you to capture and store the current metadata for the application as well as to add enhancements to the metadata that are archiving specific.

You also will need to maintain versions of metadata over time for a single application since the archive will contain data that originated at many different times. This is a characteristic not present in most metadata management tools.

Data modeling *Data modeling* is a primary tool used in database archiving design. The data needs to be modeled as it appears in the operational system and as it will appear in the archive. Data structures from nonrelational databases will generally have to be converted to relational, normalized forms in the archive. This requires standard data-modeling features.

Most IT departments currently use data-modeling tools. Most of them provide sufficient functionality to satisfy the needs of database archiving.

Data profiling A data-profiling tool might be needed to study the operational data to determine the level of data quality. Poor quality data stored in the database archive can be a serious problem. Understanding the level of quality that currently exists in the operational database can lead to data quality improvement projects important in implementing the database archiving application. The results of data profiling can be used to cleanse data or to screen data headed to the archive.

There are a number of data-profiling tools in the market, with varying degrees of effectiveness. Be sure you get one that satisfies your requirements for database archiving projects.

6.7 DISK STORAGE

The amount and type of physical disk storage needed for the database archive is always one of the first concerns of a database archiving project. It is really an operational issue that does not come into play until after the design is complete and archiving begins. However, planning for storage in the early stages of the project is crucial.

Most database archiving projects will end up with a design that puts the archived data on different disk storage than that used for the operational database. One reason for this is that the cost of disk storage per terabyte is much lower for storage area network (SAN) devices than for front-line disk storage used for operational systems. Another is the sheer volume of data.

The most popular destination for archived data today is SAN devices. Most companies are employing them already for one or more applications.

It is important to identify the storage systems that will be used to store the archived data and possibly get access to one already owned by the company, or get a small one for the archiving project design and development phases. Since the use of these devices is considerably different from usual storage, you might need to use your device to conduct tests and do prototyping and benchmarking.

Acquiring storage devices usually takes some time. This should be included in the initial resource plan, particularly the amount of time needed for developing the archiving application.

SUMMARY

This chapter outlines the important resources that are needed to begin work on a database archiving application.

The most important resource required for a successful database archiving project is a dedicated, full-time archive analyst and an equally committed large number of other people who will participate on a part-time basis. Getting all the stakeholders involved in the project early is crucial for achieving success.

CHAPTER

Locating Data 7

Your archiving project begins with finding the data that applies to the mandate set forth in the organizing effort. The project mandate can be very specific, as in targeting a specific operational database, or very vague, as in a mandate to retain a type of data. Even if your mandate is specific, care must be taken to not miss a pocket of data that is related to the mandate but is not part of the mainstream operational processing.

It is important to find all the data related to the application, including copies of data. As you will see, sometimes these need to be considered in building a comprehensive archiving and discard plan for the application, taking into consideration all the requirements.

The logical process of finding the data starts with the people in the business area who are responsible for the application under consideration. These people will lead you to the business processes that generate the data. The business processes will lead you to the operational databases in which the data originates and where it is updated. The managers of these databases will lead you to other databases that hold subsequent versions of the data and related data needed to fully understand the complete data picture. This path is shown in Figure 7.1.

7.1 INVENTORYING DATA

The first step is to inventory all data that might be relevant to the mandate. This process must be thorough. The work should also be reviewed by the archive committee that was, ideally, formed to work with the project.

7.1.1 Process Examination

The best place to start is with the business processes that generate data. The origins of data are very important in determining data authenticity. It is also important in understanding the update activity that might occur against the data

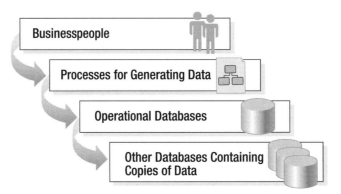

FIGURE 7.1

Search path for the data.

after it originates. You should document the processes you discover, to support your understanding of the data.

Business process examination is best done by consulting the business process analysts who are responsible for building and supporting the business processes for the application at hand. A checklist is helpful in conducting these interviews. Examples of the questions you need to ask are included in Figure 7.2.

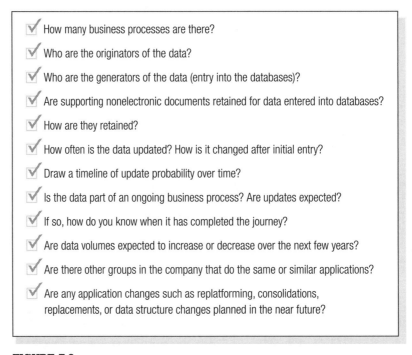

FIGURE 7.2

Process examination checklist.

If you can obtain an entity-relationship diagram (ERD) of the application's data from a data modeler or data architect assigned to the business area, then do so.

Make it clear to the business people you consult that you are pursuing a database archiving application and that you need to keep in close touch with them regarding any future plans to change the data generation and update processes.

Process examination might not seem necessary if the purpose of the project is to unload some of the volume of data cluttering up operational systems. You are charged with a specific goal that does not appear to require much investigation. However, several of the questions noted in Figure 7.2 apply to this case as well. For example, knowing the probability of expected updates as related to time; knowing when no more updates can occur is critical to effective archiving. Furthermore, data volume projections are very relevant to this case.

Multiple parallel applications   The question about related applications is very important. Large enterprises often have multiple business units that have parallel applications doing the same thing. They may be implemented differently and can be managed by different IT groups. Part of the process examination is to determine whether the archiving mandate stretches to these other implementations as well. It is not unusual to assume that the one large implementation is the only one and to ignore other, lesser-known applications that fall under the same requirement.

For example, one very large, worldwide bank was trying to implement a database archiving practice on customer account transaction data. The group in the United States looked beyond the border and discovered that other units of the bank in other countries were also either trying to solve the same problem against different requirements or were not trying to archive data at all. They decided that it would work best if the enterprise had a single database archiving strategy and implementation across all banking units that would satisfy the requirements of all countries in which it did business.

If there are multiple implementations in which the different systems use different applications on different system types and have different data models, the project might need to be split into multiple parallel paths for planning and implementing the archive.

Find the entry points   The last part of process examination is to determine where the data enters IT operational databases. The specific system and database names are required. Find the name of the data steward, if one exists, and the database administrator. If there is a data architect assigned to this application, that person needs to be identified as well.

7.1.2 **Database Topologies**

It is important that you do not assume that identification of the entry operational database automatically determines where the data for the archive will come from. Sometimes it does and sometimes it doesn't.

We were all taught that the basic concept of databases systems is that data has one and only one instance in the enterprise, and all users come there. However, this concept is often violated to create a maze of database instances that support a single application. In large, complex applications, the same data might be replicated across a number of different database systems to support a variety of operational requirements.

Many of these situations reflect bad database management practices. However, they are in common use and the archivist must work with them since they are not likely to go away anytime soon.

For our purposes, we will refer to the collection of data stores that support a single business application as its *database topology.* It is the physical landscape on which the data lies. This can be as simple as a single database instance or as complex as dozens of operational replicates containing much the same information. Figure 7.3 shows a generic schematic of what you might find when you map the database topology for a single application. The same data may occur in multiple locations of the topology.

The primary purpose of mapping the topology is to help locate the node or nodes that will be the source of data for extraction and placement into the archive. It is extremely important for you to get this task right; remember, the location might not be obvious.

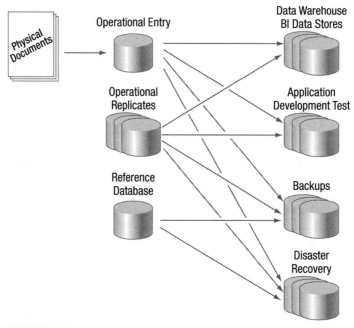

FIGURE 7.3

Database topology schematic.

Nodes of no interest to the archivist   Many of the nodes in the topology are of no interest to the archivist. They are clearly backups used for recovery when needed, test databases, or copies of data stuffed in BI repositories for use by business analysts. These are clearly not the official versions of the data that the archivist is looking for.

That said, it is often helpful to identify these nodes in the design process because some of the topics of archiving may apply. For example, if you have a hard discard policy, data that sidesteps this policy and is retained beyond the enterprise's discard policy is there for the picking for any e-discovery request that might come down later. You also might have to explain at a later time why data in a nonarchive, nonoperational store differs from data in the archive.

Multiple-entry operational databases   Sometimes data for a single application is not all entered into the same database. This can be true in cases where the transaction rates are very high, causing overload on a single entry point. Another example is where regional systems are desired for some reason. Sometimes this emerges through historical evolution by means of mergers of entities that had their own systems.

Sometimes these databases are pass-through, used only to capture data. The data is quickly moved on to another operational system that serves as a collector system. If this is the case, it is important to note whether the move action leaves a copy behind, causing the data to occur in both systems for some period of time.

Operational replicates   Operational replicates are the most troubling structures to deal with. I coined this term to indicate cases where operational data is replicated into databases beyond the originating database into one or more other databases that have operational status. This means that the data is not just a copy; it could be updated or extended in the replicate database. When this situation occurs, the same unit of information might be inconsistent between the various copies.

I learned of the concept of operational replicates through reading a study performed by the Data Quality Research Project at MIT. The study indicated that a problem of managing data surfaced at an insurance company because it had "official" versions of customer data in 30 different databases. As customer data was entered or updated in some of these databases, the changes were propagated to the others. The propagation process took several days, causing the replicates to be inconsistent at various times.

Each of the replicates served a single business function using its copy of the customer information. The purpose of the replicates was to isolate transaction processing by type of transaction.

This was a poor database design by any measure. It made no sense to create this situation in the first place; however, it is easy to see why the urgencies of the moment in IT lead to this type of practice. The data archivist has little power to unravel this situation and cause an expensive reengineering of the application database landscape. The archivist must deal with what is there.

I now make it a practice to ask IT departments I visit whether they also use operational replicates. I was stunned to learn that the practice is widespread. The high-water mark of 30 in the MIT study turned out to be far from the largest number I found. At this time the number of 55 replicate databases for a single application is my high mark.

In discovering this situation, you need to document all the databases. The information you need to collect for each node of the topology is as follows:

- Where is the data copied from?
- When in its life cycle is it copied?
- Is all the data replicated, or only some?
- Is it updated in the replicate node?
- Are these updates propagated backward?
- Does the replicate node have additional data elements not present in other nodes?

The data archivist uses the operational database diagram to determine where to archive from; which version is the one to use? This question gets more complex if no one copy contains all the data elements needed in the archive. It is also necessary to determine what to do with copies of the data being archived that exist in the replicates.

Reference databases   Some companies have implemented reference databases to relieve operational databases of some of the data loads. The data in the reference database is not expected to be updated further but is needed for expected query or reporting purposes.

The important point of these databases is that they could be the logical place to archive from or not, depending on decisions made later. The archiving study may indicate one of the following:

- Archive from the reference databases.
- Archive from the operational database at the same time data is copied to the reference database.
- Eliminate the reference database and go directly to the database archive instead.

In documenting a reference database, you need to capture the rules for when data will be moved there from the operational database, whether it will be purged from the operational database or not, and whether all the data will be moved or only some of it. What happens to the rest of it?

7.1.3 **Finding Reference Data**

Finding the data for the application might not be sufficient for archiving. As you will see later, the archive needs to be complete; it has to contain all the needed information. This means that anyone requiring information from the archive need only look in the archive. This condition might not be possible to create using only the data directly created by the application. Additional reference data might be needed to augment the data of the application.

For example, a sales database might include the salesperson's personnel ID, to identify who made the sale. Looking at an identifier field might not be very useful 10 years from now. The translation of this ID to a real person's name might be what is required in the archive. That translation might be possible only by using a table of data in the personnel application. Thus that table becomes a reference data source for the sales archiving application.

It is not always possible to identify all required reference data sources when you're initially creating the data inventory. Metadata has not yet been gathered and studied. This means that as you learn more as you do the design, you might need to revisit this issue and expand the data inventory accordingly.

Where to break the reference chain Reference chains can extend a long way. Studies have shown that all data in an enterprise is connected to all other data through chains of connectors. I saw one of these studies myself for an oil company and noted that connectors through personnel IDs, part-number IDs, order IDs, and the like did, in fact, extend to everything.

This does not make sense. The archivist must make some judgment calls on where to break the chains. The most logical place is one level off the actual business object.

7.2 PICKING THE ARCHIVIST'S DATA

After locating all the data for the application, you then need to determine which databases you will use for the project. This is a critical point. There are multiple issues to be considered.

7.2.1 What to Put Into the Archive

The most important question is which database or databases will be the source of information extracted and stored in the archive. Hopefully this will turn out to be just one database; however, if parallel operational databases are used, there can be many. If operational replicates are used, one must be chosen. If data consistency varies by data column, it might be necessary to create an archive record using data from more than one of them.

The key is to determine where in the data topology the "official version" of the data exists. This is the data you would deliver if asked to satisfy an e-discovery request. It is the version that the company would want you to present for any important purpose.

It is surprising that picking this version from multiple choices is not always easy to do. Database topologies have gotten ugly in many shops.

7.2.2 **What to Purge From Databases**

Knowing where to get data for the archive is not the only concern. Another issue is what to do with copies of the data being archived that exist in other data stores. The concerns include data integrity issues and discard policy issues.

Data integrity issues When you archive data, you normally also remove it from the data source you are archiving from. If there are replicates of this data in other databases, pairs of databases could be inconsistent relative to this data. If reports are done from both, the outcomes can differ. This can create a situation in which users become alarmed when the number of customers as reported from one database differs from the number of customers reported from another database.

If it is important to keep databases consistent, it might be necessary to have an expanded archiving process that removes the copies from the other databases at the same time. This can become an interesting process since most cases where operational replicates exist already have inconsistencies in the data between them.

Discard issues If the company has a policy of discarding data after a period of time, the existence of data in any node of the topology can cause a violation. Although it might not appear to be the archivists' responsibility to purge data from nonarchive target databases, it is the right place to identify the need to have data purged.

The way to do this is to identify those nodes where the data will naturally disappear before the discard policy goes into effect, such as in backup, disaster recovery, or business intelligence databases. The only ones to be concerned with are those that could persist for longer periods of time.

If the data archivist does not create processes to delete data from these other databases, at least the owners of these databases should be notified of the archiving activities planned for the primary operational database. They can then decide if they need to take some action to compensate for records being taken from the database through the archiving process.

7.3 **DOCUMENTING DATA SOURCES**

It is important to document everything you have collected and learned.

It is also important to retain documentation on what you discovered to support the archive for as long as it lasts. Ten years after the fact, it would be unacceptable to not know the source of the archive data in relationship to all other data being collected, copied, and stored for the application.

The archive repository is the correct place to put all this documentation. Do not depend on external instantiations. For example, if the data architects have a good ERD, copy it into the archive repository. Their copy cannot be depended on to survive over time either in its current form or at all.

Copy everything.

Diagrams   Appropriate models of the databases and their data entities are required.

ERDs are great if you can get them. If not, generate them because they'll illustrate the relationship between parts for a specific implementation of the business application. For replicates, you'll either need to be creative in extending the ERD or you will require a separate diagram that only shows these relationships.

SUMMARY

Archiving database data is a complex topic. The complicated database topologies that have emerged in our IT departments make it challenging, to say the least.

After reading this chapter, you should fully understand the need to be thorough. Look at every possible place the data exists and determine the extent to which your archiving mandate applies to each database.

It is ironic that the more complex database topologies are generally for applications that have the highest data volumes and the highest amount of stored data and that are generally the primary targets of regulations. They are the most likely to be in need of archiving and are generally the first ones to have archiving implemented for them. There is no time or opportunity to develop skills and experience by doing smaller applications first.

You might be able to get considerable leverage from prior efforts at enterprise data modeling or other good practices used in data management. Whenever possible, you should use what is available. However, you should never assume that it is accurate or complete. Things can change rapidly in critical application areas, and updating such objects is rarely a priority. It is very likely that at the end of your search for data, you'll have better data models than the other groups. You should have the best of all of them, at least at that point. You might want to share your output with the other data management groups so that they can benefit from your efforts as well.

Now that you know where to find the data, you'll need to find the metadata that matches it. This is the topic of the next chapter.

Locating Metadata

Metadata is critical to the success of any database archiving project. You simply cannot succeed unless you have complete and accurate metadata. Keeping data with no explanation of what it means will result in storing data for years that cannot be used if needed during the archive period.

Archiving has a greater need for good metadata than any other application of the data. This is because it describes data in today's form that will need to be interpreted years from now. Other current applications can depend on knowledge in the heads of various people who created the application, operate it, or maintain it. This can make up for the shortcomings of the metadata. In addition, the application programs themselves can add sufficient information for the user to understand data elements that are not backed by solid metadata. For the archive user many years hence, neither these people nor the application programs can be relied on to exist. The only interpretation tool available is likely to be the metadata.

Metadata is also notoriously one of the worst-managed parts of database management. If metadata exists, it is generally incomplete and/or inaccurate. Many companies have attempted to get this situation under control over the years. These efforts have had minimal success in establishing and ensuring a best practice for this topic.

Archiving *requires* that you be successful this time.

8.1 METADATA DEFINITIONS

There are countless definitions of what database metadata is made up of. For our purposes, the definition of *metadata* is the design artifacts that describe how data facts are organized to reflect real-world business records in physical databases. It is the data blueprint for laying down data on database structures. Metadata represents the governing rules for the way the data should be formulated, grouped, and stored to accurately reflect business objects.

Anyone needing to know how to interpret data stored in databases should be able to consult the metadata and learn all they need to know. This is an exact parallel to blueprints of buildings, machinery, or other physical objects.

Metadata should describe the structure and meaning of the business object. It does this at multiple levels:

- Business object
- Data element/column/field
- Data row/record/segment
- Data table/file/segment type
- Data relationships
- Data integrity rules

As you can see, there are multiple terms used for most of the levels. This is because some database systems use one set of terminology and others use other terminology for the same structural elements. Relational databases have columns that are grouped into rows, which are collected into tables, which have relationships that connect the tables. Hierarchical systems have fields that are grouped into segments, which are collected into segment types, which are connected by the physical database definition (DBD). Some of these relationships are implied by the hierarchy definition. File systems have data elements, which are grouped into records, which are stored in files. Relationships between files are generally only known in the application programs.

8.1.1 **Business Objects**

A *business object* for a database is a collection of data that describes either a business entity or a transaction against a business entity. Examples of entities and transactions are shown in Figure 8.1.

The difference between transactions and entities is that transactions occur only once and the data description becomes complete either on initial entry or at the completion of the transaction, usually in a short period of time. It then becomes an official record of the transaction. Entities, on the other hand, persist

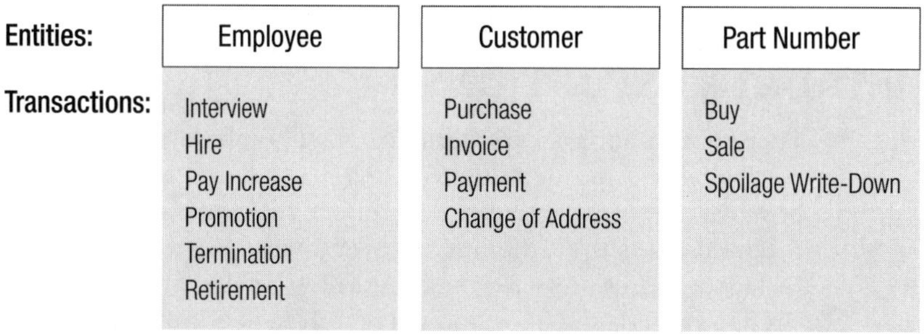

Entities:	Employee	Customer	Part Number
Transactions:	Interview Hire Pay Increase Promotion Termination Retirement	Purchase Invoice Payment Change of Address	Buy Sale Spoilage Write-Down

FIGURE 8.1

Examples of business entities and transactions.

for long periods of time, often for years, and are subject to change at any time during their lives. There is no point at which they are "complete" except when they stop being an entity for the enterprise.

Archiving transactions is an easy concept: You archive only completed transactions. Archiving entities is not an easy concept. There is no point at which archives are considered "final," since they can always be changed.

It is important that the archivist identify all the business objects stored in the database for the application under consideration and to classify them as either transactions or entities. The most important step in archiving design is to identify which business objects are to be preserved in the archive and which are not needed in the archive.

The archive analyst needs to document the business objects with an identifying name and a full description. This description should be thorough. It should include what the object is and why it exists. It should include who creates the object, how it enters the operational database, and its update possibilities. For entities it should include a description of when the archive stops being of interest to the enterprise (becomes inactive) and whether or when it is deleted from the database.

A diagram should be created showing the relationship among all business objects in the application. Figure 8.2 shows a simplified diagram of a loan application.

8.1.2 **Data Elements**

Data elements are the building blocks of databases. Each data element should describe a single value that provides a part of the data definition of a business object. Each data element should have a name, an explanation of what business fact it represents, a data type to indicate how it will be stored, and any rules or constraints that would apply to its use in real business records. An example of a data element's metadata is shown in Figure 8.3.

Sometimes data elements have more rigorous definitions, such as belonging to a universal domain definition or a master data definition. These are constructs used to create data elements that will be used across many business objects and thus ensure consistency from one application or database to another. Whenever these are used, their descriptions should be captured in the metadata for archiving.

8.1.3 **Data Rows**

Data elements are grouped into rows to describe portions of a business object. Depending on the database system, these may be called rows, segments, or records (or something else), depending on the type of data store that will be used to house the data. The scope of a row is determined by the process of normalization of business objects. It is not the intention of this book to define the normalization process. There are many good books available to do this for you.

The metadata defines each row of business objects it cares about with a name, an explanation of its role in the business process, and the data elements

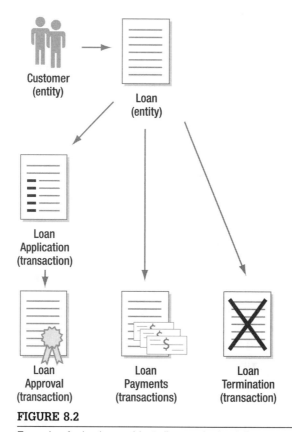

FIGURE 8.2

Example of a business object diagram for bank loans.

NAME	UNIT_PRICE
EXPLANATION	A numeric value that represents the intended sale price for a single unit of the product before discounts or taxes are applied. Unit prices are always assumed to be in US$.
TYPE	Decimal number with two decimal positions.
RULE 1	Cannot be zero or greater than 1000.00.

FIGURE 8.3

Example metadata for a data element.

that make it up. If the data elements have any specific limitations as defined for the row, they should be defined. For example, if a data element of a purchase order only exists for some purchase orders and not others, such as shipping instructions, then it should be noted.

8.1.4 **Tables**

Rows that have the same definition are grouped into tables. This is the relational context. For IMS all segments using the same segment layout are referred to as a *segment type*. The collection of all segment instances having the same segment type is the same idea as a table.

There are two characteristics of tables that often get confused with characteristics of data elements. One is uniqueness. A data element definition does not have this characteristic. A data element may acquire the unique characteristic when used in a table. It is a table characteristic. For example, PART_NUMBER might have uniqueness in the Parts table but not in the Purchase Order table. The other attribute that has this characteristic is nullability. A data element may be permitted to assume the null value in one table but not when used in another table.

Examples of data row definitions and the tables they are stored in for a purchase order business object are shown in Figure 8.4.

TABLE NAME	ORDER_HEADER
EXPLANATION	A single row is created and stored in this table for each order received. It identifies when the order was placed, the customer, the salesperson, and current status of satisfying the order.
DATA ELEMENTS	ORDER_RECEIVED_DATE CUSTOMER_ID ORDER_NUMBER
RULE	Must be unique SALESMAN_ID STATUS

TABLE NAME	ORDER_DETAIL
EXPLANATION	A single row is created and saved for each unique item number ordered. An order can contain as many item numbers per order as desired.
DATA ELEMENTS	ORDER_NUMBER ITEM-IDENTIFIER QUANTITY_ORDERED UNIT_PRICE

FIGURE 8.4

Data row metadata examples.

Another note on terminology is that many data-modeling products use the word *entity* to refer to what I call a *table*. Even when they're connected in an ERD, you still cannot identify specific business objects from the real world. It makes sense for the word *entity* to be associated with business objects and the word *table* to be associated with fragments of data that constitute a portion of a business object. In the real world this is what you see. For the archivist, this is the picture you want to portray.

8.1.5 Table Relationships

We do not archive data elements or rows in tables. We archive the data of complete *business objects*. Business objects are described in databases or file systems as data structures made up of instances of table rows, which in turn are made up of data element instances.

Tables are connected in the structure through various mechanisms. In relational systems these are referred to as *foreign key relationships*. In hierarchical systems these are the *structure definitions* of the hierarchy. They do not require field values in the segment definitions to determine relationships between segments. In file systems it is through the application programs that may use a variety of mechanisms to connect records in different files.

Business object relationships In the end, there is always a hierarchical structure to business objects. One table contains rows that describe the top of the tree for each object. It is connected to children rows in other tables that provide additional information needed to describe the complete object.

All these relationships need to be part of the metadata. The business object tree should be a diagram that shows the relationships in hierarchical order. Each path should have the method of connection spelled out (whether through data values or database structure enforcement). These paths should also show whether the relationships are one-to-one or one-to-many.

Reference relationships These are relationships that cross over business objects. For example, a purchase order can include a data element for PART_NUMBER. This tells a viewer of the purchase order nothing about what was purchased. The value in the data element can be used to connect to another business object, the INVENTORY object, to get additional descriptive information such as the part description, unit of distribution, unit price, or transport handling restrictions.

Common reference relationships that cross over business objects are PART_NUMBER, EMPLOYEE_NUMBER, CUSTOMER_NUMBER, and ACCOUNT_NUMBER.

Another common use for reference relationships is connections to an object that is used solely to explain a shortened, encoded value for multiple business objects. This is commonly referred to as a *lookup table*. For example, you might have a table that expands ZIP codes into CITY and STATE values. All business objects would include only a data element for ZIP. The application programs would use this value to expand to CITY and STATE if needed.

Each business object should identify in its metadata all reference relationships needed to fully explain to a viewer of the object's data the information associated with it.

8.1.6 **Integrity Rules**

Metadata often has several rules that describe relationships between data elements. For example, your birth date should appear earlier than your hire date. It is useful to collect these rules if they are available. However, their usefulness to an archive analyst is minimal. They exist for the purpose of checking data as it enters the database to ensure that data quality rules are not violated.

The archivist's job is to move data that is already created and exists in the operational databases. Any data quality checking and remediation should already have occurred. As we will discuss later, data quality presents a special problem for archivists. Should data be archived as it exists, or should attempts be made to improve the quality of data when it is moved to the archive?

8.2 **WHERE TO FIND METADATA**

Using the blueprint analogy for metadata, IT departments have never had a method of describing metadata that is as precise and universally excepted as blueprints. An engineering student will learn the rules of blueprint specification in an early college course and can be confident that it will work when she's confronted with real-world blueprints. Ah, that we should be so lucky in the database field.

There have been numerous attempts to define a universal standard for metadata: what it is and how it should be specified and stored. However, none of these standards has found wide acceptance.

It is not this book's intention to call for a universal standard or to suggest that companies should create complete and consistent metadata in a uniform format. The archivist could never expect to be successful in demanding that complete metadata be given to him to do archiving. It won't happen. You have to work with what you can get.

You should find all metadata that exists for the application, consolidate it into one set, fill in the missing parts, and validate it with appropriate experts in the company.

So, where do you look? Some of the more common places to find metadata are as follows:

- Formal metadata repositories
- Vendor tool metadata repositories
- Packaged application metadata repositories
- Database definitions

- Application source code
- Application displays and reports
- People

Let's take a closer look at each of these.

Formal metadata repositories   Many enterprises use vendor-provided metadata repository tools for application development, whereas other companies built their own centralized metadata repositories for application development. Some companies launched efforts to capture metadata into a formal repository after applications were already built and deployed for some time. This was part of the objectives of the enterprise data-modeling projects undertaken by many companies in the early 1990s.

Finding formal metadata repositories is generally easy since the application development people are generally very familiar with them.

A common problem with these tools is that they tend to be out-of-date and out-of-step with the actual application currently in operation. This is due to the fact that the definitions in them are not enforced in the operational programs or DBMS. They are *passive* repositories. If they are out of step, no one knows they are.

Even if these metadata repositories are not current, they can often provide some valuable information.

Vendor tool metadata repositories   Many vendor tools that work with operational databases for back-end functions have metadata repositories built into them. This is very common for ETL, extract, and data-profiling vendors. For their products to work they need to know the correct descriptions of data as it exists in the operational databases.

Even though these repositories are generally not considered to be the primary metadata definitions for the applications, they often have the most accurate and complete metadata. They are always developed from the data as it is deployed in the operational databases. Therefore they will always be at least structurally correct. They are not passive repositories since functions of the tools use the information in the repositories to execute against the data. If the information is wrong, the functions do not work properly.

Packaged application metadata repositories   When you buy and install a packaged application, you will normally get a metadata description of the business objects used in the application. This might be a document or a formal electronic repository that you can search and review online.

Most of the time this metadata does not refer to the data as stored in the underlying database tables. It is a virtual description of the business objects as they appear to the user of the product through reports, displays, or application programming interfaces. It is very important to understand if this is so. Most vendors do not want you to mess around with the underlying database tables and therefore will keep their structure definitions secret. This is generally okay, since for packaged applications you will generally be performing archiving activities through the external application program interfaces using these "virtual" database definitions.

If you capture metadata from this source, you need to know whether it is metadata for the application as shipped to you or whether it is metadata after you have completed customization of the application. Customization can alter the definition of data elements, introduce new data elements, and change the structure of the objects by virtue of not using some of the tables for your installation. You might not use all the potential data for business objects, and you might not be using all the business objects defined by the vendor. Determine whether customization changes the descriptions and whether there are parts not used.

Database definitions   When creating database objects in the operational database, you define a certain amount of the metadata to the DBMS. The DBMS will then enforce these definitions for you when data is created or updated.

The most universally understood of these is the Database Catalog of Relational Database Systems. These tell you what the tables are, what the data elements are (columns), and some of the relationships between tables (primary/foreign key relationships). They also might tell you some of the integrity rules.

This is valuable information because these definitions will accurately define the metadata components for physical storage layout. The DBMS will ensure that all data entered and updated conforms to them.

Metadata from database definitions is always incomplete metadata. It does not identify business objects and does not provide descriptive information on anything. Relationships between tables are often missing for performance reasons. Those that are defined cannot be differentiated between business object internal relationships and reference relationships. Often this is the only information that you have available to use as metadata.

Hierarchical database systems like IMS also have some limited amount of metadata. The DBD contains the full description of segments and their relationships within the hierarchy. It might also have some segment key and data element definitions, although these are not required by IMS.

Business objects in IMS are not distinguished. A hierarchy can describe a single business object or it can describe multiple business objects, or it can define only a part of a business object. The DBD will tell you nothing about this. Reference relationships can be defined as *logical relationships*. However, a logical relationship can indicate a connection to another part of a single business object instead of being a simple reference relationship. Many relationships between database hierarchies are simply not defined to IMS.

If you are taking metadata from the DBMS, be sure to use the definitions established for the operational systems and not those of test or development systems. They often differ.

If you are planning to use a "virtual" database definition for archiving, you do not need to harvest the metadata available from the underlying databases. It is of no use to you and would probably just confuse you.

Application source code   Another source of metadata will appear in the source code of the applications. For file-based databases such as VSAM, this might be the only metadata you can find. For all database types it might offer additional information beyond what is maintained in the other metadata sources. The area to look for in the source code is the data structure definitions and the output specifications.

The most widely available source code descriptions of database data is the *COBOL Copybooks* for mainframe applications. These are used to provide overlays of IMS data segments, VSAM records, and DB2 buffers returned from SQL calls. For older systems these are probably more current than other repository descriptions simply because they are used to compile application programs. Even though the original applications might have been developed years or decades ago, the copybooks need to be somewhat current to support maintenance and enhancement of the applications. As such, they will be as current as the applications that come from them.

This does not mean that copybooks are accurate or complete. They are notorious for not defining new fields and letting the logic of the program do plus-displacement processing of unspecified data in filler spaces or past the end of the record. Also, sometimes fields are assigned to new uses, and thus the copybook description of a field could be inaccurate and misleading. However, regardless of any disparities, the copybook will be mostly current and can be used by the archivist.

Use the copybook for all it's worth. The field names, the field data type and length specifications, and any comments that the programmer might have generously provided are all useful information to harvest.

Similar information can be garnered from PL\1 Data Sections, Assembler Language DSECTs, or C .h files for Web applications.

Application displays and reports   Another place to look for explanations of data stored in databases is in the visual output of application programs. Printed versions of business objects or display forms used for data entry, update, or display can be used to gather metadata information. The headings associated with data fields and the placement within the presentation can provide valuable insights into what the database fields mean in the business context.

You should gather examples of these in electronic form if possible as well as in printed form for use in validation, as described in the next chapter. For packaged applications, this might be the only metadata you have available.

People   Of course, a final source of metadata information is people who work with the applications every day. They include application developers, data modelers, data entry staff, and business planners. If the application has a BI practice associated with it, you can bet that the business analysts for the application will know the meaning of the data elements.

At this stage of the project you want to identify the people who can help you validate and complete the metadata package you will need to include in the archive.

8.3 **SELECTING A VERSION OF THE METADATA**

So, why is it so hard to get accurate and complete metadata? People who define metadata do not know all the stakeholder requirements or interests when doing so. They work from a narrow focus of what the metadata will be used for. When someone else needs to use the metadata for another purpose, it falls short. This situation is shown in Figure 8.5.

Another factor that leads to poor metadata is that it gets defined too early in the process of defining a new application, and the natural process of completing the application changes the data definitions. The person who defined the metadata is not engaged in the development steps, and thus the metadata does not get updated to reflect the final data structures.

Another factor is that the metadata is not used for operational control. Some of it is used for relational database systems, but only a small portion of what should be considered complete metadata. The fact that it is not a part of the database operational environment means that if the real data definitions drift from the metadata descriptions, no one knows.

These are three very powerful explanations for the reason that metadata tends to be poorly managed. There are doubtless others.

Because metadata sources tend to each have a limited view and since most of them are highly subject to being outdated or inaccurate, you need to collect metadata from all available sources. It is tempting to select one that looks like a very official version and run with just that. This is a mistake and will lead to problems later on. Take the time to locate all the sources and gather from each of them.

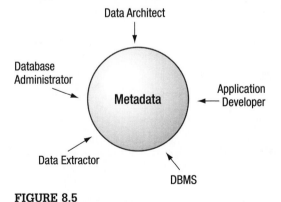

FIGURE 8.5

Multiple views of metadata.

8.4 **CLASSIFYING DATA**

Another useful activity that will enhance your metadata is to classify the various units of metadata by several characteristics or requirements. The purpose of this classification is to ensure that you end up using the right version of the data and that you know your requirements for storing and protecting the data.

This should not be a complex nor time-consuming step; however, it is important to get it right. If you end up archiving from the wrong data source, the archive could lose its authenticity when it's called on to represent facts for the enterprise years later.

8.4.1 **Classification Elements**

Data should be classified according to parameters that are relevant to database archiving; nothing more. The goal is to ensure that you are getting the right data, that you protect it in the archive, and that you document for the archive any characteristics that may aid someone in the future in understanding what they are looking at. Figure 8.6 shows the circle of classification.

Getting the right data   The first part of classification is identifying one or more databases as the source for archiving. This is the same as classifying the database as the "official corporate record" of the data.

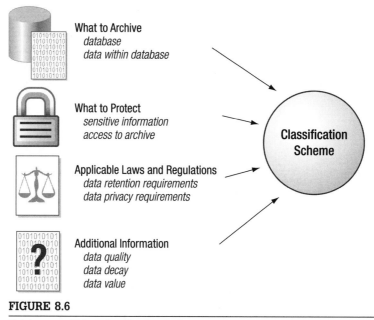

FIGURE 8.6

Database archiving classification factors.

Sometimes it is obvious what database you will draw on to get the data for the archive. Other times it is not so obvious. It might take awhile to figure out a complex database topology.

The data you pull must have the authority to represent itself as the official version of the business objects. This principle should not be compromised. This is the criterion you should use in selecting the source of the data.

In addition to selecting the primary business object for the archiving application, you must also select the data to be included in the archive as reference data. This can come from the same or different databases. The criteria for selecting among options are the same: the data that represents the enterprise's official version of that data.

The database you get data from might be the initial operational database (the place where data is created), a secondary operational database that holds a more complete version of the data, or a reference database that is used to keep data in the operational setting.

Timing Time in the database might be a factor used in selecting where the data comes from. Indeed, timing can be part of the classification. For example, in dealing with financial transactions, the place and time for the most "official" version of the data is the entry database at the time of entry. At that time the data has had no chance of being compromised by unauthorized or authorized users. The longer the data sits in the database, the longer it is exposed to mischief.

Most archiving applications are not this strict in requiring that data be pulled so early.

8.4.2 Protection of Data in the Archive

Data security classification This is a classification scheme that identifies the archive as to its treatment as data within the enterprise. A typical scheme would include *top secret, secret, confidential, business confidential,* and *public.* It sounds like a military scheme. Some companies will be dealing with the military and so need this classification. Other companies use a comparable scheme to segregate data for access control.

The security scheme can be applied to the entire archive, to the business object level, or to a subset of data elements within the business objects.

Sensitive data classification Another element of classification is identifying data that is sensitive to unauthorized exposure, such as customer names, addresses, credit card numbers, account numbers, and Social Security numbers. Identifying sensitive information is a common practice these days in light of data privacy laws and dire consequences of compromise. Archiving does not add a new dimension to this scenario. Archiving must adhere to the same rules of sensitive data protection as the operational databases.

Sensitive data classification generally applies to data elements and, specifically, to groups of data elements. Whereas a Social Security number by itself might not be sensitive, a group of data elements that includes name, address, and Social Security number would be.

The implication of sensitive data classification is that the identified data must be protected in the archiving process and in the archive as strongly as it is protected in the operational databases.

Archiving process protection   The archiving process must not expose people to sensitive data they are not authorized to see. This includes any part of the archiving process. It includes protection of temporary files, execution logs, diagnostics routines, and the like.

Archive store protection   Once data is in the archive, sensitive data must be protected from unauthorized viewing. This means that the data at rest must be encrypted or otherwise protected. It also means that people authorized to get data from the archive must have the proper credentials to see this information.

We are not designing the protections at this stage of archive application design; we are merely classifying data elements so that we know what will need to be protected as we design processes later on.

8.4.3 Laws and Regulations

Data should be matched to applicable laws and regulations. This process should yield the legal requirements for data retention as well as data protection requirements to guard against unauthorized access.

8.4.4 Additional Information

It might also be useful to identify other characteristics of data that would be helpful to readers of the archive in later years. The list provided here is limited. You can expand on these categories with other factors that apply to a specific application.

Data decay   *Data decay* means that the identified data elements are subject to change after they are included in the archive for a specific business object. For example, names, addresses, and phone numbers are subject to change. This notifies readers that the data they will be looking at was correct for a business object at the moment it was archived but might have changed afterward.

Identification number reassignments   An identified data element (such as an account number, phone number, or part number) can be reassigned in the future. The number is used to identify an object. This can create special problems with data archived over long periods of time where the identifier used can refer to different business objects, depending on the time it was archived.

Data quality   *Data quality* refers to classifying data according to the expected quality of the data (accuracy of values). It would normally use an index of expected data quality, such as 95 percent.

The problem with this category is that most companies do not know what value to use and, if they did know, would be reluctant to admit this through documenting this index in the archive metadata.

Value This category would classify data according to expected value to the enterprise. The value would normally be expected to be expressed in terms of the consequences of its loss or compromise.

8.4.5 **Granularity of Classification**

Your classification scheme needs to separate classification parameters at the database, business object, table, and data element levels. Sometimes the same classification parameter applies to more than one level, in which case the higher level takes precedence.

8.4.6 **Who to Get It From**

Classification might already exist. Some companies have performed data classification exercises to support IT compliance directives. This fits nicely with database archiving since you are doing the same thing, only for a subset of the data and a subset of the classification categories. If this has already been done, you need to gather the results and use it for your purpose. If a classification project is currently going on, join the team and add your requirements to the exercise.

If you need to initiate the classification exercise, it is best that you form a team of people who can provide the necessary input or easily get it. This team would consist of data stewards, business analysts for the application area, someone from the IT compliance office, someone from the IT risk analysis office, a representative from the legal department, and a database administrator responsible for the operational database or databases involved.

There are consulting firms that offer data classification as a practice. IT departments have been using them to identify sensitive data areas and to match data to laws and regulations for compliance purposes. You might want to consider enlisting one of these firms if the classification is complex enough and important enough.

8.5 **DOCUMENTING METADATA**

You must capture a snapshot of the metadata from its source during the archive project development process. The sources might change on you, change their location, or simply disappear. Never depend on a source you do not control yourself; otherwise it might not be there later.

In gathering metadata, note that many of the repository-based sources have the ability to output metadata into an industry-standard XML format. It is a good idea to use this facility since that makes metadata easier to store for both current and future uses.

You should keep your metadata in the archive repository. Remember that all of it should be kept, not just the final version you develop and choose to work from.

You need to build a classification scheme to work from. This should be tailored to the archiving application being studied. You will probably end up with a big spreadsheet cross-referencing classification parameters with data structure pieces.

Another way to document the classification scheme is to annotate the metadata, although the original spreadsheet should also be retained.

The archiving project will need to maintain a history of changes to the classification and be able to relate classification versions to units of stored archived data. The corporate classification scheme only needs to maintain the latest version, whereas the archive needs to keep all versions.

8.6 KEEPING UP WITH CHANGES

Metadata changes. The most important data structures tend to have more frequent metadata changes. These are the data structures that you are most likely to be archiving.

Many of the changes impact the metadata. As noted earlier, often these changes do not get reflected in the latest version of the metadata.

As an archivist you need to keep up with changes to metadata, since archiving is a long-term continuous activity. To keep up with it you need to get wired into the groups that make and control changes. The archivist needs to become part of the application change process as well as the change process for moving changes from development to test to production.

You should also establish a method of checking metadata periodically for changes. Your repository will be yet another passive metadata repository, and thus changes might get by you (and the change control process). You must have a very high probability of catching changes when or shortly after they occur.

The application programs might have no need to maintain old versions of metadata; they only need the most current: the one used in operational applications. They will generally have no facility for maintaining versions. This is another strong argument for capturing metadata in the archive repository instead of pointing to metadata artifacts in the application development or operational environments.

Classification of data does not change often. It changes much less frequently than metadata. Classification is not a normal part of the application development change process for minor changes but could be a part of the planning for major reengineering changes, application replacement projects, or restructuring of operational database deployments.

The data archivist should set up periodic reviews to revisit the classification scheme to ensure that it is current. This can be on a quarterly, semiannual, or annual basis. Usually it can be combined with other review or archiving audit activities without generating an additional meeting.

SUMMARY

Metadata is the foundation for good archiving. It is the hardest part to gather, to make correct, and to maintain; not surprisingly, metadata is often inaccurate and incomplete.

Metadata can be found in many places for a single application. Each place will probably contain only a fragment of what is needed.

Metadata is always changing, so it is critical that you keep up with the changes, and you need to maintain versions that match archive units of data that have been stored in the archive.

You need your own repository for metadata; it needs to be part of the archive repository. Your metadata must be usable by people years into the future. The development and operational people only need the current version of the metadata; the archive needs all versions.

Classification of data is a step in the process that is easy to miss. It might not seem important to every archivist in the beginning. However, failure to nail down factors can lead to serious mistakes later. Classification will generate requirements that have to be met by later design steps. The classification scheme you develop should be treated as additional metadata. It should be stored in the archive repository and versioned with links to units of archived data to which each version applies.

You will see in later chapters how to validate the metadata, use it in archive design, and use it for archive data access years later.

Data and Metadata Validation

We have presented a lot of information about the application's data and metadata. Before charging ahead to use it, we need to evaluate its accuracy and completeness.

It is not uncommon for metadata to appear to be correct and authoritative, only to have us find out later that the data doesn't match it. This must be found and corrected early in the process.

It is also important to determine the usefulness of the collected information. Will people who are not on the project be able to interpret the documentation you have produced and use it to access archive data? Users of the archive years into the future will be such people.

There are a number of steps in the validation process, which we examine in this chapter.

9.1 MATCHING DATA TO METADATA

Any metadata you have gathered was probably correct at the time it was generated. However, poor data management practices often cause changes to the operational systems to be made without going back and changing the metadata. Some of the common errors in changes are:

- Adding a new column to a table and not adding it to the metadata or to the application program data definition
- Changing the use of a column that is no longer needed without changing the column name to reflect the new use
- Denormalizing a pair of tables into one table
- Changing the encoding scheme of data within a column, possibly changing the granularity of reporting
- Using unused bytes or bits within a column for another purpose, creating an overloaded field
- Defining a column in the metadata but never using it in the data
- Defining a column that is used for a period of time and then ceasing to use it

There are probably many more examples of practices that render metadata incompatible with the data. In short, you must not trust the metadata.

In addition, the metadata is often incomplete or lacks clarity. Some of the reasons for this are:

- Using short column names that have structural meaning, not business meaning
- Specifying columns as *character* of length *n* without describing how data is structured within the column when, if fact it contains nontext information
- Failing to specify how the null condition is to be entered into the column

9.1.1 **Looking at the Data**

The simplest test to perform for validation is to print or display some of the data by column and compare it to the metadata that you think is correct. Go column by column and ask yourself if the data you are seeing is truly representative of the description as given in the metadata. Is this what someone else would expect?

You should look for encodings that are not evident from the metadata. For example, if the metadata calls a column JOB_TYPE as character 1 and you discover by looking at the data that it contains values of *A, B,* and *C,* will someone else know what *A* means? What *B* means? What *C* means?

Determine how missing values (null) might be represented. Are they simply left blank, or is something else put in the column to indicate that the true value is unknown or not applicable?

Mismatches and misleading metadata generally become highly visible after you conduct this simple test. It clearly shows empty columns, columns that have been repurposed, and columns that are overloaded.

Be sure to access a sufficient amount of data to satisfy your review. You should also select data randomly to get a better perspective over multiple time periods and other factors. For example, having data from only one time period might skew the data or hide other problems.

Use the raw data, not a version that has been processed through an application. The application programs might change or embellish the raw data values. The raw values are the ones that will be stored in the archive, not the processed ones.

Relational data People often make the mistake of assuming that data in relational databases is accurate because the relational catalog is used to enforce data inserts and updates. This can be a false assumption. It is true that the basic data element shape (data type, length, precision) is enforced; however, there is nothing that ensures that the column name has any valid business meaning. There is nothing that says that the content has any values in it. There is nothing that says that a 30-byte column has only 1 byte used in every row. Bad database design is still alive and well in the relational databases.

Check the data.

9.1.2 Comparing Data and Metadata to Reports and Displays

A similar approach is to use the application programs to print some business objects or to display them in forms on a computer screen. If you know what values are in the columns, try to match them to what you see after they are output.

This approach will reveal misused columns. The column name in the database might say one thing and the headings on the reports or display indicate something entirely different. This is one way to expose the encoding scheme for encoded columns. This disparity should be captured and documented.

This approach will also reveal display fields that are derived from database columns. It is important to know what they are and how they are computed. If this is an important output field, can you compute it from the source data? Is the method documented in the metadata?

The test that you need to apply is whether you could generate the same outputs from the underlying data without using the application programs. If not, you need to work on the metadata some more.

9.2 ASSESSING DATA QUALITY

The question of data quality brings a new dimension to the analysis of data for archiving. The data is already deemed the enterprise official version of events. As such, it is expected to have accurate values recorded for each business object. However, it is well known that corporate databases, even the most important ones, often contain inaccurate values.

Most IT departments are unaware of the quality of their data until they launch a formal data quality assessment program to determine whether they have a problem. Invariably when they do this they uncover problems—often very serious problems. At this time only about 40 percent of IT organizations have a formal data quality assessment practice. The others just believe that their data is correct though, in fact, it is not.

Though it is not the responsibility of the data archivist to uncover or solve data quality problems, the data archivist is responsible for collecting information to understand data quality and, if appropriate, encourage IT management to either perform data quality assessments or to take actions to remedy known data quality problems.

Launching a database archiving project might be a convenient time to step up to the plate on data quality as well. If the archive is the place where the enterprise's records are to be kept, every attempt should be made to ensure that the data is accurate.

9.2.1 Data Profiling

Data profiling is a formal process of examining database data to determine whether the data has quality problems, whether the metadata has quality problems, or both. If a data-profiling effort has been performed recently on the data targeted for archiving, the data archivist should collect and document results of that assessment.

If problems have been reported and are in the queue to be addressed, the data archivist should determine whether any of the problems will present difficulties in developing and implementing a database archiving solution. All problems should be documented and tracked until resolved.

If the data archivist has reason to believe that data quality is a problem with operational databases or that the risk of quality problems could reduce the value of data in the archive, a formal data quality assessment program should be called for on that data.

9.2.2 Looking for Data-Cleansing Activities

Something that remains sort of a mystery to me is that many IT organizations have efforts to clean up data when they move it out of operational databases and into data warehouse or business intelligence data stores. They do not consider cleaning the data at the *source* so that it will be correct in the operational databases. It's as though it is okay to be wrong in the operational databases but not okay to be wrong when used for business analytics.

The data archivist can examine extract and data integration processes to see if data cleansing is going on in them. If so, the specific cleansing activities and statistics on amount of data changed should be examined.

If the data archivist finds that cleansing is occurring excessively, this should be brought to the attention of IT management and a plan drafted to clean the data in the operational databases or to improve the data entry processes to get data right when it is first entered. The goal should be better operational data that becomes the source of data for the database archive.

9.3 ASSESSING METADATA QUALITY

You need to determine whether the metadata provides sufficient explanation of the data to serve its users in the far future.

An impartial test is needed that uses people who are not part of the archive design process and who are not connected to the business area or development of the application. Assemble a group of people who are representative of potential future users by skill set but who have no knowledge of the business area being studied. Give them some sample data and the metadata and have them assess their ability to understand and work with the data.

This is a simple process that can yield valuable insights. The data archivist must not be defensive in taking criticisms. Any problems raised by this group need to be addressed by beefing up the metadata with additional explanations or more structure.

9.4 VALIDATING DATA CLASSIFICATION

The last validation exercise is to test the data classification scheme. This is probably the most accurate component of information you gathered, since you would have gathered it using the experts who know the area most.

However, it is useful to hold a review of all the people on your application archive committee. Show them all the diagrams of data topologies and business objects, including those that show data stores that you will not be using. Indicate what you intend to use.

Go through the data classification spreadsheets to ensure acquiescence on the data you will be using and its applicability to the various classification parameters.

Always conduct this meeting as a group. Do not allow absentees or substitutions. Do not do this by sending results around and having them review it individually. The group must all agree to the plan at this stage.

9.5 DOCUMENTING VALIDATION ACTIVITIES

By now you should have realized that I am a proponent of saving documentation on everything in the archive repository. Keeping a complete record of all your findings and decisions can help others in years to come. This philosophy extends to validation activities as well, so you should document what validation activities you performed as well as who was involved.

Many of the validation activities will surface problems that cannot be immediately addressed. These should be encapsulated into problem tickets and entered into a formal problem ticket resolution and tracking system.

You may get some pushback from IT management on documenting shortcomings in data quality. IT management generally does not want to make such information widely known.

If you go through the exercise of comparing data to reports and displays, it is a good idea to retain the results. This can be done with hardcopy paper documents that show the reports and screen prints of the forms with annotations on them about what data fields the entries came from as well as how they might have been derived. If possible, keep this in electronic form so that everything can be kept in the archive repository. This is something I would want to see years later if I were confused about what the metadata meant.

9.6 REPEATING VALIDATION ACTIVITIES

You might want to repeat some of the validation activities after the archive design goes into operation. This would not normally be required unless there was a known change to the metadata, data encodings, or classification scheme. This could be the trigger you need to conduct a new validation.

SUMMARY

Metadata often looks very authoritative but in fact might not match the data. It is essential that you verify that it does. The ultimate test of the metadata is whether someone outside the project can use the metadata you have developed against real data and make sense of it.

Data quality is a sleeper issue that should be examined to determine if you will be archiving inaccurate data—data that could be unacceptable for legal use. If so, the quality should be addressed through a separate organization within IT.

Designing Database Archiving Applications

It's time to dig in and explore the way database archiving applications are designed. The topics of metadata and data models are discussed in great detail, and we define how to establish policies for archiving activity. These topics showcase the major efforts that the data archivist will undertake on a daily basis. They also demonstrate the major difference in implementation between database archiving and other forms of data archiving.

CHAPTER

Designing for Archive Independence

10

Independence is the single most important objective to achieve in a long-term database archive. The archive must be independent from the operational environment unless you are willing to maintain the operational environment in its entirety forever.

Dependencies run as deep as relatively minor changes to data structures where some data is created under one definition and other data created under a newer definition. The dependency comes down to a "version" of the application. Archive units of data may also be tied to versions of operating systems or hardware.

When you have data retention requirements of many years, the number of separate configurations of the application and operational environments used to generate the data can be very large.

Maintaining dependencies is very costly to IT departments, causing them to retain old systems and applications long after their usefulness or long after it would have been better to switch to newer technology. If the archive design retains the dependencies, it compounds the problem. If it eliminates the dependencies, it frees up resources that can be used to modernize systems and applications.

The archive design process described beyond this point assumes that achieving independence is a major goal of the design.

The goal of independence is that once data is in the archive, all access needs for that data can be satisfied from the archive without moving the data back to the original application environment. This includes accessing data and understanding what it means.

In essence, you are moving the data to a new application and operational environment, *the archive,* which will be held constant over time.

10.1 INDEPENDENCE FROM APPLICATION PROGRAMS

The application programs are usually depended on to provide reports, displays, and interpretation of data stored in the operational databases. For many applications this is the only way that the data can be externalized.

10.1.1 **Is operational Data Independent of the Application?**

The first question to answer is whether the data in the operational database can be used without its application programs. Is the data independent from the applications as it sits in the operational environment? This is often true for data stored in relational databases where a data consumer can use ad hoc SQL to access and present data through standard report writers. If you can do this to handle all the information needs beyond transaction processing, the data is independent in the operational environment. This is a big plus if true; it will make archiving much easier.

However, this is often not the case for data stored in nonrelational databases or file systems. It is also not true for relational database applications in which the underlying data models are not reflective of the business objects or are complex and not understood by the user community. This is very often the case with packaged applications. The vendor does not want the user to meddle in the underlying databases and thus shields them from the knowledge necessary to directly access the databases.

Storing coded data instead of understandable data in the database is also a frequent cause requiring applications to be kept. Of course, this can be mitigated by transforming the codes to understandable data when archiving, by adding a code table to the archive that describes the meaning of the codes, or simply by documenting the code descriptions in the archive metadata.

10.1.2 **Version Independence**

Over time, all applications undergo changes. Operational systems never deal with data stored under different versions of the application. They only deal with data that is stored under the current version in operation. If old data is to be used with a new version of the application, it must be transformed to match the data definitions of the new version. This process creates "fuzzy" data values whenever the changes involve new columns or changes in encoding of older columns. For example, if a new column is added to a table, the data rows added to the table prior to the event would contain a null indicator for that column, not the true value that would have been used if the row had been added after the addition of the column.

A properly designed archive will retain data as it existed when archived. This means that it will maintain versions of data for the same application. This gives a much truer picture of the data. It essentially becomes independent of application versioning.

10.1.3 **Transforming to an Independent Form**

The goal of archiving is to transform the data to a form that makes it independent of the applications. This form will always be relational. We do this today when we build data warehouses and business intelligence analytic stores. Every ETL tool on the market transforms data from virtually any type of database.

10.1.4 **Special Processing Concerns**

Arguments are often heard that the application programs add understanding beyond what is stored in the databases through data transformations, data expansions, triggers, stored procedures, and other means. The underlying data is not the complete story of the data. The application programs, including program fragments stored with the DBMS, are needed to present true information to the end user.

The implication is that the archive must preserve these program fragments as well if it is to achieve application independence. In reality most, if not all, of the arguments fade away when examined closely.

Most of these special processing routines referred to are used only during transaction processing. They are process fragments used to complete the transaction or to trigger other data events in other places. However, the archive is storing data that is beyond transaction processing. In essence, the data has already reached a mature status. It is complete. Data in the archive is only looked at. It is not expected to be changed; it is not allowed to be changed.

When you take away the transaction processing functions, there is little left. The remaining concerns are about data transformations that occur to make data more presentable or understandable when externalized. These could be important concerns.

An important characteristic of these processes is that they are data driven. The visual outcome is determined by data values in the database. Therefore the user can easily replicate this processing in one of two ways. The first is to make the archive data reflective of the presentation form of the data. Create virtual data columns in the archive data structure and do the transforms when putting data into the archive. The second approach is to use SQL SELECT clause functionality to replicate the transformation process when you're accessing the archive.

10.1.5 **Virtualizing the Operational Data**

If the processing done by the application is so extensive as to make the underlying database structures unrecognizable, the best approach to independence is to create the archive from a virtual view of data through the application outputs or application programming interfaces, if available. This approach should eliminate even the most troublesome cases.

10.1.6 **Metadata**

This might seem repetitive, but you cannot achieve application independence without complete and accurate metadata. To be independent you cannot rely on application programs to add meaning and understanding to the data. It can come only through the metadata you capture and store in the archive.

10.2 **INDEPENDENCE FROM DBMS**

The operational data will be stored in a DBMS or a file system. Most of these are very proprietary in the way they represent data structures, data relationships, and data elements.

The archive should be a DBMS neutral storage place. It should support industry-standard JDBC processing that can be achieved through a variety of data storage implementations.

10.2.1 **Relational Data Sources**

Even when RDBMS vendors claim to be using industry standards, as most of them do, they all have unique differences that make them nonstandard.

Relational systems also change on a regular basis. They add new data types, new output functions, and new relationship capabilities. They have always been downward compatible, thus preserving the ability to work with older data.

In moving data to the archive, it is important to get to a true industry-standard storage format. This can usually be done within any relational system by restricting data element definitions to industry-standard JDBC formats. You must resist the temptation to use structures that are not pervasive. For example, the TIMESTAMP construct of DB2 is unknown by most other relational DBMS systems.

Another area of difference in relational systems is the handling of large data objects (BLOB, CLOB, and others). Examine the implementations that you use and ensure that you can get to a standard implementation in the archive. LOB data structures are becoming a more common part of operational database applications. They must be carefully considered when you're designing an archive application.

10.2.2 **Nonrelational Data Sources**

If the operational systems use nonrelational DBMS stores, the need to change the data is even more critical. DBMS systems such as IMS, ADABAS, M204, and IDMS all have this requirement. The users want nothing more than to retire the applications that use them from service. They run on expensive mainframes. They require expert staff that is getting harder and harder to find.

If the archive data is stored in their operational formats, the systems must be kept indefinitely. If it is transformed to relational, they do not. Most companies have plenty of experience is transforming data from these systems to a relational format.

10.2.3 **Multiple Data Sources**

Another reason to strive for DBMS independence in the archive is that data will most likely come from more than one DBMS type. This might be true in the beginning because you have parallel applications. If not, it might become true in the future when the applications are moved to other DBMS types.

Again, you do not want to have to deal with the archive when you make the decision to move an operational database to another DBMS type. If the archive is DBMS independent, it won't matter.

10.2.4 **The Archive Data Store**

The archive data store needs to be able to handle all the independence factors described in this section. That tends to rule against any of the industry-standard DBMS systems from being used for the archive store.

10.3 **INDEPENDENCE FROM SYSTEMS**

The data you move to an archive might come from multiple types of systems. There might be mainframes running z/OS, distributed systems running Unix, Linux, Windows, or AIX, or there may be other lesser-known systems. The elements of a system that are of concern are the hardware, the operating system, and the native file system. As discussed for DBMS independence, you want to have the archive system independent of the original systems and be situated on a platform that is likely to survive over time.

One mistake is to assume that you will host the archive on the same system the data comes from. If you do this, you will be hosting archives on a multitude of systems. Your company then becomes dependent on those systems to maintain and access the archive. You do not want that dependency.

The file system is significant in that file systems often impact the way data files are formatted. File systems have differences in blocking factors, end-of-record markers, end-of-block markers, or end-of-file markers. Some of these limitations end up being restrictions for the DBMS. For example, maximum row size can differ between relational systems. This is almost always a consequence of the file system used by the RDBMS to store data. They also might support data in different encoding schemes such as EBCDIC or ASCII.

The ideal design is that the archive be housed on a system that is universally recognized, that is low cost to maintain, and that is likely to have a long life. To the extent that this can be virtualized is also a valuable characteristic. For example, hosting the archive on a Linux operating system gives you the ability to move it to many different hardware bases.

10.4 **INDEPENDENCE FROM DATA FORMATS**

Designing for independence gets down to the consideration of actual data values. We'll cover this topic in greater detail later in the book, but it is worth mentioning here. Figure 10.1 shows the concept of archive independence.

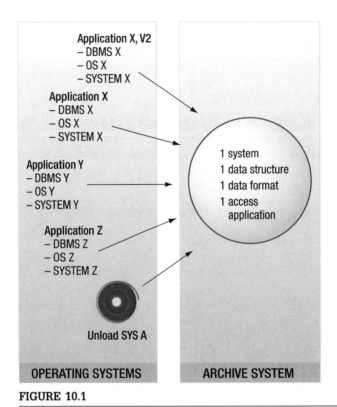

FIGURE 10.1

View of archive independence.

Data in operational systems is often encoded in ways that are specific to the origin. Examples are code pages, the mainframe packed decimal format, floating-point formats, date formats, and time formats.

In putting data into the archive, it is very helpful to change the format of the data elements to a more universal format to aid in later access. The intent of such changes is to change the storage format of the data and to not have data loss. For example, changing all character data to Unicode format will preserve all meaning of the data while putting it into a universally accepted format that all systems would be expected to recognize.

One common mistake is to encode a data element as *character* when the content is truly *binary*. This is often done without concern since most DBMS systems treat them the same. However, when you move data that has different character-level encodings from one system to another or move data from non-Unicode to Unicode, the binary data will become meaningless if character transforms occur. You must ensure that all data elements containing binary encoded data are labeled *binary* and handled as such when moving to the archive.

SUMMARY

Many writings about archiving data from databases talk about the need to preserve the applications and systems to process the archived data. This book takes the opposite approach: Change the data so that you do not need the applications or systems it came from. The first approach is simply not feasible for long retention-period requirements.

If there is anything the archive analyst can do to help the IT bottom line, it is this: The data archivist should look for opportunities to assist IT in using the archive to solve other problems.

Independence allows a single archive to be a consolidation point for data coming from multiple sources over time.

Achieving independence through archiving can simplify IT decisions and systems. It can remove roadblocks to application conversions and system migrations as well as the need to maintain obsolete systems and staff knowledgeable about them.

Keep independence in mind throughout the design process. It is a major factor in designing the archive location, the archive structure, and the data transformations needed for storing data in the archive.

To achieve application independence, the data structure definition in the archive often needs to differ from its representation in the operational database. The next chapter takes us to designing data structures for the way they will be stored in the archive.

CHAPTER

Modeling Archive Data

11

The database archive stores data coming from structured databases. It only makes sense that it would be a structured database itself. This means that the archive for any specific application is logically a database and must be architected just as the source database was originally architected. There will be differences between the model of data in the source system and the model of data in the archive. These differences may be minor or significant.

The data archivist must model two data structures and relate them to each other. One is of the data in the source operational database that are impacted by the application's archiving activity. The other is the structure that the archived data will take in the archive data store.

This information is very specific about what data is moved to the archive, what data is deleted from the source data store, and how data moved to the archive is restructured for long-term independence.

The input to this process is the metadata developed in earlier steps. The output diagrams will be used later to define the extraction process for the operational databases and the storage processes for putting new data into the archive.

11.1 THE SOURCE DATA MODEL

The *source data model* is a model of business objects, as defined earlier in Chapter 8. You don't need to model everything in the source database, just the tables that constitute the business objects you will be working with. The purpose of modeling is to indicate what is impacted when a business object is moved to the archive: what gets selected to be moved to the archive and what gets deleted or modified in the operational database.

Figures 11.1 and 11.2 show examples of source data models for two common source database types: a standard relational database and a hierarchical database such as IMS.

Data Source: DB2A on z/OS System 10
Database: ACCOUNTS

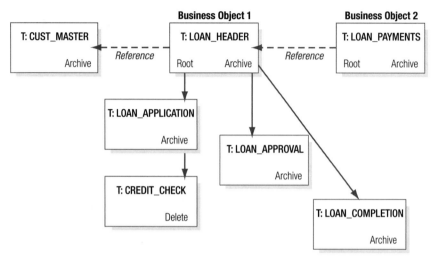

FIGURE 11.1

A relational database example of a source data model.

Data Source: IMS ABCD on z/OS System 10
DBD: CUSTOMER

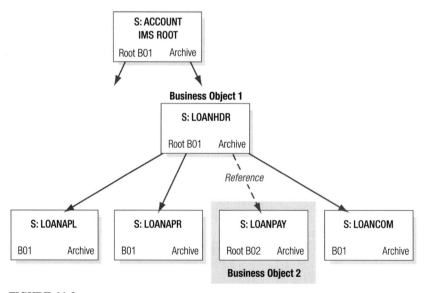

FIGURE 11.2

An IMS database example of a source data model.

11.1.1 **Data Source**

The data source should be identified on the diagram for reference purposes. It should come directly from the metadata and should identify the computer system and the database instance where the source operational database resides.

11.1.2 **Business Objects**

You archive business objects. A *business object* is the data that describes an event (transaction) or a long-standing business entity. Archiving anything less than a business object isn't logical.

You carve business objects out of the tables and relationships described in the metadata. Start with the metadata ERD you created earlier in finding metadata and select tables until you are done. This should correspond exactly to the table structure implemented in the database. Sometimes ERDs show the true normalization, which may differ from the materialization in the database. The point of the diagram is to guide the extract designer on what to do with database constructs. It must model the real table structure as implemented in the database.

Selecting the archive root table All business objects are hierarchical. They have a single identifying value that makes them unique. You need to find the table (the archive root table) that contains one entry for each object of the business object type, which will contain a data element or elements that uniquely identifies each object. If you cannot find this table, you cannot archive; at least you cannot do selective database archiving.

After you have identified the archive root table, you then proceed to complete the definition.

If there are multiple business objects that you want to archive on different schedules and thus create separate archiving streams, you need to designate which tables contain the archive root for each business object. This is shown in Figure 11.1, with the table LOAN_HEADER containing the root entries for one business object and the table LOAN_PAYMENTS containing the root entries for a second business object. If the designer felt it was better to wait until all payments were made and the loan closed before archiving anything for the loan, this would be redefined as one business object and not two.

Object relationships You need to find the other tables that contain entries that are needed to fully define the business object. These should have been identified in the metadata-gathering function. The relationships between tables should also have been defined earlier.

All relationships that are children to the archive root need to be identified, whether they are going to be put into the archive or not. This is because once a root is removed from the operational database, all children are automatically deleted as well. At least this is what should happen. Most DBMS implementations will do this automatically if the relationships are properly defined. This is sometimes referred to as *cascade delete*.

If you discover data that should be part of a business object but no relationship exists between its table and one of the other tables in the object, you must find the relationship. This can only mean that the metadata definition is incomplete. Find the relationship and complete the definition. If it is a part of the business object, a link in the data must exist.

11.1.3 Reference Tables

The business object relationships contain only table references that make up the object. Often parts of the object definition are linked through relationships to other data in other tables that expand on some of the information of the data elements of the table. This is very common, linking customer-id to expanded customer information, part-number to expanded product description, personnel-id to identify the actual person involved. The tables linked to are not part of the business object; they merely provide expanded information. These are referred to as *reference tables*.

You should look at the metadata and discover where expanded information is useful or needed to make the business object meaningful in the archive. When this is true, you need to include the tables containing the reference information in the diagram and link them to the business object table that contains the reference identifier. They need to be marked as reference links.

There are two distinct cases for reference information. The first case is where the referenced information is not part of the application. This is shown in Figure 11.1 for the CUSTOMER_MASTER table. It is not part of the loan but does cross-reference the customer ID stored in the LOAN_HEADER table to the customer's name and address.

The second case is where the application structure is divided into multiple streams to archive transactions earlier than master information would be archived. In this case some of the master information might be designated as a reference for a subordinate table. This is shown in Figure 11.1 where Business Object 2 points back to the LOAN_HEADER table to find expanded information on whom the loan payment is for.

Relationship links   All connectors between tables must be supported by underlying links in the database. These must all be known and specified in the metadata or in the source data model.

For relational databases, these are *primary/foreign key pairs*. That means that column values are needed to connect them. They must exist. They may not be specified as links to the DBMS. In fact, often they are not, since database administrators either never defined them or removed them to achieve better performance in executing maintenance utilities. However, the relationships still exist and must be found, whether defined to the DBMS or not.

For hierarchical systems, they exist by virtue of the database hierarchical definition. Data values are not needed to navigate. The hierarchical relationships are used instead.

The top of the business object must have a unique key that identifies each specific business object instance. This value is normally a part of all object links to tables below it. It is not part of reference links.

11.1.4 **Archive Actions**

It is important to annotate the model to show which tables have data that will be put into the archive and which ones will not. In Figure 11.1 this is shown in the lower right corner of each box. The entries indicated are ARCHIVE and DELETE.

The ARCHIVE function indicates that the data for this table is moved to the archive. That is a primary purpose of the source data model but does not indicate what will be done with the data in the operational system. The disposition of data in the operational database is determined later in the process. It might be deleted, marked for delete, or left undisturbed.

The DELETE parameter indicates that the data is not put into the archive. Again, it is not a reference to what happens in the operational system.

This is used if you have entire tables that contain superfluous information that is not needed for long-term storage. Figure 11.1 presents an example in which credit check information on the loan applicant is done and saved in the operational system. The archive designer chooses to exclude this data from the archive since it serves no purpose, contains privacy information, and will probably be invalid by the time the records are archived.

Hierarchical rule   All nodes in the business object tree must be marked as ARCHIVE or DELETE. If any node is marked DELETE, all tables connected underneath it must also be marked DELETE. If this is not what you want, you need to move the table you want to keep to connect to another table that is going to be kept. The purpose of this is to force you to define a relationship with data links that will be needed in the archive. Otherwise you end up with an orphan in the archive.

11.1.5 **Hierarchies of Business Objects**

Figures 11.1 and 11.2 show a case where the application has more than one business object and the business objects are connected. This is not an unusual occurrence. If parts of the application's data are to be archived using one set of rules and another part using another set, this situation will occur.

Two business objects for an application do not need to be related through structure. It just turns out that they often are.

When you do define a hierarchy of connected business objects, there are some rules that must be followed, as outlined in the following subsections.

Order of definition   It is much easier to identify and specify business objects from the bottom up. Identify the transactions you want to archive first, since they will generally always be at the bottom of the tree.

No overlap for archive A single table must *not* be listed as an ARCHIVE node for more than one business object. This is an absolute rule. You cannot tolerate some of the rows being archived in one archive stream and some in others. It makes no logical sense for this to occur.

A table can be listed as a reference table in as many other business objects as wanted. However, if a reference table is in the same hierarchical structure as one of the business objects, it must always be higher in the hierarchy than the archive root node of that business objects. This rule simply makes sense.

Order of execution When you specify archive execution criteria in Chapter 12, you need to include a test within any business object for the absence of rows of junior business objects that are archived separately. This means that to archive Business Object 1 in Figure 11.1, you cannot have any Business Object 2 occurrences connected to the ones you select.

If you do not follow this rule, instances of Business Object 2 will be deleted from the operational database when the higher-level object is archived and the data will be lost forever.

11.1.6 **Data Elements**

At this point we are assuming that all data elements within entries in the table are moved to the archive when the selection criteria identifies the business object. Generally this is what you want to do. However, there are times when specific data elements are not needed or wanted in the archive.

It is possible to selectively delete data elements from the rows during the archive process. For example, you might include a BLOB data element in a row that has a picture image of the applicant. You decide that it would be unnecessary to move this to the archive.

If you want to selectively delete data elements from being moved to the archive, you should specify this on the data source model as well. This could be done within the diagrams shown by adding additional text or could be done with a separate schedule showing which data elements are moved and which removed. For our purposes it will be reflected on the primary diagram since you generally would delete only one or at most a few data elements from any table.

If there is any doubt at all, you should retain the data element. It is hard to anticipate the future and what might be useful to someone. Unless there are strong reasons for omitting a data element, it should be saved.

11.2 **THE TARGET DATA MODEL**

The *target data model* shows how data will be represented in the archive after it is moved. For relational data sources these models will look a lot like the source data model. For others they could be more complex.

11.2.1 **Business Objects in the Archive**

The source data model tells us which business objects will show up in the archive. The purpose of the target data model is to show how relational tables in the archive reflect the business models pulled from the source. An example of a data target model is shown in Figure 11.3.

Each table in the source data model will appear as a table in the target data model. This is a rule that should always be followed. As we will see later, sometimes a table in the source data model will require more than one table to be used in the target data model.

Data Source: IMS ABCD on z/OS System 10
             DBD: CUSTOMER

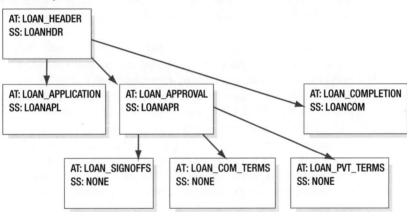

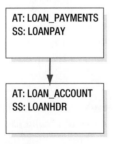

FIGURE 11.3

Example of a target data model.

11.2.2 **Names**

Table names, segment names, and column names in operational databases often convey little meaning as to what they contain. Names in the archive data model do not have to be the same as they are in the source databases.

Your archive implementation should allow for changing the original name to a better one in the archive. It might also be necessary to change the name if the archive table is to contain data from more than one data source (as in a distributed strategy).

If you are changing a name, show the source table name and the archive table name in the diagram. This is shown in Figure 11.3 where the short, meaningless IMS segment names are changed to more meaningful names.

11.2.3 **Normalization**

For relational sources it should not be necessary to normalize any of the data, since it is already normalized within the source data. Even if it is not in third normal form, it is a good idea to keep it at the same normalization level as it is in the source database.

For other types of data sources, such as IMS segments or VSAM data records, the content of the segment or record may contain structures that need some normalization done to them to represent them as relational structures in the archive. The two constructs that cause the most problems are REDEFINE and OCCURS clauses. In neither case is normalization automatic. You need to apply some knowledge of the data to make that call.

A REDEFINE clause overlays one or more data elements with one or more other data elements. They occupy the same space in the source segment definition. This structure is common for COBOL written application programs. It can mean one of two things: (1) redefinition of the same business fact or (2) definition of a different business fact based on some value in a different data element within the segment.

In the case of redefinition of the same fact, no normalization needs to be done. However, the user needs to pick which representation will be used in the archive structure. You cannot use both. For example, if one definition defines CREATE_DATE and the REDEFINE over this includes three data elements CREATE_DAY, CREATE_MONTH, and CREATE_YEAR, you would probably pick the first definition.

The second case calls for normalization. For example, if the segment contains loan term information that differs between commercial and retail customers, the fields used for commercial customers might include data elements for LINE_OF_CREDIT_ID and RATE_REVIEW_PERIOD, whereas fields used for a private individual might instead use data elements APR and LOAN_DURATION. The IMS segment defines these as using the same space since one segment can only be one type of customer or the other. Some other data element in the segment contains an indicator as to which type of customer this is—for example, CUST_TYPE.

When this type of REDEFINE is used, it is necessary to normalize this structure into two additional tables: one containing data for commercial customers and one for retail customers. Each of these tables needs key information included with it to connect them to the higher-level table. This idea is shown in Figure 11.3 for the LOAN_COM_TERMS table and the LOAN_PVT_TERMS table.

Another way to handle this is to merely expand the relational table LOAN_APPROVAL to include all data elements. When you do this, population of the rows with data would leave one set of data elements null and would fill in the other with values based on the same logic. This approach does work but is not relationally correct.

The second construct is the OCCURS clause of COBOL. This is a repeating group of one or more data elements. Again, there are two conditions to consider.

In one case the repeating parts are merely different business facts for the same row, but the data designer chose to use a repeating group instead of separate data element names. For example, a group of MONTHLY_SALES OCCURS 12 TIMES would really mean that the construct is truly 12 different data elements—one for Jan, one for Feb, and so on. When this is the case, the row does not need to be normalized; it merely needs the repeating group decomposed into 12 column definitions with unique names.

In another example of COLLEGE OCCURS 6 TIMES containing data elements for SCHOOL_NAME, DEGREE, DATE_RECEIVED, the only right way to handle this is to create a subtable with these columns and populate it with one row for each instance that has data in it in the incoming segment. If you do not normalize it, it will become difficult to search the denormalized rows for colleges or degrees. The new table needs to also contain a key to define the relationship between it and the parent table the values are extracted from.

This situation is shown in Figure 11.3 where LOAN_SIGNOFFS are normalized into a separate table. Possibly the loan approval process could have multiple signoffs, each with a NAME, TITLE, and SIGNOFF_DATE.

11.2.4 **Keys**

Relational database structures need key fields to identify business objects and to connect tables that contain parts of the object definition. If you are coming from a relational data source, this will generally not be a problem; they already exist in the data and you know what they are. However, this is not always the case for nonrelational data sources.

Reusing identifiers Business object identifiers are always *unique* within the operational database. This is how you distinguish one from another. However, this does not always translate over to the data archive for the same business object. The problem arises when an enterprise reuses an identifier after the original user has disappeared from the database. There are many examples in which account numbers, phone numbers, or part numbers get reused. In the operational database it is not a problem. In the archive it is, since the older, retired business objects can still exist for years and the new user of the identifier might also appear in the archive before the first user's data is discarded.

You need to ensure that this situation does not exist for the business objects you are working with. If it does exist, you need to solve the problem in some way.

One way is to change the operational system to *not* reuse identifiers. This is a proper solution, albeit one that will often meet with resistance. It might require that the identifier increase in length. Operational folks will be very upset if they are required to make this change.

Another way is to pick a different data element or a set of them to use as the business object identifier. This is often possible since identifiers are just shorthand for uniquely identifying something that often could have been identified by something else.

If none of these solutions is possible, it can be handled in archive access through a complex process that will be described in a later chapter. That process works on the assumption that you copy reference information with each archiving run and that the scope of a *join* is restricted to the archive objects sent to the archive together. This last approach should not be used unless you cannot get a better resolution.

Database archive stores that do not deal with this problem and that put all archive data into a single database will not work for applications that have this problem.

Duplicate keys   Putting reference information in the archive will result in reference objects having nonunique keys in the archive database. This is true even if duplicates are eliminated for each execution of the archive function. The referenced object will exist only once for a specific archive run but might be duplicated across multiple archive runs.

This is justified on the basis that each occurrence is a version of the information that is stored at the time the object that references it is archived. In essence it is subordinate to the business object that references it. The true identifier is the key to the referenced table plus the archive run date or a generated sequence number.

Using this logic results in a versioning of the reference information, which could be very useful in the future.

For example, for an archive of banking transactions, a transaction that connects to a reference table row by the CUSTOMER_ID may contain the name "Kathryn Young," whereas a different transaction connects to a different row using the same CUSTOMER_ID but the name is "Kathryn Olson." This reflects that Kathryn changed her last name in the time interval between the occurrence of the two banking transactions.

If you do not want to have this situation occur, you can eliminate duplicates in the archive by having the *store* function not store a referenced row if one already exists. This would be useful if the referenced information cannot change over time.

Hierarchical key generation Hierarchical systems such as IMS often have complex key structures that depend partly on data values and partly on positioning within the hierarchy. When you convert these to a relational system, the positioning assumptions must be converted to actual column values. Often columns need to be added to the tables to accomplish this goal.

There are two situations in which positioning comes into play. One is where the child source segment does not contain the parent segment's identifier (key). It is assumed by its definition to be a child segment. In this case, the table representing the child segment must be expanded to include the parent's identifier field or fields as well. In IMS parlance this is referred to as the *concatenated key*. It will not likely be in the segment received at the archive entrance.

The second condition is where a segment has no key to uniquely identify it within a set of multiple segments connected to the same parent segment (called *twins* in IMS parlance). IMS does not need these, since positioning will accomplish the ordering of segment instances. When this segment type is translated to the archive relational table, a sequence number column needs to be added to create uniqueness for each row.

All the changes and conditions noted in this section need to be included on the target data model. It provides guidance for designers working on later steps.

11.2.5 **Data Transformations**

Any data transformation that will be performed on the data needs to be annotated on this diagram. These transformations were discussed earlier and involve such things as *character* to Unicode, numeric structure changes, null indicator recognition and redefinition, floating-point structure changes, and similar things.

11.3 **MODEL REPRESENTATIONS**

Diagrams for the source data model and the target data model should be created and stored in the archive repository. They should not be simply marked-up ERDs used for operational metadata. They need to be separate, kept simple, and show specifically what is happening when archiving occurs. It might make sense to do these in an XML format since this has a long-term survivability expectation.

The models need to be reviewed by the archive review committee before you launch into later design steps.

SUMMARY

The data archivist essentially becomes a data modeler at this point. A background in data architecture or data modeling is very helpful.

The archive data store is almost always represented in relational format. If the source data is relational, the mapping between the two is straightforward. However, some source databases will not be relational and will require some work to make them relational.

This exercise is not dissimilar to designing a data warehouse or a business intelligence analytic database from the same data sources. In fact, most of the time, the exercise of normalizing a nonrelational data source has already been done at least once for the targeted data. It is unlikely that an important database has not been tapped for extraction to a relational target at some point in the last 10 years. The data archivist can get a head start on modeling by examining the previous work done or, better yet, having the staff that did it before help out if possible.

This should not be a complex nor time-consuming step. After the metadata for the operational database is collected, the creation of the source data model and the target data model is fairly straightforward.

These models are extremely useful in later steps, where the design of the action processes will occur. Now that you are armed with this knowledge, let's get to the business of setting archive policies.

CHAPTER

Setting Archive Policies

12

The next step in designing database archiving applications is to set the archive policies. An *archive policy* is a statement that stipulates the way the flow of data into and out of the archive is to be managed. There are three basic policies that need to be set and approved:

- *Extract policy.* This defines when a business object qualifies to move from the operational database to the archive.
- *Storage policy.* This defines which rules need to be enforced for data while it is in archive storage.
- *Discard policy.* This defines when a business object is removed from archive storage.

Archive policies serve as the requirement statements for programs and procedures that will subsequently get built to implement the archiving processes for the application. A clear, complete, and unambiguous statement is what you want to develop.

The scope of a policy would normally be a single business object. This could result in multiple policies for a single application. They can share a common storage policy and possibly a common discard policy, but the extract policy will normally be different for each business object.

12.1 EXTRACT POLICIES

The extract policy drives the development of processes to read the operational database, find inactive business objects, move them to the archive, and delete them from the source database.

The key elements of the extract policy are:

- Selection criteria for what determines inactive data
- Disposition of data in the operational database
- Determination of when and how often to execute the extract process

12.1.1 **Selection Criteria for Extraction**

The selection criteria are logical expressions that identify inactive data eligible to be moved to the archive. They are expressions in terms of data values that can be tested by a program. The selection process needs to be automated so that it can run against millions of database records and find the ones that can safely be moved to the archive.

The selection criteria is used to qualify the business object, not to actually perform the selection of rows to be moved. This is an important distinction. Trying to combine the two into a single expression will only limit your ability to express the needed criteria. Execution of the selection criteria will return identifiers of business objects that qualify for movement. The actual gathering of the data for them is performed in a separate process.

Some common criteria The most common element of a criterion will be *time since* some event—for example, 90 days since the transaction was made, one year after the account is closed, 120 days after the claim was settled. The amount of time should include sufficient opportunity for all expected uses of the business object to have been made. Setting this amount is a business judgment that only the application business owners of the data are qualified to make.

A common indicator is a *completion status,* such as account closed, order received, or employee terminated. Another common indicator is that *no exception condition exists,* such as lawsuit pending, part back-ordered, or payment not received.

Often multiples of these selection elements exist for the same criterion, such as 90 days since the claim was submitted, the claim is settled, and there are no pending lawsuits.

Format of selection criteria The selection criteria need to be expressed in a form that is easily understood by anyone needing to see, understand, and approve them. An archive analyst's temptation is to express these criteria in terms of the form they will take for execution; for example, as an SQL statement. However, this might not be understandable by all individuals who need to know and approve them.

It is better to write the selection criteria out in text form first, then express them a second time in terms of a logical expression that incorporates the data elements of the business object itself. SQL is not a bad choice, although it might not work for some data sources such as IMS. A generic logical expression is all that is needed for this level of documentation. Providing the program implementation form of expression at this point is premature and not useful for getting the criteria defined and approved.

After the technical expression is generated, it can be tested against the text expression to ensure correct conversion. The text expression is the business statement. Even though it is written in business language, the test expression should show which data elements will be used to satisfy the criteria. Examples of expressions are given in Figure 12.1.

Example 1: Simple Criteria for LOAN_PAYMENTS
90 days after payment received
```
IF DAYS(CURRENT_DATE — LOAN_PAYMENT.TRANSACTION_DATE) > 90
```

Example 2: Multiple Table Criteria for LOAN_HEADER
Loan closed over 120 days and title documents received by client
```
IF LOAN_HEADER.STATUS = "C" AND
(DAYS (CURRENT_DATE — LOAD_HEADER.CLOSED_DATE) > 120) AND
LOAN_COMPLETION.TITLE_DOCS_RETURNED = 'YES'
```

Example 3: Use of External Criteria for Loan Header
Loan closed over 120 days and account not in default
```
IF LOAN_HEADER.STATUS = "C" AND
(DAYS (CURRENT_DATE — LOAD_HEADER.CLOSED_DATE) > 120) AND
LOAN_HEADER.ACCOUNTID NOT IN DEFAULT_ACCOUNTS.ACCOUNTID
```

FIGURE 12.1

Examples of selection criteria.

Source of data values The data elements that will be used in the evaluation can come from anywhere. They do not need to be restricted to testing values in the rows of tables included in the business object. Generally the tests will be applied to data elements in the archive root node of the business object; however, other times they might use data elements in child nodes or look to a completely external data source to qualify the objects.

Multiple sources The source of data for use by selection criteria can come from multiple sources, as shown in Figure 12.1, Example 3. It requires that a condition exist within the data elements of the business object and also that another, exception condition exist in a database table outside the business object (the accounts in the default table).

Basically the selection criteria can come from anywhere as long as they return a list of unique identifiers of objects to be archived.

12.1.2 Data Disposition on Extraction

The second part of the extract policy addresses what to do with the data in the operational database when an object is moved to the archive. The user can do one of three things:

- Delete the business objects from the operational database.
- Mark them as having been archived.
- Leave the objects without change.

Delete   Deleting the selected objects from the operational database is the most common action to take. This includes removing the root row and all connected rows of child tables as specified in the source data model for the business object. Any rows connected by reference relationships would not be deleted.

Mark   The mark option is used if the application wants the data moved to the archive but is not ready to remove it from the operational database. In this case the extract program will need to have a place in the business object's data to leave a mark. The mark can be a simple flag (*A* for archived, "blank" for not) or a value such as a time stamp of when the data was archived.

One reason for using a mark instead of deleting is a case where it is beneficial for the data to arrive in the archive before it becomes inactive. For example, if the data is highly sensitive, it might be important to copy it from the operational database before any mischief can be done to modify it. This is referred to as *early archiving*. It protects the authenticity of the data if the archive storage is better protected from mischief.

The mark may be placed in only the archive root node of the business object, or it might be placed in every row of all tables that make up the business object. Rows within reference tables would not be marked. They are not yet officially in the archive; only a nonfinal version is used to add information to the business objects.

The archivist must provide for a separate process to remove marked items from the archive when the time is appropriate. This process needs selection criteria apart from the extract criteria for determining which marked items are ready to be deleted.

Selective marking   It is possible to implement a policy of selective marking. This means that some selected business objects will be extracted and deleted, and others will be extracted and marked. This is a very unusual policy but one that could be implemented. This might be used for objects that contain exception status conditions requiring them to remain in the operational database but that are also required to be in the archive to maintain consistency with other data objects in the archive.

If selective marking is performed, additional selection criteria must be added to the policy to determine which business objects are marked and left and which are deleted. The concept of the selection criteria is the same as the general criteria. The documentation should be handled in the same way.

Leave the data with no changes   This policy option states that items selected by the extract selection criteria are to be copied to the archive with no change to the data in the operational database. This can be used to collect versions of business objects. This option should never be used for early archiving, since the user has no way of knowing whether an object is in the archive or not. Marking should be used for early archiving. A template for selection criteria that use selective marking is shown in Figure 12.2.

```
IF  (selection criteria)
    THEN IF (marking criteria)
        mark business object as archived using current date as mark
    ELSE
        delete business object from database
```

FIGURE 12.2

Example of extract selection criteria with selective marking.

12.1.3 **When to Execute Extracts**

The third part of the extract policy is to state when the archive extract function will be executed. The *archive extract function* is a program that will scan an operational database looking for business objects on which to act. It is executed periodically, much like running backups. It can be viewed as a database maintenance function.

Periodicity   The policy should state the intended periodicity of execution. Will it be once a month? Once a week? Daily?

The selection criteria determine whether a business object is eligible to be moved but do not state how long it might have been in the eligibility state. The length of time between archive extract executions will impact how long an item might be eligible before it is "discovered" by the selection criteria.

Having items in the operational database that are eligible for the archive might not be a problem; however, for some applications it could be an important factor to consider. For example, if you want to establish data authenticity and reduce exposure to unauthorized modification, it might be important to archive as close to the eligibility point as possible. This could dictate a frequency of once a day.

Another factor to consider is the impact on the performance of operational systems of leaving inactive data. If the interval between archive extract executions is too long, a large amount of inactive data can accumulate. This not only affects the operational systems' performance but results in a larger archive unit of data to handle at one time through the archive store function. Thus a three-month interval might be a poor choice and a weekly run might be more appropriate.

The decision on the interval policy must not be left to the operations staff. This is a business decision the archive analyst must reach with input from the business owners of the data and consultation with the operations staff.

Continuous archiving   It is possible to build extract routines that archive data on arrival in the operational database. This is the extreme case of early archiving. It would only make sense if the disposition policy called for *mark* or *do nothing* and not *delete*. In this case the selection criteria are not used and a trigger is placed on the INSERT function of the DBMS.

Implementing a continuous archiving policy should be avoided if at all possible. Maintaining consistency between the archive and the operational database across interruptions and recoveries can be difficult. It also might negatively impact operational performance during peak operating periods.

Relationship to normal operations   Another issue is whether the execution needs to be performed when the operational database is not running (such as in IMS Batch Mode) or whether it can be run while normal database activities are occurring. This will determine how the extract function gets constructed.

This policy should also state the relationship of executing the archive extract function to other operations on the database. The ideal situation is to allow the extract function to tolerate normal operations, much like any other online application; however, it will always cause some degree of impedance to normal operations. Thus the policy may restrict execution to certain hours of the day or days of the week so that it runs only when loads on the operational database are expected to be minimal, most likely during the Saturday night second shift.

There might also be a need to restrict the amount of time the function executes. For example, it may be restricted to no more than one hour due to other work that needs to be done in the same time period allocated for database maintenance. These restrictions can influence the frequency of execution.

Interruptions   A final part of this policy is to state how tolerant of interruptions the extract process needs to be. If it fails to finish execution during one of its periodic sweeps through the operational database, does it store what it collected up to the point of failure, does it roll it back, does it restart until finished? How important is it to finish 100 percent of the extract process each time? To answer this question, you need to consider the impact of data remaining in the operational database after it becomes eligible for archiving.

12.2 ARCHIVE STORAGE POLICIES

It is important to specify rules for storing data in the archive. The policy does not include all the details of implementing the policy; it simply specifies the requirements. This policy should be used in later years to audit the storage activities for the archive to ensure that they continue to conform to requirements.

The storage policy needs to be developed with the business application people and the storage management group. It needs to be validated, approved, and stored in the archive repository.

The goals that need to be achieved through the storage policy are protection of the data from physical or logical loss and prevention of unauthorized access or modification.

12.2.1 **Form of Data**

The storage policy does not deal with the detailed structure of the data in the archive. However, the macro-level view of the way data is structured is important to consider in making storage decisions. Our concern here is the way different forms of data representation affect storage decisions.

It might not be known at this stage of application archive design which form the archive data buckets will take and the dynamics between them. The policy might have to evolve throughout the design phase. If you are using a packaged archiving solution, it will be known and so the policy can state with certainty what the form of data will be.

Database If the archive is going to be stored using a standard vendor-supplied DBMS, the storage decisions are limited. The DBMS will require that the entire database be on front-line storage and available to receive new data or to satisfy access requests. It is not possible to store the archive in a DBMS and use tape or other offline storage. It is also not possible to keep portions of the archive in one place and portions in another place.

There are many reasons to avoid storing the archive in a DBMS. Managing storage is just one of them. However, if that is the choice for an application, the storage policies become simple although highly restrictive.

Files A more likely view from the storage policy is that the archive is a collection of files. The files may contain data in UNLOAD format or some other format that can be processed by an archiving application. The fact that the storage component will be managing files opens up many beneficial storage options, which we'll discuss later.

If a file scheme is used, it needs to be understood whether adding new data to the archive requires access to previously written and stored files and, if so, how many of them. In other words, the storage policy should state the impact on retrieval of files required for inserting new archived data. It should also have an idea of how many of the archive files might be needed for query access.

12.2.2 **Location of Data**

The question of location has three components: type of devices, where these devices are attached in the user's computing map, and geographical placement. The choices you make should be a result of your opinion of the value of the data and the consequences of data loss. For high-profile data being kept for legal reasons, you want to consider a fully protected policy. For less important data, you can pick a much simpler strategy.

Device types The primary concern in selecting device types is whether you want to save money on storage costs. Define whether you want the archive stored on the front line, in always accessible storage, in low-cost semi-online storage, or in even lower-cost offline storage.

Some common types of storage are tape, write-once/read-multiple (WORM) devices, SAN devices, network-attached disk storage, or normal computer-attached disk storage. Of course tape is very cheap, but recovery of data takes a long time and accessibility can be a real problem. Searching data is mostly impractical. Tape also has a shorter life span, requiring copying to new tape media at frequent intervals. WORM devices appear to have an update prevention advantage. Although this is true, it prevents selective discard of data, requiring disposing of the entire media to accomplish discard. As such it is generally not appropriate for database archiving, since there are other ways of achieving protection from updates while putting the archive on updatable devices.

SAN devices seem to offer the best place to host a database archive. They have large capacity, are accessible online (although slow), have longer media life spans, and are lower cost. However, acquiring a SAN and developing the expertise to manage the devices can be an obstacle. Most IT departments are already using SAN devices, thus making them a logical choice.

Computer-attached storage is the most accessible but also the most expensive option. In addition to cost, managing the storage in an operational setting will make life more difficult for the storage administrators.

Device connections   The best place to attach archive storage is over an IP connection. Keep it independent of the system that is storing and accessing the archive so that the storage can live unattended for many years while the managing systems change with new technology. Direct attach to any system is not usually desirable.

Geographical   Another component of the storage policy is how many copies of the archive data you want to maintain and whether geographical dispersion is desirable. This is critical for establishing a recovery and disaster recovery strategy for the archive. You would never want to have only one copy. Media rot or malicious overwriting of data can render the archive useless. Even though these threats might be small, any possibility is too large to risk loss of the archive.

You will generally want a minimum of three copies in three geographically separate locations. It might be possible to rent space on someone else's systems to store one or more copies. This is a way to achieve geographical dispersion without building a new data center.

12.2.3 Protection from Wrongful Access

The storage policy should stipulate whether the archived data needs to be protected from wrongful access. This could require that the data be encrypted while in storage. It should indicate the degree of encryption required. This raises the need for encryption key management and the archiving of these keys. It could also require file-level signatures that would allow for determining whether a file has been overwritten or not.

12.2.4 **Protection from Data Loss**

For long-term storage, protection from data loss could require that data be tested from time to time to determine whether any data loss or corruption has occurred. I refer to this as a *ping*. The ping should include reading the entire archive file and checking a file signature, if one exists. This should be done for all copies of the archived data, not just the primary copy. You might have to depend on a backup at some time in the future, and ensuring that the copies are alive and well is just as important as testing the primary version.

In addition, the policy could specify a time interval for copying the data to newer media. This is especially important if the data is going to be stored on tape.

12.3 **ARCHIVE DISCARD POLICIES**

The discard policy states when business objects should be removed from the database archive. The policy may be as simple as "never" or as complex as you want to make it. The discard policy is a business decision and should be made by the application's business owners.

Once data is discarded from the archive, it is lost forever, requiring special care in setting the discard policy. If the criteria is too liberal, it could cause problems later on. If possible, the discard policy should be set with some extra time beyond the absolute legal requirement for keeping data.

12.3.1 **Discard Criteria**

If the criterion is not "never," criteria should be developed and stated in terms of the data elements stored in the archive. This is very similar to the extract function selection criteria. The criteria must be executable by a program. An example of a discard criterion is shown in Figure 12.3.

The discard criteria are generally based on date values in the data objects. They are almost never a function of how long data was in the archive.

If the criteria are based on the age of the business object, it is possible that when archiving begins objects are placed in the archive that are very close to the discard criteria. They have aged in the operational database. Thus even if

---

Discard Criteria for LOAN_PAYMENTS

Discard loan transactions that are 10 years after the payment was made

```
IF YEARS(CURRENT_DATE - LOAN_PAYMENT.TRANSACTION_DATE) > 10
```

FIGURE 12.3

Example of a discard criterion.

you have a 10-year retention period, the discard function could find data that qualifies for discard as soon as archiving begins.

The criterion of "never" is very tempting to use. However, almost every IT department I visited says that they want to discard data as soon as the law allows. I often heard the phrase, "It is only in there to be used in a lawsuit against us" in this context.

12.3.2 Exceptions to the Criteria

The policy should state whether there are any exceptions to the criteria that need to be honored. The obvious exception is the legal HOLD function that comes into play when the archived data is the target of an e-discovery request. In this case the requirement to retain the data trumps the legal discard criteria. It must be held until the HOLD is released by your legal department.

You can implement a HOLD on the entire archive stream for the application or just the specific business objects that are relevant to the discovery request. Most legal departments will want you to hold the entire archive for the application instead of being selective. You need to work with your legal department to determine the policy for each HOLD request. You cannot afford to wait for a lawsuit to arrive and then decide what to do. Implementing a selective HOLD function could take some time.

On the other hand, if the application is frequently subjected to lawsuits, holding the entire archive stream when any suit is open could result in never discarding anything.

12.3.3 When to Run Discard

The discard function runs periodically against the archive, looking for business objects that qualify for discard. The policy should stipulate how often the discard function should be executed.

The longer the interval between runs, the longer some objects will be in the archive beyond their discard qualification date. This would normally not be a problem if the interval is short. However, if you execute discard once a year, this can create a risk. Remember that discard is not used to free up space; it is used to remove data before it is caught in an e-discovery request. A typical policy will have the discard function executed once a week or once a month.

12.3.4 Disposition of Data

The discard process should identify business objects to be removed from the archive and then delete all data for this business object. It does not make sense to remove the header for a loan and leave transactions. Thus a discard execution can involve more than one type of business object.

The policy should stipulate that data for identified business objects should be removed from all archive copies maintained as backups.

The policy should stipulate whether the removal process needs to do "electronic shredding" of the data to make it undetectable by forensic software. Most SAN devices have electronic shredding features, but they will not be used unless you specify that you want them to be.

12.3.5 **Record of What Is Discarded**

You might want to keep a record of what business objects you discard from the archive. This would normally be a list of object identifiers and the dates removed. This is a function you do not want to use unless you're required to do so. However, for credit card accounts or bank accounts, it might be necessary to do so. One reason for doing this is to use the list to locate and remove data from nonarchive data stores.

12.4 **VALIDATION AND APPROVAL**

It is important to get validation of the policies from all relevant stakeholders. This can normally be done through the archive committee.

The policy statements should be widely distributed and easy to access. They should be stored as documents in the archive repository. You can expect to be asked what the policies are on a frequent basis.

Remember that archive policies should be periodically reviewed to ensure that they reflect the organization's current needs.

SUMMARY

Specifying requirements as a set of policies helps the implementation process immensely. It also makes audits of the archive practice easier to conduct. The components of your policy should be a part of every archiving application.

Mistakes in archive policy can lead to loss of data through inadequate storage rules or early discarding of data. An unbalanced extract policy can lead to either performance problems in operational systems because inactive data is held too long, or operational difficulties because data is moved to the archive too early. It is critical to the success of the project to carefully consider the policies before executing them. It is equally important to periodically review the policies in place to ensure that the archive is effectively serving its intended purposes.

Changes to Data Structures and Policies

Earlier chapters outlined how to design an archiving application with the assumption that everything stays the same over time. The operational applications, the rules for archiving, the decisions that are made, all were assumed to be constantly going forward from the time of initial design. As we all know, however, changes are bound to occur, and change is the one constant for IT departments. In fact, changes might occur while you are doing the initial design, before you get a chance to implement what you are doing.

This chapter explores how changes to the design objects impact the database archiving application. Dealing with change is one topic that can distinguish a good database archiving application from a bad one.

Since the data archivist cannot prevent changes from happening, the best course of action is for the archivist to become a part of the change process and have the archiving application change in concert with the operational and business decision-making changes.

Changes to the operational applications impact only the data at the time changes are made. Beyond that point, the data conforms to the new definition, not the old. It is as though the old data structures never existed. For the archive, the old data captured using the old structures could persist for many years. The archivist has a special problem to address that the operational folks do not.

We'll now turn our focus to changes to data structures in both the operational view and the archive view and explore how these changes impact data that has previously been stored. We'll also discuss changes to archive policies for an archiving application and how that could impact data archived under previous policies.

13.1 ARCHIVING SYSTEM STRATEGIES FOR HANDLING METADATA CHANGES

Recall that a single application can have multiple archive streams generated based on multiple parallel applications or serial upgrades or replacement of applications. A single structure change to an existing operational application could also generate a separation of archive data streams based on the scope of the change. The first thing to consider in any change is whether it requires generation of a new archive stream with the new structure or whether the old stream can tolerate the change.

When the metadata of the source data changes, this is referred to as a *metadata break*. This means that data archived before the break conforms to one metadata definition and data after the break to another. The scope of the metadata break can be very minor, such as changing the length of a single data element. However, it can also be very major, such as replacing the entire table structure. Many degrees of metadata break significance are possible between these extremes.

A single change event can include a number of changes. It is normal for application developers to collect changes over a period of time and make them to operational systems all at once. The application may have a periodic change cycle once a quarter, semiannually, or annually.

The changes you make in a single event might have nothing to do with each other. If many changes are done at one time, it is still just one metadata break. The metadata break severity would be set to the most severe change of each of the individual metadata changes implemented in the event.

There are two approaches an archive application can take in regard to metadata changes. One approach is to keep an archive stream consistent in metadata definition throughout time by changing the previously archived data to match the most current metadata definition after a change. The other is to never change data after it is archived, leaving the archive data stream with many distinct archiving units, each having its own version of the metadata associated with it.

13.1.1 **Single Data Definition Strategy**

In a single data definition strategy, the data will become suspect after some period of time if data values are modified or manufactured to maintain a single archive of data that is consistent with a single metadata definition. However, it will make it easier to manage the archive data store and to access data archived over long periods of time.

Using this strategy will ultimately require an archive stream to end whenever significant data structure change occurs that makes it impossible to modify the old data to match the new definition. It will force the end of one archiving data stream and the beginning of another.

13.1.2 **Multiple Data Definition Strategy**

The second strategy will lead to a larger number of stream variations. It basically introduces a stream variant within an archiving stream: a minor change that does not invalidate the stream but does require some special handling when accessing data on both sides of the minor metadata break. The archiving stream has a time-ordered sequence of archive data units, each of which has a single metadata definition to cover it. The archive units have metadata variations between them that do not violate the basic structural definition of the archiving stream.

With this strategy the data has more authenticity. You can claim that the data is in the archive exactly as it arrived on the initial entry. It has never been modified. The metadata that matches any archive unit of data is also frozen over time. An investigator would have more work to do to extract data from the archive stream but would have an assurance that the data is correct.

Using the multiple data definition strategy is facilitated if you have special software that can process extract and query requests across metadata breaks without corrupting the meaning of the data. If you have the ability to do this you would always want to use the multiple data definition approach.

This strategy will also break down when the scope of changes is too great. If the data structure of the business object does not maintain structural consistency across the break, you must end one archiving stream and start another.

The impact on the archive stream map will be different depending on the strategy you use. This concept is shown in Figure 13.1. For the single data definition strategy there will be no metadata breaks, but there will be more archive stream ends and starts. Not every change will result in a new archive stream, since some will be resolved by modifying the data in the previous stream and continuing to use it.

For the multiple data definition strategy, there will be fewer streams, but streams will have metadata breaks within them—possibly a lot of them.

13.2 METADATA CHANGE CATEGORIES

It is important to understand how changes that are commonly made to metadata can impact your implementation of both single definition and multiple definition strategies.

13.2.1 Minor Metadata Changes

Minor changes to data structures are very common, especially for custom applications created in-house. A minor change does not alter the basic structure of the business object as defined and implemented for the operational database. The basic table structure and relationships between tables remain the same. The key fields that uniquely identify the business objects and that make the relationships work stay the same as well.

Examples of common minor changes are:

- Increasing the length of a column
- Decreasing the length of a column

Single Data Definition Strategy

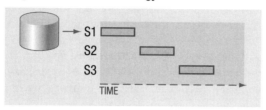

S1 = Loan Payments
S2 = Loan Payments Version 2
S3 = Loan Payments Version 3

Multiple Data Definition Strategy

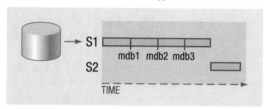

S1 = Loan Payments
S2 = Loan Payments Version 2

FIGURE 13.1

Impact of strategies for handling metadata breaks.

- Changing the precision of a numeric column
- Changing the data type of a column to one that is compatible with the old one
  - Changing an integer to a small integer
  - Changing a fixed-length character column to a variable-length character column
- Adding a new column that is not a key column
- Dropping an old column that is not a key column

No-impact changes Some of the changes have no impact on the data stored in the archive. The old data could accurately be stored in the new structure. For example, lengthening a column, shortening a column (if all the old values were short enough), many data type changes, and many precision changes are all easily handled.

To address this type of change, you can either convert all the data already in the archive to the new definition or, if your archive access routines are tolerant of these differences, you can merely leave the data already stored as it is. If you do leave it as it is, you would still mark the changeover point as a metadata break.

The ability to tolerate differences between data stored under slightly different definitions is a unique feature of some archiving solutions. This is a valuable feature since archive data can grow up to very large volumes, and having to convert older data to new definitions can be very time consuming.

Minor-impact changes These changes are similar to the ones just described but could require more attention. For example, changing the precision on a numeric column could cause a small problem with previously stored data.

If the precision is reduced, all the old data is able to be adjusted to the new precision on access. If you do this to all stored data, no problem will occur. On the other hand, if your access routines do the conversion dynamically, it must always use the smaller precision since that is the only one that produces consistent results.

If the precision is increased, the old data cannot be correctly converted to the new precision. It can be "fudged" by adding zeroes in the lower positions, to make it appear that it is accurate. However, the data is slightly wrong. If possible, you could keep the old data as it is and have the access routines that process data on both sides of the break always convert new values to the smaller precision.

Another minor impact change may occur in converting nonstandard dates to standard dates. The values are all convertible, although access routines would not normally be able to know this. It might be necessary to convert all previously stored values to the new format to allow for consistent and meaningful access across the break. In this example there is no data loss, just a big task in converting old values, similar to the Y2K problem.

Some of the Y2K solutions involved leaving two-digit years on dates and using a crossover value for the year to determine which century the data value applied to. For archive data expected to survive several decades, this approach presents a serious problem waiting to happen. At some point the application will need to be changed. When it is, the problem shifts to the archived data. It would have been better to anticipate this problem and perform data value conversions when moving data to the archive all along. Then, when the new change is implemented in the operational system, only the conversion routine needs to be changed (or dropped).

Adding and dropping columns Adding a column to an existing application is probably the most common minor change made to an application. These are almost always nonkey columns since no change to the business object structure is generally involved.

When a new column is added, the old data has no values for this column. For operational systems, a value is "plugged into" all rows. Sometimes this is a null value indicating that the true value is unknown. Other times a constant is used instead. Blanks and zeroes are commonly used. No matter what value is used, the true value is not known and the database is not trustworthy when it uses this column to select data from old rows.

The same approach could be used for the archive: Plug in a wrong value to all old rows and pretend it is right. A better approach is to leave all old data as it is and start archiving the new data under a modified metadata definition. In other words, force a metadata break in the archiving stream. In this way, queries can be done on either side of the break with the knowledge that some rows have data values missing for that column. You know exactly which rows have the column and which do not.

It would be better if the operational systems did the same thing: identify which rows have no value for the column and which rows do. Unfortunately the DBMS systems in use do not allow for this and thus invite the plug-in approach. Some of the plug-in values will get into the archive simply because the business objects were in the operational system before the change and archived after the change. There is not much the archivist can do about this situation.

If you try to "plug" the archive every time that a new column is added, after several years the authenticity of the archive will be suspect. You would be surprised at the number of columns added over a 10-year period, let alone a 50-year period. Each column is added at a different time. Figuring out which rows have plugged values for which columns will become a nightmare. This argues against the single data definition strategy.

If a column is dropped, all values in operational databases will be thrown away on implementation. The archive rows still have the column. One approach to dealing with this is to delete the column from the archive store as well. Another is to keep the rows in the archive as they are and treat the boundary as a metadata break to be handled by the access routines. The handling by the access routines will be the same as in the case of adding a row, since some rows have the value and some do not.

The best approach is to never change the data in the archive, leaving it as it was when it was initially stored. Make the consumers of the data deal with the breaks. This forces them to be aware of the breaks and they can factor it into their use of the data. At least they will know that all values in the archive are authentic. Chapter 17 will discuss handling data access requests across metadata breaks.

Semantic changes   A *semantic change* is one in which no metadata change is made to a column but the use of the column is modified and the content follows a new set of rules. These changes should be outlawed since they mess up the archive. However, the practice of changing the way a column is used is a common practice, even though a bad one. Some examples of semantic changes include:

- A column is no longer used; all new values are null, blank, or zero
- A column that was not used before begins to be used
- A column used for one business fact is changed to begin storing values for a different business fact

- The encoding of values in the column is changed
- The granularity of expressing values in a column is increased or decreased

You can probably come up with more examples of semantic changes that do not get reflected in the metadata.

When a semantic change occurs, old data has values that are inconsistent with new values. The archive has rows of data containing the old values and will begin receiving rows that use the new values.

The correct way to handle semantic changes is to *drop* the column and *add* a new column. In this way the values are not mixed. Everyone knows where the break occurs and can adjust their access and use of the data accordingly.

When you begin an archiving application, it is important to stress to the application development staff that all changes of this sort need to be made with *drop/add* columns instead of simply changing the use of an existing column. Enforcing this rule could be difficult since the archive analyst has no authority over the application development staff.

If the archivist becomes aware of a semantic change before it is put into operation, a metadata break can be implemented in the archive data stream just as though a *drop/add* column had occurred. The trick is to know when it will be implemented. Of course you also have to know what the application staff is going to do with rows that are in the operational database at the time the change is made. If they do nothing, the archivist might not be able to avoid a consistency problem.

13.2.2 **Minor Structural Changes Within an Application**

This category of change involves keeping the basic structure the same while making some minor structure changes. The application is the same; the structures are very close to the same.

Examples of structure changes that fit into this category include:

- Adding a table
- Dropping a table
- Combining tables
- Splitting tables
- Changing the column used as a primary or foreign key
- Changing the internal representation of a primary or foreign key

The primary issue when you encounter one of these is whether a new archiving stream needs to be started or whether you can continue the old one while tolerating the change.

Adding a table   Adding a new table can be a minor change or a major change depending on where the table is added in the structure of the business object. You would never create a new table in an existing archive stream and then populate every column with plug-in values for old archived objects (single data definition strategy). However, you could keep the old archive stream and let some business objects in the stream have rows in the new table and others not. If you do not create a new stream, you still need to record the metadata break so that future readers of the archive will know whether rows might have applied to older business objects or not.

A table added to the bottom of a structure would have minimal impact. This means it does not change the root table of the business object nor does it change any downward relationships between other tables. It merely adds a child relationship to one of the existing tables.

For example, an HR application could add a new table that records the results of a background check on employees assigned to sensitive areas. This new table becomes a child table to the EMPLOYEE_MASTER table and has no relationship to other HR tables. It is simply additional information collected and maintained for employees. Some employees will have rows in this table and some will not. This type of change could easily be accommodated without generating a new archive stream. Most table additions are similar to this scenario.

If a new table is disruptive to the business object structure, a change to a new archive stream will be warranted. For example, if our loan application added a table between LOAN_HEADER and LOAN_PAYMENT that indicated payment agent information for loans that were farmed out to collection agencies the business object would have a fundamentally different structure, requiring a new archive stream.

Dropping a table The impact of a *drop-table* change is very similar to the impact of an *add-table* change. If the dropped table is not an archive root table or not in the middle of a string of related tables, it might be easy to accommodate within an archive stream. You would simply have new business objects that had no rows in that table. Again, you need to record this as a metadata break so that future readers of the archive will know when this table stopped being used.

Again, if you drop an archive root table or an intermediate table, the data structure will change sufficiently to require a new archive stream.

Combining or splitting tables Combining or splitting tables is often done by database administrators or application developers to improve performance. If there is no change to the columns recorded and the structure could be represented either way, it might be possible to accommodate this change in the existing archive stream. For a single data definition strategy you might be able to make the structure change to all data previously recorded in the archive. For a multiple data definition strategy you would create a metadata break and archive data according to the new definition after the break. The access routines would have much more work to do in making it look consistent to readers across the metadata break. However, it is possible.

If the combining or splitting table change is also accompanied with *add* or *drop* column actions, clearly the structure has changed enough to warrant a new archive stream.

Changes to key columns   Changes to key columns almost always result in a new archive stream. Trying to bridge data archived under one object identifier definition with data archived under another is most likely going to be unworkable.

A change to a key column could be physical or semantic. Physical changes are obvious but semantic changes might not be known. For example, if the column is the same but the values recorded in it are different, it might be possible to treat old and new data the same way in the archive. For example, if an identifier column was six characters in length and is changed to seven, the archive would not be impacted as long as all values are unique.

13.2.3 Major Application Restructuring

Every few years applications get a major makeover. They are redesigned from the bottom up, replaced by either another custom application, or replaced by a packaged application. When this occurs, always treat this as a new archive stream.

There are some things the archivist should do when these changes occur beyond simply initiating a new archive stream.

Determine what happens to data in the old operational database. Does it get converted and loaded into the new application, or is it left in the old database? If it is not converted, the old data should ultimately end up in the archive under the old archive stream. It might be necessary to run the two archive streams in parallel for some period of time until all the old data is archived.

If the old data is converted to the new application and loaded into the replacement database, the archivist will have a specific cutover point between the two archive streams. It might be a good idea to adjust the archive extract policy for the last archive run against the old database to be more aggressive, to get as much data into the archive as possible under the old definition. This will result in fewer business objects having questionable data values that ultimately result from conversion to new structures.

The archivist should also seek a conversion map used to move data from the old database to the new database. This map should be retained in the archive repository as information that might be useful to a future user of the archive data in understanding how data values transitioned the two archive streams. These maps should show structure relationships between the two business object structures, column relationships, and data value relationships if data values are encoded differently.

13.2.4 Upgrades to Packaged Applications

Packaged applications periodically distribute updates to their products. When this occurs, the data archivist must get involved early to study the changes made by the vendor and determine the impact on archived data. All changes to virtual data structures need to be analyzed in the same way as data from custom applications.

13.3 CHANGES TO THE ARCHIVE DATA MODEL

On some occasions, the data archivist needs to make changes to the target data model. These changes assume that there is no change to the data structures in the operational database. For some reason, possibly an error in design, the archivist wants to change what gets put into the archive and how it is structured there.

These types of changes are rare. However, there could be good reasons for occasionally making them.

13.3.1 Changes to the Extract Model

The extract disposition policy includes the ability to include data from a table in the archive stream (ARCHIVE) or to not include it (DELETE). Since the table is part of the business object, failure to include it in the archive model will result in the data being deleted from the operational database but not included in the archive.

From the archive view, changing from DELETE to ARCHIVE is equivalent to an *add-table* change. Changing ARCHIVE to DELETE is equivalent to a *drop-table* change. It would be analyzed and implemented accordingly.

The operational databases do not change; however, the change to the extract logic will result in either a metadata break in the existing archive stream or the establishment of a new archive stream.

Making a change from ARCHIVE to DELETE would be rare. When data is deleted from the operational databases and not archived, it is lost forever. It cannot be recovered in the future if you change your mind again.

13.3.2 Changes to the Archive Transformed View

There should be little reason to change the way data is represented in the archive if there is no change to the operational systems. However, if an error was made on specifying a transform for data or for not specifying one when it would have been appropriate, a change might be indicated. The intention is to change the form of data, not the content.

For example, if a date field was stored in the archive with two-digit years, it might be wise to correct this oversight by changing all old values to a more correct four-digit year. This could be a lot of work, but it would make the archive stream useful for many more years. With long retention policies being imposed, it might be a necessary change.

A more mega-change would be to change the encoding of character data from EBCIDIC or ASCII to Unicode. For example, if your archive is serving only U.S. business units but is going to be expanded to include worldwide customers, it might be necessary to change over to Unicode to accommodate new data. At the same time it might be useful to convert old data in the archive to Unicode to make it more consistent.

These changes should be recorded in the archive repository.

13.4 MANAGING THE METADATA CHANGE PROCESS

Changes to data structures of operational systems can have a major impact on archive applications. They are generally more far-reaching than they are on the operational applications themselves. They can render an archive worthless if not handled properly.

At the core is the absolute requirement that the data archivist be an integral part of all data structure changes. Also at the core is the requirement that the change process be formal, disciplined, and never violated. Database administrators cannot be permitted to make changes on their own without the consultation and approval of the data archivist.

Knowledge of changes   The data archivist must know about *all* changes to data structures before they occur. This includes structural, column, and semantic changes. Any committees, email lists, change order distributions, or other artifacts used to communicate changes must be modified to include the archivist so that the archivist is directly involved in the planning process.

The person who wants to make a change is unqualified to understand the impact the change could have on the application's archiving streams. Only the archivist should be allowed to make that determination.

Planning process   The archivist should be involved in planning all changes. It makes no sense to have one group plan a change for weeks only to bring the archivist in at the end, near the cutover point, and expect him or her to get ready in only a few days.

The archivist might be required to make design changes to portions of the archiving process and policies to accommodate the changes. These could be extensive and require great effort to achieve.

The type of change planning that may be involved includes:

- Routine, minor changes
- Application replacements
- Bringing new business groups into the archive
- Mergers that bring new data stores to the archive

Data design process   The archivist should be involved in data design changes. The archivist's experience can influence the way some of these changes are made. This can either simplify or frustrate the impact on the older, archived data.

Archive strategy for changes   The archivist needs to create a strategy for implementing archive changes for each data structure change made to the operational database. Decisions need to be made about whether metadata breaks are generated, whether new archiving streams are created, and how the changes will impact access requests. Metadata changes need to be documented so that they are available to archive readers whenever new data flows to the archive.

The archivist may discuss the desirability of not converting old data to new definitions in the operational databases but rather let it work its way to the archive under the old archive stream definition. The archivist is the best-qualified person to make the call on whether or not this is the wisest strategy.

Cutover planning   The implementation of the changes in the operational databases needs to be coordinated with the data archivist. If new extract or transformation policies are to be used, the data archivist needs to know when to use the new rules.

The important point to remember is that the new rules should be executed at the time of the next archive extract after the change. This event does not need to occur exactly at the time of the cutover, only sometime after. The archivist's planning should include suspension of archive extract under the old rules and allow for a time gap to occur before executing archive extract under the new rules. This will give the operations staff a window within which the change must be made. The archivist must be made aware of when the change is complete in the operational database in order to schedule the next archive extract.

The archivist might need to get involved in the test environment for the change, to test changes to the archiving processes. If IT has a test process for the changes, the archivist should work with IT instead of creating an independent test environment. The outcomes will be more accurate if both teams are using the same test data.

13.5 CHANGES TO ARCHIVE POLICIES

The archive policies as well as the data structures will change from time to time. However, unlike data structures, changes to archive policies tend to have less effect on the data, the archive stream map, or database operations. They generally do not need the involvement of other groups and cutover coordination for implementation that data structure changes require.

This is not to say that others are never impacted by such changes. Change to archiving policy can impact operational system performance (positively or negatively), business user access, and others. Although these changes might be small, the archivist cannot plan and implement changes to archive policies in a vacuum.

13.5.1 Changes to Extract Policies

The extract policies cover determination of when a business object is ready to be moved to the archive, how often searches of the operational database are performed to find them, and how to deal with interruptions in the extract process.

In changing these policies, one rule needs to be maintained: Once data is moved to the archive, it stays there. Implementation of a policy change should not cause data to be moved back to the operational databases. It would be rare for you to want to do this and it should be avoided if at all possible.

Policy for when an object is ready   This change should apply only to data that has not yet been archived. If you change the policy in regard to already archived data, you might have to move data back to the operational database and delete it from the archive. This is not something that you want to do.

An argument for making a policy more aggressive (archive objects earlier) would be to reduce the amount of data carried in the operational database in order to impact performance. This could increase the need for accessing data from the archive, since you are moving the line more toward the active data side.

An argument for making the policy less aggressive (archive objects later) would be because too much access against the archive is being made. The data is not as inactive as you thought. When you do this you increase the amount of data kept in the operational database.

It might take some time after an archiving application is put into production before you get the right balance between operational database access activity and archive access activity.

Other reasons for changing the policy could be that management wants to protect data better, necessitating a more aggressive extract policy. Each proposed change should be measured against the two competing goals of lower amounts of data in operational databases versus lower access demands on the archived data.

An error in the original policy might be another reason for change. You discover that business objects are appearing in the archive that are clearly not ready or are left in the operational database when they are clearly inactive.

Putting a new policy into action should be harmless. You simply do it at the next archive extract event. If you made the policy more aggressive, you could get an unexpectedly large amount of data. This should occur only once.

Conversely, making the policy less aggressive could lead to an archive extract event that returns few or no business objects. It could take some time before the new policy reaches a normal state.

Policy for frequency of extract execution   Changing this policy could be used to get inactive data out of the operational database closer to the time it first qualifies for extract. The extract policy is not the problem; the period of time between extract executions is the problem. Executing extracts more frequently can reduce the amount of data in the operational database by a measurable amount.

A reason for making the interval longer is that it allows for fewer times that the extract process is running and potentially causing overhead or disruption of operational activities. This could be an important factor if the extract is run when the database is not available online.

Changing the frequency of execution will not have much impact on the time to execute but will have an impact on the amount of data that comes out of the database each time. The most noticeable change will be observed during the first execution of data extraction following the change.

Like the extract policy, the frequency of execution policy could take some time to tune to the dynamics of the operational database activity levels.

Policy for interruption handling   The policy for handling interruptions during the extract process can also be changed. If interruptions are frequent and the policy is to force it to restart and run to completion, a change in the policy might be needed. If interruptions are rare, keeping either policy in place could be acceptable. The impact of a change will directly affect the operations staff who must deal with planning how restart will be done when disruptions occur.

13.5.2 **Changes to Storage Polices**

Changing storage policies can require some planning to execute but should be transparent to users of the archive. You might need to find a period of time to make the changes when the archive will be unavailable for adding new data or for accessing data. This will almost always be a requirement.

Changing storage format   Changing the way data is stored in the archive is always a major change. For example, if you were storing data in a DBMS and wanted to change to an XML store, you would be facing a major conversion. Major conversions can come about because the choice you made at the beginning turns out not to be the best choice.

Changing the software you use for archiving is another reason for format change. You might want to move the data archived under one solution to an archive managed by a different solution.

Cost and time required need to be factored in when you're deciding whether or not to move the data. It might be a better choice to leave old archived data in one format and begin new archive streams in another. This places a greater burden on the users of the archive data, but if access is rare, it might be worth doing.

If you have built custom access routines against your archive data structures, you could be creating a serious problem by changing the storage format of the data. These must be considered when you're implementing this type of change.

The cutover point for implementing a change must be carefully planned since the cutover activities can take a long time to develop, need to be tested, and might not work as planned. Changing the format of archived data is just as complex as changing the format of operational data.

Changing devices   A change to the device type on which data is stored is a less disruptive change. For example, if you decide to keep the archive in a SAN device instead of on tape, you merely have to copy the data. If you decide to put it on a WORM device instead of disk storage, you simply copy it. If you need more backup copies, you simply make them.

It sounds easy, and generally it is. You do have to consider the volume of data involved when you're planning this move.

The motivation for making a device change is to save money by using cheaper devices, provide more security of data, provide more protection from disasters, and so on. You are typically trying to make the archive more effective, not less.

The cutover to the new copies can be held off until all the copies are made and tested. Archive users can use the old storage locations up to the point of cutover. You only need be concerned about new data coming in. This would typically be handled by suspending archive extract activity during the cutover period.

Changing geographical locations Your policy for storage can include the need to keep copies of the archive in multiple geographical locations for the purpose of disaster recovery. You might need to switch locations from time to time as your corporate data centers move around. You might also want to add new recovery locations to provide for better protection.

Implementing this change generally involves nothing more than making copies of existing files. Since these are backup copies, it should have no impact on users of the data.

Changing encryption/signatures You might also want to change the policy for whether data is encrypted or carries dataset signatures. This would normally be done to make data more secure. These changes can be implemented by copying the data to files with the desired capabilities. This is normally a nondisruptive action.

13.5.3 **Changes to Discard Policies**

Discard policy changes would normally be made to satisfy a new requirement to keep data longer than it was required to be kept before the change. That normally has no impact on the archiving process other than the discard function. These changes are entirely implemented by the data archivist.

One vital fact to remember when changing this policy is that you cannot bring back data that has been discarded. Let's explore how this affects change.

Discard policy If you change the discard policy, causing objects to stay in the archive longer, there will be no immediate impact when the change is implemented. However, some data that would have still been in the archive under the new policy might already have been discarded under the previous policy. You cannot do anything about that; the data is gone. However, you should document this fact in the repository so that an investigator can be made aware of the fact that some data is gone that might still be there if the new discard policy had been in force earlier.

If you shorten the discard policy, you would merely discard more items on the next run. There would be no data caught in the middle.

If you change criteria other than time, you might or might not have data that is missing that otherwise might have been there under the new policy. If this is the case, it should be documented to alert investigators that data might be missing.

Frequency of execution   You might change the frequency of execution of the discard process to avoid data staying in the archive longer than necessary. If the enterprise is serious about discarding data when eligible, the interval between discard executions should be short.

Record of what was discarded   You can change the policy regarding recording the identifiers of discarded data but will end up with inconsistencies.

If you had a policy to record identifiers and then drop it, you might want to discard the earlier lists as well. Since you will not be adding new entries, the list will be incomplete. Since the new policy calls for no list, dropping the old list is not a violation of the new policy.

If you are adding a provision to begin recording discarded identifiers, the list will start when implemented. You cannot go back to business objects discarded before the implementation and retrieve their identifiers. You should record this fact somewhere in the repository.

13.6 MAINTAINING AN AUDIT TRAIL OF CHANGES

The user of the archive data needs to understand the content of each archive unit of data and the differences that occur between them. To provide for this audit trail, the archivist must maintain a considerable amount of documentation about changes. The place for this documentation is in the archive repository.

The documentation that needs to be kept for data structure changes includes:

- Metadata definitions for all streams and metadata breaks
- Bridge documentation across streams and breaks
- A map of the streams and breaks
- Dates on which changes occurred
- Reasons changes occurred

You need to keep an audit trail of all changes to policies. You need to record the change made, the reason for the change, and the implementation date.

This information could be used in a court case if there is some issue over the company's record-destruction policies. Maintaining consistent policies, executing them diligently, and recording when and why changes are made to the policies are important attributes to defending the destruction of records.

SUMMARY

The data archivist will spend the most time and do the hardest work in handling changes. Keeping up with data structure changes is the most difficult task for a data archivist.

Once archiving begins for an application, the change process must be planned, managed, and controlled with a discipline that is uncommon for IT departments.

IT management must adopt a stricter attitude toward changes for applications that are archiving data for long-term retention. It is not possible for the data archivist to control changes; only higher-level IT management can do that. Changes to operational systems must include only those that are necessary and must be designed with archiving in mind, and the cutover must be coordinated with the archiving application.

The archivist needs to think through the impact of each policy change in regard to changes that cannot be reversed. Once data is removed from the archive, it is gone forever.

A diligent archivist who is constantly monitoring the archive and striving to make it as efficient as possible will look for opportunities to use policy changes effectively.

Clearly, an archive is not something you set up once and let run by itself. Managing changes alone requires extensive monitoring and adjustment of the archiving design of a single application. There are no applications that will not undergo changes; most of them will experience significant change over any period of a few years.

Database Archiving Application Software

4

Up to this point we have been gathering data, designing data structures, and developing archiving policies. The next chapters discuss the software components needed to implement the design decisions that have been made for your database archiving application.

Many software products on the market address database archiving requirements, but there are wide differences in how these products are architected. Each solution is good for one or more types of applications and not so good for others. There are also many ad hoc, locally developed solutions presenting a variety of approaches.

The following chapters focus on one software component of a complete solution at a time, discussing the strengths and weaknesses of various approaches. It doesn't matter whether the software is internally developed or acquired from a software vendor. The requirements of the various components can be understood and used as criteria for determining whether a specific solution fits the needs of an application or not. It is possible that different software solutions will be needed for different applications within one enterprise.

The components covered are:

- Archive data store
- Archive extractor
- Archive discard
- Archive access

The Archive Data Store

The data being archived comes from databases. It has the same characteristics in the archive that it had in the operational DBMS that managed it before it was moved to the archive. You cannot change that. It is highly structured and consists of many instances of each structural element. It stands to reason that the archive data store should also have the same basic organization and functions as any DBMS.

That said, the archive data store can benefit from having other desirable features that are not applicable to the operational database environment. These features call for different optimization characteristics than those used to construct the DBMSs used for normal operations. You don't construct these DBMSs; vendors do. They are not optimized to the needs of the archive. They are optimized for transaction processing, which includes heavy insert and update activity.

You will see a lot of constructs offered as solutions to the archive data store as database archiving vendors seek optimal solutions. Most of them in use today have shortcomings in regard to satisfying requirements, some of which are severe. You need to understand them.

If you are building your own software for an archive solution, you are limited to using storage structures that are commonly available. These could be satisfactory for some archiving applications and not for others. It is important to know the strengths and weaknesses of each choice available to you. You need to pick a solution that fits your requirements.

Vendor-provided database archiving solutions use a wide variety of data structures for the archive store. This is symptomatic of the early nature of this technology in that a best-practices solution that applies to most or all applications is still emerging. You can expect a lot of changes in this area in the near future. What is needed is a storage structure for holding a very large archive database that is optimized for that purpose alone.

Also consider that the archive data store needs to include the metadata as well as the data. They cannot be separated. It needs to include all the metadata—an enhanced version that goes far beyond what a relational database catalog would contain.

14.1 ARCHIVE DATABASE CHOICES

Vendors have chosen only a few forms to use, and implementations created in-house also are commonly built around only a small number of solutions. These are discussed in the following subsections. In addition, the metadata may be integrated with the storage solution or separately managed. Let's explore some of these choices.

14.1.1 Data Stores

The data can be stored in a DBMS, database UNLOAD files, XML files, or what I call a *custom archive* DBMS. The custom archive DBMS is a sketch of a data store that's designed to provide the most efficient capabilities for an archive data store.

DBMSs of same type   It would appear that storing the archive data in a DBMS of the same type that the data comes from would be the best choice. After all, the data would already be structured appropriately, and it would take little effort to implement. In fact, this is often the choice of homegrown archiving solutions. It is always the choice for archiving solutions delivered by traditional DBMS vendors who want you to continue using their software.

When this option is chosen, it is important to put the archive in an instance of the DBMS that does not compete for resources with the operational system. This generally means putting it in another physical system.

There are a number of problems with using operational DBMSs for archiving, as discussed in the following sections. Problems include such limitations as not being able to deal correctly with metadata changes, inability to guard against unwanted updates, and efficiency problems on writing new data to ever-growing archive stores. When serious thought is applied to the requirements, this choice, which is usually the first choice, begins to fade until it finally becomes a choice that's not viable.

For some small applications that have little requirement for maintaining a trail of authenticity, using the same DBMS type could be a correct choice. However, this is almost never the case for the most important applications that you want to archive.

If the operational database is a legacy database such as IMS, ADABAS, IDMS, or M204, this is always a bad choice. It is unrealistic to assume that these systems will persist for the life of the archive.

DBMSs of different types   Implementing DBMSs of different types has the same appeal as the prior choice. You are using a DBMS to store the data; what could be more natural? This option can be used to replatform data where the operational data is stored in a legacy DBMS type. It can also be used to move data to other system types—for example, moving from mainframe DB2 to a Unix-based database such as IBM's DB2 LUW.

This choice has the same problems as using any DBMS, as will become more apparent in the comparison sections that follow. One example of such a problem is data loss in transformation. All DBMSs have limitations on the size of data elements and variations in how they handle specific constructs such as BLOBs. Conversion to data types when you're moving data from one DBMS type to another can result in truncation or other data loss that could be unacceptable.

The UNLOAD files are a common choice for homegrown solutions. You use an UNLOAD utility or your own application program to select data you want archived and put it into an ordinary UNLOAD file. A common UNLOAD format is comma-delimited character files.

Some of the UNLOAD formats are generic and will allow loading the data into different database systems than the one it came from. Others are specific to the DBMS the data came from and can only go back to that same DBMS type.

The UNLOAD files are convenient and do have some advantages over using a DBMS. For example, you can push data to very low-cost storage. You simply keep adding to the archive without having to update previously written units of data.

The files are more easily protected from update by storing them on SAN devices.

However, UNLOAD files are not easily searched. For DBMS-specific UNLOAD files they are not searchable at all without reloading all of them into a DBMS. You have to manage reloads separately for UNLOAD files generated from data having metadata differences. You cannot tell from the files which belong to which version of the metadata. That has to be managed separately.

XML files   Converting database data to XML files is a common, intuitive choice. It tends to make sense. You are converting data to a common form that can embed the metadata with it and can be stored as a document. Some vendors have built their archiving solution to do just that.

Using XML documents to store the archive data is another form of UNLOAD files. You are moving the data to a neutral form that can be reloaded to another DBMS later.

XML enthusiasts will claim that it is not just another UNLOAD file. It can be searched more easily than UNLOAD files. It also embeds the metadata and thus is understandable.

The downside of XML files is the amount of storage required to store them (can be as much as six times that required of other forms), the inability to do searches over large volumes of data, and the lack of sufficient metadata. The tags in XML hardly constitute sufficient metadata for archive use.

XML can be a useful form for archive storage for applications with small to moderate volumes of data. It cannot compete with other forms when the volume of data grows to large amounts.

Custom archive DBMS   What is really needed is a new DBMS type that is custom built to serve the needs of a long-term database archive holding very large amounts of data. It is very unlikely that you would build something like this in your own IT organization. Some vendors are beginning to recognize the need to move in this direction. Don't expect the traditional DBMS vendors to do so or to admit that it is something worth doing. It would mean moving data from their DBMSs into a different DBMS.

The next section explains several requirements for a database archive data store, shows how the previous choices deal with them, and explains how a custom archive DBMS solution might provide better solutions.

14.1.2 Metadata

Metadata must be a part of the archive. All vendor solutions recognize this fact. Metadata will change over the life of the archive. The original places that capture the metadata could disappear at worst or become out of date at best. The archive needs to become independent of any external representation of metadata.

There are four possible choices for keeping metadata: use the database capability, embed it in the database, keep it in an external metadata repository, or keep it in standalone documents that are archived with the data.

Use the DBMS capabilities   Most DBMSs come with a catalog (relational systems) or have an associated data description facility. If you chose to use a DBMS as the archive database engine, you will need to populate these constructs as well. These could serve as your metadata repository in the archive.

The downside of this is clearly that the DBMS metadata constructs are insufficient in conveying to future generations of data users the true meaning of the data elements. Having merely a column name is often not enough to explain to someone what the content really is.

Another problem with this approach is that the DBMS supports only one version of the metadata: the one used to store the data. It cannot handle versions that go back through changes made over the years.

Embed metadata in the database   You can use a DBMS to store metadata as data by developing your own data architecture of the metadata as application tables. You can use this approach to store all relevant parts of the metadata as well as metadata versions and even a metadata change audit trail.

Clearly, you can solve the problem completely this way. The downside is that you have created a dependency on a DBMS in the archive. A more serious problem is that you have created a construct that cannot be stored with the data unless you are also storing the data in the same DBMS—a good choice along with a bad choice.

Use an external repository   You can implement the preceding choice by using a packaged metadata repository solution. You still have the same problems with this approach as with building your own solution in a DBMS. In addition, you will discover that most metadata repository tools are not designed to support the needs of archiving but are designed instead to support the needs of operational databases—for example, having the capability to match metadata versions to individual units of stored data.

Store metadata in documents in the archive   Another choice is to convert the metadata for a unit of archive data to a common, understandable form and store it as a file in the archive storage device along with the data. This is an ideal choice since it creates an automatic affinity between metadata and data. It can handle versioning. As a document, it can express any level of understanding that's needed.

The obvious choice for the document format is XML. Whereas XML is generally not a good choice for storing the archive data, it is a perfect choice for storing the metadata. You can use this choice along with all the other choices available for storing the data.

A number of metadata XML formats have been created by vendors or standards groups over the last 10 years. It might be useful to follow one of them. However, they will all need extensions to handle archive-specific information. A perfect standard that fits the needs of archiving has not yet emerged.

14.2 **IMPORTANT FEATURES**

This section discusses a number of features that need to be considered in making the choice of where to store the archive data and metadata. It shows how previously described choices satisfy or fail to satisfy the requirements.

14.2.1 **Independence from Operational Systems**

The issue for the archive database is to not create or perpetuate a dependency that you might not want to maintain in the future. It might be expensive to keep a license of a DBMS for very long periods of time if the only reason you are doing so is to house the database archive. Some database systems require specific hardware as well. For example, IMS requires an IBM mainframe and the z/OS operating system. If you plan to drop mainframes from your future plans, you do not want to house the archive in a mainframe-constrained DBMS.

DBMS solutions all have some dependencies. Relational database systems have the fewest dependencies. If you do use one, do not use the features that make the DBMS different from other ones, since conversion to a different relational DBMS could be problematic. For example, avoid using data types that are uniquely defined for just one DBMS, such as the TIMESTAMP data type of DB2.

UNLOAD files can be tied to a specific DBMS or generic. The best approach is to make them generic, such as a comma-delimited file, so they can be used to load into a variety of DBMS types in the future.

XML is clearly an independent solution. If independence were the only issue, XML is an ideal choice.

The custom archive DBMS would have a proprietary database solution that is capable of storing data in a variety of places and could be accessed by standard SQL. It would become system independent by design.

14.2.2 **Ability to Handle a Large Volume of Data**

Any archive database must be able to handle large volumes of data. The archive data store for an application with a 25-year retention requirement will be many times larger than the operational database for the same application. It stands to reason that if you are having trouble managing the operational database because of size, you will have larger problems handling the archive database if the same DBMS solution is used.

The ability to handle size is not restricted to whether the database can physically store the amount of data; it also has to do with how well it performs when accessing data from it. For example, DBMSs can store enormous amounts of data, but common functions such as indexing, backup, recovery, nonindexed scans, and multitable join queries become inefficient as the amount of data increases. Some older DBMSs have size limitations on physical datasets and the number of datasets that will easily be exceeded for large archive applications.

Oddly enough, DBMSs tend to be a problematic choice for archive databases when faced with staggeringly large amounts of data. They tend to manage data holistically and thus are susceptible to ever-growing inefficiencies as the data volume grows. They also require that the data reside on front-line disk storage, which can be a problem for very large amounts of data. These are some of the reasons for moving data from operational databases. You might just be moving the problem, not solving it.

UNLOAD files are a disaster for dealing with large amounts of data. This is because the data has to be staged back to a DBMS to use it. The staging time will only get longer and longer, eventually running into several days to get it all back to a usable form. The amount of front-line disk storage needed to restage the data will also grow. You will have to keep that amount of disk storage available all the time, even though it will not be used most of the time.

XML also has problems with large amounts of data. XML explodes the size of storage required. In addition, its search functions become extremely slow and unusable when the data volumes begin to get very large.

The custom archive DBMS would be designed to allow for unlimited amounts of data to be stored. It would not require front-line disk storage. It would be able to efficiently search the data using standard SQL without having to restage the data.

14.2.3 **Ability to Store Enriched Metadata**

Enriched metadata is a must for any archive application. The metadata that is stored in relational database systems or the tags of XML are insufficient to describe the data elements. They are also in a form that is difficult to use. This means that the metadata must be stored in a separate place from the data. This might be in XML files that are devoted only to metadata.

All archive database storage types can accommodate this requirement if they store the metadata separately. However, there is a strong temptation to believe that the relational catalog or XML tags are sufficient. They are not.

The custom archive DBMS will store enriched metadata in the archive along with the archived data. It would be the only solution that embeds them together.

14.2.4 **Ability to Store Data in Units with Metadata Affinity**

The archive database will contain data from many versions of metadata over time. Metadata changes, and thus the data will not be consistent throughout the archive data store. It is imperative that the metadata for any unit of data be associated with that unit.

This is very hard to achieve in a DBMS. DBMSs support only one version of data definition: the current one. If you have data that is from different definitions, you have to have separate sets of tables for each version. Data for two different versions cannot coexist in the same tables. Managing an array of tables is awkward at best. Another obvious problem is supporting queries against the array of tables. There is no easy way to do this: especially if the number of versions gets into the hundreds.

Managing metadata versions for UNLOAD files or XML files becomes a book-keeping problem that can also be difficult to manage. For XML, you could embed the metadata into the data XML files, thus creating many more tags in a single metadata file. This can cause problems on searching XML documents.

The custom archive DBMS would maintain the association of data and metadata versions internally to the database without requiring external recordkeeping.

14.2.5 **Ability to Store Original Data**

When data is stored in an archive database in a form different from the way it is stored in the operational database, it could become an issue of whether the transformation routines changed the meaning of the data. It might be necessary to be able to show the original storage representation of the data.

Since the receiving DBMS might not be able to support the original representations at the field level, it would be necessary to store the original representation of data as a BLOB or in some other type of sequential file that does not understand the content. DBMS or XML solutions for this problem are very difficult if not impossible to create and manage.

The custom archive DBMS would keep the original data representation along with the transformed representation and would be able to associate the two together, at least at the row level.

14.2.6 **Ability to Store Everything Needed**

You ideally would include in the archive additional information that will be useful to people in the future. This includes design information, execution information (when specific data was moved to the archive and possibly error logs showing transformation problems), originating system identification, and audit trails of file activity after data lands in the archive.

None of this is easy with a DBMS solution. It requires separate administrative tables. This is especially true of UNLOAD or XML files, which require that the data be maintained separately.

For a DBMS solution, there is no easy way to associate this information to specific rows of data in the archive unless a new set of archive tables is created with each execution of the extractor. This is extremely impractical.

The custom archive DBMS will have the capability to encapsulate this information with each unit of archived data.

14.2.7 **Ability to Add Data Without Disrupting Previously Stored Objects**

The archive database will become very large very soon. The design of the data store should permit new data to be added to the archive without having to update data stored from previous additions.

For example, a DBMS solution receives new data as INSERT or LOAD functions. The process will update all existing indexes and will require that a new set of backups be created—backups for the entire database, not just the portion just added. Prior to backing up it might be necessary to reorganize the tables and indexes, since they were disturbed by the addition of new data. These operate against the entire database, not just the portion added. If you designed it to use a new partition for each add, you would need the partitioning data element to be a new token column indicating the add number. This would result in a seriously large number of partitions. It would also not help in indexes that span the entire database.

The preceding scenario describes a condition in which inserting new data into the archive will cause it to run slower and slower as the amount of previously stored data increases. Eventually the overhead of dealing with the entire database will become too excessive. This scenario makes a DBMS a poor solution for large archives.

For UNLOAD files and XML documents, this is not a problem; you simply add more files without having to do anything with previous files.

For the custom archive DBMS, inserting new data will require no impact on existing stored data, stored metadata, or backup files. The process only deals with the new data. The insert process time should become nearly constant over time.

14.2.8 **Independent Access Authority**

Authority to access the archive data needs to be independent from the authorities granted for the operational data. This can be achieved quite easily through any of the solutions. A DBMS solution requires a DBA be authorized to manage the database, causing an authority to exist that might not be needed for the other solutions.

For UNLOAD files and XML files, file-level protection needs to be implemented that will require considerable bookkeeping and management. There will be lots of files.

For the custom archive DBMS, access authority will be managed completely within the DBMS. Since the data store will never require reorganization or backing up beyond backing up data additions only, the services of a DBA would not be needed.

14.2.9 **Search Capabilities**

It is very important that the archive be searchable to find data. Even though the data is inactive, it has the potential to be needed and, when it is needed, must be capable of responding.

Searching can be complex since often it involves using columns that are not identification columns. For example, a request for information could include searching for values between two dates and originating at a specific branch office.

Searching an archive often involves search conditions that would not normally be seen in operational systems. Thus the index scheme of an operational system is usually not the optimum for an archive.

DBMS solutions have good search facilities. That is a foundation function for them.

UNLOAD files cannot be searched efficiently. They usually need to be restored to a DBMS before they can realistically be searched. There are search packages available that search through flat files; however, they are very inefficient and will collapse under heavy volume, as is expected for database archives. You cannot do a multiple table join using UNLOAD files.

XML documents have search capabilities. These work well on small amounts of data and not well at all on larger amounts of data.

There are search engines for databases, flat files, and XML files that index data externally and then use search results from these indexes to select data from the source files. They cannot join data across multiple UNLOAD files containing data from different tables or segments. They do not work against native UNLOAD files of legacy DBMS types.

Working with an external search engine requires additional software and a great deal of effort to be effective. They are not designed for use against structured databases that involve complex business object structures.

The custom archive DBMS would provide both internal and external indexing to achieve efficient searches. You can search using SQL, which will satisfy all join condition searches. It will support some form of generic search that does not require SQL.

14.2.10 Ability to Query Data Without Looking at the Whole Data Store

This is a must. The archive will become very large. The query capability needs to have the ability to scope a query and determine the specific units of data that need to be looked at to satisfy it. Unqualified scans of the entire archive are not realistic over very large amounts of data.

DBMS solutions accomplish this task only if the predicates reference columns that are indexed. If they have appropriate indexes, this goal can be achieved. It is less important for DBMS implementations since all the data is on front-line disk storage anyway and does not require restaging to search.

UNLOAD files simply do not satisfy this requirement. To make it so, you would need an elaborate external index on multiple columns. You are not likely to implement something like this. XML files also would require an external index to accomplish this task.

The custom archive DBMS would keep the data segregated in separate data units according to when they were archived. It would have both internal and external indexes on columns that are likely candidates to be used in predicates. The external indexes would point to individual units. It would also have a simple scoping construct to substitute for an external index for columns that are well ordered by time.

14.2.11 Access from Application Programs

The data in the archive should be able to be queried directly from application programs. This does not mean transparent access via the original application programs. It does mean that the user can write new programs or modify old programs to access the archive. It also means that common query and reporting tools should be able to access data in the archive without difficulty.

This goal is accomplished by having an industry-standard SQL capability. The archive should provide the driver for this capability. A JDBC driver would be ideal. It would allow any program anywhere that is connected via the Internet to query the archive data.

All relational DBMS products have this capability. Nonrelational databases can sometimes have a collection of products cobbled together to accomplish this goal. Generally this works only on well-behaved data in those database types, which is generally not the case.

This approach does not work with UNLOAD files.

For XML, you can get this access by using software that is obtainable. It will not be efficient.

For the custom archive DBMS, this capability would be automatically provided and would be efficient.

14.2.12 Ability to Restore Data to Any Desired Location

Although data should be accessible directly from the archive, it is also often desirable to extract large amounts of data from the archive and store it in another location that is more useful for the intended use. For example, if an enterprise receives a lawsuit that requires working with a large subset of the archive data, the best way to handle it is to select the data needed and replatform it on a standard DBMS for use by the investigative staffs. This same requirement could be appropriate for an internal business study that is directed against a specific subset of the archive data.

Archive data, by its very nature, is slow to access. Much of the data will be on low-cost, low-performance storage. You do not want to run a large number of queries over the archive. If you know you will need to extensively massage the data, it is better to move it out of the archive first.

The archive system should be able to select, move, and store data in alternative places. The location and target DBMS type would not necessarily be the same as those in which the data originated. In fact, it is best if it can be redirected to any relational DBMS.

To accomplish this task from a DBMS archive store is easy if the DBMS is relational. It is difficult if it is one of the legacy DBMS types. All relational systems have UNLOAD capabilities to generic formats that can be loaded into other relational DBMSs.

UNLOAD and XML files require some work. You will need a method for executing extraction criteria and putting the result into load files. Some XML data requires reformatting to get it into a loadable format.

The custom archive database would have built-in extraction criteria capability with output that includes load files and DDL scripts for the target DBMS. It also would handle data type transformation issues needed to load the data. For legacy-originated data it would provide the ability to get a file of loadable data in a format that is acceptable to the specific legacy DBMS from which it originated.

14.2.13 Protect from Unauthorized Updates or Deletes

You want the archive to be protected from updates or deletes that might be made for improper reasons. You want to be able to claim that the archived data is unchanged from the time it was put into the archive until it is accessed, no matter how long it has been there.

Operational DBMSs all have the ability for updates and deletes. Privileged users such as DBAs always have the ability to perform these tasks. You cannot satisfy this requirement if you are using a DBMS.

UNLOAD files are somewhat easier to protect since you can push them to a disk location and set them as read only. However, privileged users can retrieve them, delete them, and write a new version without being detected. The support here is only slightly better than that of a DBMS. The same is true of XML files.

The custom archive DBMS will have no functions available to update the data. It would use hash counts to verify that the data is the same and would keep copies of the hash counts in multiple places to ensure that no one developed a Rube Goldberg way of changing the data. It would use multiple dispersed backup copies to be able to find and retrieve the correct version of the data if such an action did occur or if the data was merely maliciously overwritten with random data.

14.2.14 **Provide Encryption and Signature Capabilities**

The data should be able to be encrypted when it's stored. It should also have file-level signatures to be able to detect damage to the data.

Encryption is available for all DBMS products. Signatures are another matter. Since they assume that data will be added, changed, and deleted, adding signatures is not possible.

UNLOAD files and XML files can easily be encrypted and have security signatures created through various SAN storage devices or through explicit support you would use if storing in open folders.

The custom archive DBMS would store data in individual storage units offering both encryption and security signatures at the unit level.

14.2.15 **Selective DELETE for Discard**

The database solution must support the ability to delete records from the archive based on selection criteria, to satisfy the DISCARD function. This should be tightly controlled to prevent abuse from those trying to delete data that should be left in the archive.

A DBMS certainly can support this requirement. Security on DELETE can be controlled in most DBMSs by granting DELETE authority to only specific individuals. A more clever approach is to put a trigger mechanism on the DELETE function of the tables in question and use it to create an audit record of such transactions. Not all DBMSs have this capability.

UNLOAD files cannot be used for selective discard. To make it work you need to write an application program that reads the file and writes a new file leaving out qualifying records. The same is true of an XML solution.

The custom archive DBMS would provide an explicit DISCARD function that would accomplish the function with full auditing of what took place.

14.2.16 **Use Disk Storage Efficiently**

This is a very important issue. Since archive data stores will become extremely large, it is important to be able to offload all or parts of the archive to lower-cost, less accessible storage. It is also important to use as little space on the storage media as possible.

DBMSs do not have the ability to put data for tables into multiple layers of storage. They do not allow for offline storage, such as on tape. DBMSs do not minimize the amount of space used and actually inflate it somewhat to anticipate update and insert actions.

UNLOAD files and XML documents are ideal for pushing parts of the archive into other layers of storage. Neither is particularly good at minimizing the space used.

The custom archive DBMS would allow for individual data units in the archive to be put anywhere the user wants, controlled by policy. Effective use of SAN devices is crucial to accomplishing this goal. It would separate the main data store from backups to allow separate policies for where to put each copy. It would also allow for data compression to conserve space.

14.2.17 **Low-Cost Solution**

The archive data store should be cost effective. The cost of the data store will eventually become a major budget item.

DBMSs are expensive. They cost a lot in license revenue and vendor maintenance fees. They also require more expensive storage. They also employ expensive staff for performing database administration.

UNLOAD files and XML files have little of these costs. The custom archive DBMS would minimize the cost of operations.

14.3 **FALSE FEATURES**

In addition to these desired features, two features are often asked for that should not be. These are false requirements in that they should not be needed for an archive database and satisfying them will frustrate or make impossible providing other features that are needed. It takes some thinking about archiving to convince oneself that these "features" are not worth asking for.

14.3.1 **Transparent Access to Data from Application Programs**

The requirement for an existing operational application program to see archive data without modifying the application program is often requested. In other words, the data is still active, not meeting the requirement for archiving. This sounds like a great feature to have.

However, the cost of providing this feature is very high. The data must be kept in a form that conforms with the view of data from the existing application programs. This severely constrains the options on the underlying archive database. Generally, this means that the database must be the same or highly similar to the operational database.

It also implies that the data be readily available. This means that it is not shoved off to offline storage or to devices with low access performance. If you put the data in a SAN, you can expect the retrieval time from the SAN for most accesses to result in a TIMEOUT of the application program. To prevent this you have to keep the entire archive up front—not what you want to do.

It also implies that your application program calls the DBMS to be intercepted and rerouted to the archive access routines on NOT FOUND conditions or always if the user wants a database UNION to occur. This type of intercept logic would increase the overhead cost of executing transactions. If the archive database is not kept on the same system, the processing model gets even more complex. No DBA is going to want that type of code running on operational systems.

You cannot gain system and application independence through this feature. This means that you keep old systems and applications around long after they are needed, adding to overall IT cost.

For DBMSs, this feature is possible with a lot of work and clever programming. For UNLOAD and XML stores, it is impossible.

A custom archive DBMS would not support it. It's a *bad* idea.

14.3.2 **High Performance on Data Access**

Another requirement that comes up often is the concern over performance for access requests to the archive. After decades of concern over database performance, it is not easy to accept the fact that you might be installing something that will not perform well.

The archive contains inactive data. The number of requests per week should be very small. The urgency of getting an answer is never subsecond. Tolerance is in the minutes, hours, or even days category. If your requirement for performance is higher than this, you should not be archiving the data. It is still active data.

To satisfy this requirement, the user would have to pick the DBMS solution for storing archive data. This would give up any hope of satisfying other, more important requirements.

Note that even keeping data in an active DBMS might still not yield high performance since the amount of data could prevent high performance from being achieved.

The custom archive DBMS would give as good performance as possible after satisfying the other, more important requirements. Performance on access would not be the most critical design parameter. Users must reset their expectations for archive access performance.

	Same DBMS	Other DBMS	UNLOAD Files	XML Documents	Custom Archive DMBS
Operational system independence	0	4	2	5	5
Large volume of data	3	3	5	5	5
Store enriched metadata	1	1	0	5	5
Subset data with metadata affinity	0	0	3	4	5
Store original data	2	0	0	0	5
Store additional information	0	0	0	3	5
Add data without disruption	0	0	5	5	5
Independent access authority	4	4	4	4	5
Search capabilities	5	5	0	2	5
Query without seeing entire archive	0	0	0	0	5
Application access	5	2	0	0	2
Restore to other DBMS types	2	4	4	2	5
Protect from updates or deletes	0	0	3	3	5
Encryption and signatures	3	3	5	5	5
Selective delete for discard	5	5	0	0	5
Efficient use of DASD	0	0	5	1	5
Low cost	0	0	4	3	5

FIGURE 14.1

Comparison of archive database choices. (Scale: 5 = fully satisfies; 0 = does not satisfy.)

14.4 **HOW CHOICES STACK UP**

Figure 14.1 summarizes the strengths and weaknesses of the various archive database choices in relation to the most desired features. Of course, the custom archive DBMS gets the best score since it was the theoretical baseline for designing an archive data store that satisfies all needs.

The custom archive DBMS takes the best design points from the other solutions to create a new DBMS design that is ideal for archiving large amounts of data for a long time. It has the access power of a relational database and the storage power of dealing with files, as UNLOAD and XML solutions do. It accommodates enhanced metadata and encapsulates it into the archive. It can support multiple versions of metadata definitions tied to individual units of archived data.

SUMMARY

If you build your own solution to archiving, you are pretty much limited to using a DBMS or UNLOAD files for storing the data. These alone are not sufficient. To be complete you need to add more support to any of these solutions. Even if you do, you will still fall short of requirements.

With vendor choices you get a wide variety of data store solutions. Some are good and some are bad. If you pick one that is not complete, you can either accept their limitations or build additional, add-on support to accommodate the missing functions. You are unlikely to do that. You cannot build enough support to get to the level of the custom archive DBMS solution.

The initial, intuitive choice is a DBMS, but after analysis it turns out to be a bad choice. There are too many requirements that operational DBMS architectures cannot satisfy.

To do it right, using a DBMS, UNLOAD, or XML solution requires adding a lot of additional recordkeeping and a lot of administration. This is rarely done, leaving a weakened solution. Even with this additional work, the solutions have other limitations that cannot be overcome by simply doing more.

You can use the information in this chapter to evaluate proposed solutions. You can also use it over the next few years to prod your vendors to get their solutions more in line with the complete set of requirements described here.

A bad choice will not serve you well. It is hard to change your choices once you start archiving and storing a lot of data. In addition, some choices could transform data in a way that makes it impossible to reconstruct the data as it originally existed. You cannot recover from that. You have to decide how important this issue is for your applications.

The Archive Data Extraction Component

15

The *archive data extraction component* is a critical part of a database archiving solution. It can make or break a project. There are multiple ways to design an extractor component. This is very evident by the fact that vendor supplied software varies widely in how this is accomplished; in fact this is one component you can write your own software for.

You should be aware of the important advantages and disadvantages of different approaches. Armed with this knowledge, you can make informed decisions when you're evaluating software choices or developing your own software for a specific archiving application.

The problem that makes extraction complex is that the data you are looking for is not conveniently placed together in a separate partition or location in the database. It is randomly dispersed throughout the database. The extract process is trying to find the fragments sprinkled throughout the database that need to be processed. It has to look through the entire database to find them. This is much different from archiving solutions that archive entire files or data that has already been clustered together to make identifying and processing easier.

The goals of the extractor component are to provide:

- Minimum interference with operational activities
- Full, bulletproof integrity
  - □ No data loss
  - □ No data in both places
- Tolerance of interruptions
- Handle large data volumes

Note that performance is not an explicit goal. The more important goal is minimum interference with operational activities. The last thing a database administrator wants is another process added to the operational environment that either requires a database outage or slows online processing. It's better to give up some performance in elapsed time for archive extraction to execute in order to achieve minimum impact.

That said, the performance should be good enough to get the job done without running for hours and hours. It is a question of reasonableness.

15.1 THE ARCHIVE EXTRACTOR MODEL

Figure 15.1 shows the basic parts of the extractor component. The basic roadmap is very simple.

The extractor component is an application program. It runs against the operational database that has business objects stored in it that could be eligible to be moved to the database archive. It finds those business objects that are ready to be moved, copies the data to the archive, and either deletes the data from the operational database or marks it as having been archived. As such the process must be correct and efficient. Incorrect processing by the extractor component brings the potential of data loss. A poor implementation also has the potential to seriously impact other activities against the operational database while it is executing.

The extractor process looks a lot like an extract, transform, and load (ETL) program. It actually is an ETL process with the added burden of deleting or marking data in the operational database. Other than that, it very closely follows the ETL concept.

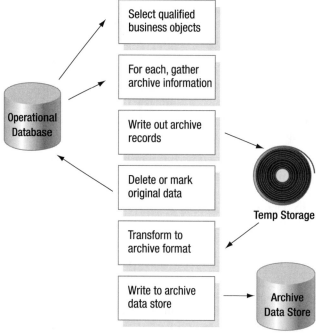

FIGURE 15.1

Basic extractor model.

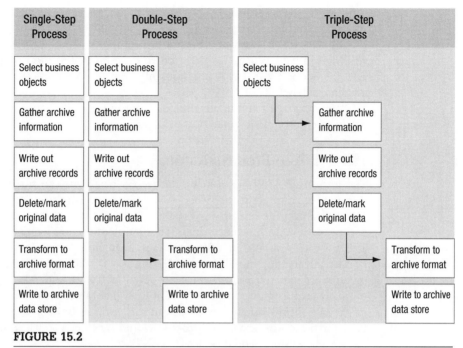

FIGURE 15.2

Extractor process models.

All these steps can be implemented as one large process or broken down into two or three processes. Figure 15.2 shows three possible models.

15.1.1 Single-Process Model

The single-process model attempts to perform all functions in one program. For it to execute, it must have access to the operational database and to the archive database at the same time. To execute correctly with integrity, it requires a two-phase commit function between the two databases.

The single-process model is best used for cases in which all processing is done on the same machine. Connecting processes on different machines with interactive communications between them and two-phase commit has the potential for higher-than-normal processing interruptions, performance delays, and data loss. The extractor program will run for a long time, making the exposure longer.

15.1.2 Double-Process Model

If the operational database and the archive database are on different machines, it is wise to separate the work done on the operational system (qualifying, gathering, copying, and deleting) from the work done on the archive machine (transforming and storing). This task is much easier to manage with integrity and will allow for fewer interruptions along with better online performance.

The data to be archived is stored in a temporary file on the source machine and then moved as a file to the archive machine when the first process ends. The connection can be a program, file transfer program (FTP), or queuing mechanism such as IBM's MQ Series.

This approach has the advantage of putting less impact on the operational database environment while it is running.

15.1.3 Triple-Process Model

The impact on the operational database environment can further be lessened through separating out the process of qualifying business objects for archiving. A separate process can be designed and implemented to do the qualifying step and produce a list of object identifiers that meet the archiving selection policy. This list can be stored in a file or a temporary table.

The advantage comes through having the qualifying step run in read-only mode with minimal impact on the operational workload. The qualifying step normally requires a database scan of at least one table. This can take some time to execute. If in read-only mode, it can run without holding locks. The elapsed time for the entire archiving process would be longer, but the impact on the operational system would be less.

Another advantage is that it will shorten the delete/mark portion of the overall process. There will be no need to look at objects that will not qualify. You also can get a count of the number of business objects that will be processed if it is important to gauge the amount of work that will be done in the delete/mark step or the amount of data that will get pushed to the archive for this cycle.

If the selection criteria consists of looking at only columns in the archive root node in the operational database, this separation is not that helpful. If, however, the criteria include looking at columns from multiple tables or possibly from tables that are not part of the archive data structure, the separation is particularly helpful.

15.2 EXTRACTOR IMPLEMENTATION APPROACHES

The extractor program is a nontrivial component of software. It must be carefully studied to ensure that it does not have a serious flaw that will make it unusable or a constant headache to deal with.

15.2.1 Form of the Program

The extractor program can be acquired through a vendor, or you can write your own. It can be a custom-written program or procedure tailored to a specific application, or it can be a generic program designed to handle multiple data structure definitions and policy statements.

Custom programs   If you choose to write your own program, realize that it is not a trivial undertaking.

To write a specific program for a single application is possible. You simply embed knowledge of the data structures and the extract selection criteria into the program logic. This is very doable for most applications.

The problem with a program that is built in-house for a single application is that it requires program changes to deal with data structure or policy changes. This means that a programmer needs to be added to the archive team. It also means that you need to write a separate program for each archiving application. If you have one simple but large data volume application, you might want to do it this way.

It is not likely that an IT department is going to write a generic program to handle parameter-driven data structure and policy definitions. This is a major undertaking that will result in a large requirement for program maintenance over time. It is possible, but it's not something that most IT departments are willing to do or maintain.

The use of scripting languages to accomplish the archiving task is fraught with all kinds of risks. The requirements are so large that it is not likely that you would be able to accomplish everything that needs to be done. Also, it would undoubtedly run much too slowly. For some small, noncomplex applications, it might be possible to fashion a satisfactory solution through scripts; however, each script would be customized to a single application.

Vendor products   Many software vendors have entered the database archiving space. They have widely varying implementation approaches to extract. Some have been built from the ground up to handle this problem, and some have been created by modifying software originally intended for other uses.

A vendor solution is generally the best approach since vendors build generic, parameter-driven solutions. However, since this is a new industry, some implementations are more robust than others; some are more complete than others.

It is imperative that you evaluate each vendor solution according to the concepts put forth in this chapter.

15.2.2 **Online or Batch**

The archive extract program can be designed to run online along with other applications, or it can be designed to run when the database is in batch mode with no competing activity.

If your application can tolerate a batch window, it is not a bad idea to use archive extract this way. Many applications already have batch applications; thus, adding another might not be considered a burden. That said, the archive extract process is not a short-running process and it will require a healthy chunk of time to execute.

Unfortunately, most applications that require database archiving have a requirement for little to no database downtime. Adding a batch archive extract is not possible for these applications.

The ideal archive extract program runs during online operations as a crawler across the database that holds few locks for short periods of time and runs at a low priority. The operational environment becomes unaffected by the process. No one knows it is there. It is like a robot quietly going about its business without disturbing anyone.

One approach that is used is to combine archive extract with a database reorganization utility. The concept is to remove qualifying data during the unload phase of a reorganization, leaving the resulting database short a bunch of records—the ones moved to the archive. This concept, illustrated in Figure 15.3, can be implemented as part of a batch, offline reorganization function or, better yet, as part of an online reorganization program. The idea is that it adds no overhead, or at least only a little bit of it. You get two functions for the cost of one.

First you need a reorganization utility that can support this function. For relational databases it will generally work only if the archive data object consists of only one row from one table. The selection criteria must also be expressed as a predicate using only columns from this one table. Reorganization utilities do not look at two tables at once with the exception of hierarchical databases such as IMS, which look at all the segments of a physical database during reorganization. For IMS databases, the entire physical data structure can be examined for selection criteria and entire business objects processed for extract during reorganization as long as they are defined to IMS in the same physical database record. An online reorganization approach to archiving makes a lot of sense in this case.

Another downside is that you get archive extraction only when you run database reorganization. This could lead you to run more reorganization than you otherwise would and any advantage is lost. If you currently run reorganizations

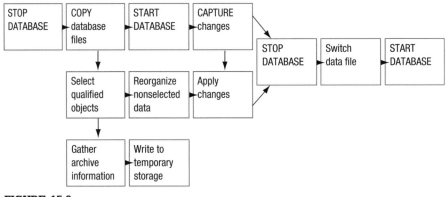

FIGURE 15.3

Archive and online database reorganization integration model.

frequently and on a periodic schedule, this might not be a problem. However, most shops run reorganizations only when they are pressed to do so.

An acceptable solution is to combine archive extract with an online reorganization. At least one vendor has done this for IMS. This allows it to run more frequently with minimal disruption of the operational online processing. Basically, you get the advantage of reorganization while doing archive extract instead of the other way around.

The downside of this is that the online reorganization consumes a lot of cycles during online processing that creates a heavier load, inhibiting smooth online operations. However, if it is run during a slow period, it can be the best of all solutions.

Another factor to consider is that removing items to the archive during database reorganization could result in deletes not being put in the recovery log. The impact of this could be that log analyzer programs or database auditing programs would not see the deletes. This might or might not be a problem for a specific application.

15.2.3 Source of Data

The archive extract program would normally access data by making application calls to the database software. For a relational database it would do SELECT, DELETE, UPDATE, and COMMIT calls.

Some vendor programs might read the underlying files of the DBMS. This is a plausible approach if the processing is done in dedicated batch mode or online reorganization mode. It could be used to provide better performance. However, it can be dangerous if not done carefully. It is better to use an application approach that runs online with low priority than to run faster using a riskier approach.

Using the application API Another approach is to use an application programming interface (API) provided by the application to perform extract operations. Most packaged applications make this possible. You do GET and DELETE functions against virtual objects instead of against the underlying physical database tables and rows.

This approach can be more straightforward than using the underlying tables. Sometimes there is a choice as to which approach to use. Using the underlying tables should be faster than using the API. When given a choice, do load testing to determine whether using the API provides sufficient performance.

15.3 EXECUTION OPTIONS

The extract program can benefit from a number of execution options that might be available for an extractor program. Some of them are discussed in this section. You won't find these in all solutions. However, they are helpful where they do exist.

Statistics   This option executes the extract program over the operational database performing the qualifying function and the gathering function. However, it does not output business objects, remove them from the operational database, nor mark them. It merely computes the number of business objects, the number of rows from all applicable tables, and the number of bytes of data that would have been extracted had a normal execution been performed. The purpose of this option is to give the archivist an idea of how much time and disk storage will be needed if the selection criteria being used is launched.

The STATISTICS run can be made during normal operations since it is read-only. Since it outputs nothing and needs no locks, it should run considerably faster than a normal archiving run.

Simulation   The SIMULATION option will perform all the steps of the archiving process except deleting or marking business objects from within the operational database. It is a test run only. The difference between this and STATISTICS is that it actually produces an archive data unit. This can be used to verify that the output is what you expected. You can also test access and discard routines on the test archive data unit.

Although you could do much of the same testing using a test database instead of the real operational database, the advantages of using the real thing make it a better test. You might want to do both. It ensures that the test criteria are compatible with the definition of the database at the operational level.

Limits on archived amounts   Archiving is all about finding business objects that are ready to be moved and then moving them. Sometimes the expected volume of data that would be moved at one time would be overwhelming to the archive storage system if it were received all at once. This condition can be determined by looking at the output of STATISTICS.

One way to handle the large amount of data expected the first time archive extraction is run for the application is to break the execution into multiple jobs that run on successive days and limit the number of business objects extracted in each run. This is very helpful in limiting the size of archive storage units and in limiting the daily impact of archiving on operations.

This is also a useful option to run with SIMULATION. It gives you a reasonably sized archive test unit for use in testing the discard and access routines.

Limits on time run   This option is similar to the preceding one except that it limits the time the archive extract program runs. This would be used to ensure that the archive extract program does not run past the end of a time period available for execution. For example, if extract is run in the middle of the night when transaction rates are low and the database administrator wants to ensure that it ends before the morning rush begins, it might limit execution time to three hours. All business objects identified and gathered up to the time of expiration would be safely put away in the archive, but no other ones would be sought.

Again, this option is valuable in controlling the process in a busy operational environment.

Runtime progress feedback   This option would provide a monitor output during execution, to show progress. It could identify the number of business objects found so far, the number copied to temporary storage, or the number safely stored in the archive. It would identify unexpected slow progress rates or complete stoppage of progress.

This feedback can be used to ensure that the process is moving along as expected. After a few weeks of operation, a notion of normal rate of progress will emerge.

15.4 INTEGRITY CONSIDERATIONS

Integrity cannot be compromised. Archive data is important data; otherwise it would not be a candidate for archive. The goal of integrity is to ensure and be confident that the process does not result in data loss or in data duplication (same data in both operational and archive databases). The extract process should be able to tolerate any interruptions during execution and recover properly.

15.4.1 Interruptions

Interruptions can always occur during processing. Some interruptions are the result of the extract process itself; some are simply things that happen no matter what. Examples of extractor-caused interruptions are programming errors in the extractor, running out of space for temporary files, lock timeouts, and data transformation errors. Examples of interruptions not attributable to the extractor are the operator pulling the plug on the job, power outages, operating system failures, DBMS failures, and disk errors. The extract process must be defensible against all of these.

Minimize window for interruptions   Breaking the extractor process into phases helps in dealing with interruptions. If the qualifying step is separated from the other steps, an interruption during its work is of no harm. You can merely start over.

If you isolate the process of copy and delete from the transformation and store functions through intermediate temporary files, the time window within which an interruption can cause a problem is minimized. You basically need to be concerned about integrity only in the one phase of delete/mark of the operational database. Every other phase can be restarted from the beginning without harm. This idea is shown in Figure 15.4. This makes a strong case for splitting the extractor component into multiple independent steps.

15.4.2 Locks and Commits

In running against the operational database and doing deletes or marks, the extractor must establish a unit of work. This is the work that will be done between commits to the database. Establishing a unit of work that is too large

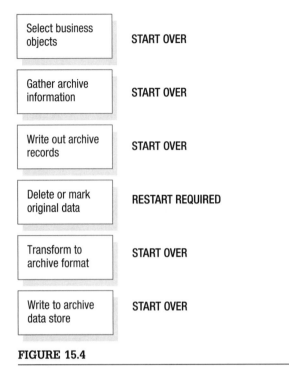

Select business objects	START OVER
Gather archive information	START OVER
Write out archive records	START OVER
Delete or mark original data	RESTART REQUIRED
Transform to archive format	START OVER
Write to archive data store	START OVER

FIGURE 15.4

Extractor step sensitivity to interruptions.

can result in serious trouble. The bigger the unit of work, the more likely lock conflicts will occur and the more extensive the impact of interruptions.

You simply cannot establish a unit of work that covers the entire execution. This will certainly cause serious operational problems.

Some argue that since the data is inactive, holding row-level UPDATE locks is not harmful to other operations. Some relational database systems do not support row-level locking but instead lock entire blocks of data that the subject row is stored in. This also locks many other rows that share that data block. All DBMSs have lock escalation logic that causes lock levels to escalate if too many smaller locks are held. This will certainly kick in for an archive extractor run. You think your lock covers only inactive data and then discover that it is locking entire tables. The outcome is clear: The database administrator will stop the job and roll back all work.

Even if only row-level locks are held on inactive data, it might cause other problems if held too long. One is that the system parameters for the DBMS could cause an automatic JOB abort and roll everything back. Another is that it could block read attempts from other applications that are doing scans of all or a portion of the database. Even if these programs would ultimately ignore these rows, the locks would stop the scan process until commit of the extractor read lock. If held too long, it could seriously impact these other programs and bog down the entire system. Short lock durations are good; long lock durations are bad.

Vertical vs. horizontal locks There are two approaches to processing that are used in commercial products. One is to process one table at a time and extract the parts of business objects from each in turn. This is a *horizontal approach* to a unit of work. The other approach is to drive *vertically* down the business object structure and gather all the data from all of the tables for one business object at a time. The unit of work becomes a business object.

The problem with horizontal processing is clear. If you commit the work done on one table before finishing another, you leave orphaned rows in the operational database (partial business objects). The only way this can work correctly is to run in batches and not release the database until *all* tables have been processed. This might not be possible in all cases. This approach cannot be used for online extractor processing.

If referential constraints are defined in the database using CASCADE DELETE, they require that tables be processed from the bottom up. Otherwise, deleting rows in the higher tables in the hierarchy will cause loss of data before it can be copied. However, if processing is done from bottom up and an interruption occurs, the business objects are left in the database but are incomplete. You lose either way.

The vertical approach of one business object at a time lends itself much better to online processing and also has benefits for batch processing. All interruptions will cause the rollback of partial work on at most one business object. The operational database is never left in an inconsistent state.

The unit of work for vertical locking can be set to one business object or to any other number to facilitate more efficient processing. It allows the user to control the commit frequency.

15.4.3 **Restarting Versus Starting Over**

The extract process must have a notion of what to do when an interruption occurs and the job did not finish.

If you have committed deletes/marks in the operational database, the logic must allow for the data from them to ultimately find its way to the archive. The best way to ensure this is to make sure you have captured the data destined for the archive before the commit to the operational database. One way to do this is to use two-phase commit logic against the actual archive data store. This clearly works. If you do this, you do not need a RESTART or a STARTOVER function. Whatever was put into the archive has had all necessary processing completed in the operational database. What's done is done; there is nothing to restart. If you start over, it is the same as starting a new job from scratch: It will find other business objects that the original process did not get to.

This is a sound plan, although it does require complex two-phase commit logic and does keep the window of interruption vulnerability open for a longer period of time.

Multistep approaches   If you have divided processing into steps and the vulnerable delete/mark step is interrupted, you need to ensure that the temporary files holding data headed for the archive are safe and consistent. This can be accomplished much more simply than using a two-phase commit approach. Write the temporary file to disk before doing the database commit. Then you only need to check the last business object on the file to see if it is still in the database. This would be done on a RESTART. If using a temporary table in the DBMS, you merely need to include it in the commit.

The RESTART could also be used to keep appending data to the temporary files, or it can be used to simply fix the last business object and send what you have so far to the archive. In other words, if you are doing vertical locking and use temporary files, any interruption can be handled very simply by using what has been processed so far, or it can be restarted to resume what it was doing before the interruption.

The other steps of multiphase processing can be handled through a STARTOVER function, provided that any inserts into the archive can be identified to that run and backed out.

If an interruption occurs during any phase after a single commit has been done to the operational database, it is imperative that the process complete. Otherwise archive data is sitting in temporary files or tables. It is neither in the operational database nor in the archive; it is stuck in temporary space.

15.4.4 **Workspace Management**

If temporary files or tables are used to separate processes, they must be managed carefully. It is a good idea to always create dual files, separating them on different disk drives. This way an error in reading a file cannot cause loss of data. Most DBMSs do dual logging for exactly the same purpose.

Be sure that enough space is available before starting execution. You don't want to get an out-of-space interruption. You can use STATISTICS to determine how much temporary space is needed. After a few extract executions, the space requirement should become clear.

Do not delete temporary files or tables until you are positive that the data on them has been safely put away in the archive. This includes creating any archive data store backups. They might be needed for a RESTART.

You might want to keep the temporary files around for a longer period of time. Possibly store them in a file-archiving system. Then if the archive proves unusable or has other problems that make it suspect, the data is in the temporary files and, with some effort, can be salvaged. You might want to do this for a period of time after a new archiving application is put into service as yet another safety valve. Of course this presents a problem if the temporary files are kept beyond the point at which some of the contents might be discarded from the archive data store. You cannot simply forget about these files. If possible, use file system auto-delete functions based on time since they are created.

15.4.5 **Data Errors**

Data errors may occur in transforming data elements to the format required in the archive. For example, the data type of a source data element could be specified as DATE but the value being delivered is not recognizable as a valid date. Data errors can also occur on column limits, such as floating-point numbers. The conversions are normally done after the data has been deleted from the operational database.

There are two strategies for handling data errors. One is to put the business object in the archive with the data value stored being a null or other default value. The error is logged and the log is stored with the archive storage unit.

The other strategy is to reject it from the archive. This would normally imply that it is left in the operational database with a log entry to the user about the error. The user must fix the data in the operational system before it can be archived. This strategy requires that data transformations are "tested" in the data object-gathering phase of extract or that the capability exists to put a business object "back" into the operational database if errors are found later in the process. Putting back might not be possible if data portions of the business object are deleted from the operational database but not moved to the archive.

You can head off data error problems by using SIMULATION in advance. If you are getting a large number of errors during SIMULATION, you can redesign the archive application around the problem.

15.4.6 **Metadata Validation**

The extract process assumes that the metadata of the operational system is the same as the metadata used to design the archive application. It is possible that the database administrator slipped in a metadata change to the operational database without notifying the archive analyst. They might be out of step.

It is a good practice to have the extract process validate that the basic metadata available at execution time matches the metadata used to develop the archive design. For relational databases this can be done through examination of the relational database catalog.

This process adds processing but is worth it if only one metadata change is caught. Failure to catch a metadata change can cause serious distortion in the archive itself.

15.5 **OTHER CONSIDERATIONS**

There remains other important factors to consider when building or evaluating archive extract software: audit trails, capacity planning, and post-extract functions.

15.5.1 **Log Output and Audit Trails**

The extractor process should produce a log that shows what happened and when it occurred. At a minimum it should record:

- Application identification
- User ID executing the job
- Date and time of the execution
- Success or failure
- Duration of execution
- Execution options used
- Selection policy used
- Number of business objects/rows/bytes sent to the archive
- Number of rows deleted or marked in the operational database
- Detailed information on failures, especially data errors
- Restart or startover events

The execution logs should be intelligible. They should not include a lot of unnecessary data; they should be short. It would be great if a program actually produced a log as an XML document.

The logs or information extracted from them should be permanently saved in the archive data store or in the archive repository or both. They should suffice as an audit trail on archiving extract activities. They should be easily read and searchable. Information in them could be useful for capacity planning or trend analysis.

15.5.2 **Capacity Planning**

The archive analyst needs to be sensitive to the amount of disk storage needed for temporary files and for the archive data store. The amount of data moved in one extractor execution can be large—very large. The analyst should also be cognizant of the amount of time that needs to be reserved to execute the extractor function.

Each archiving application will have an initial volume result and a stable volume result. The initial volume result comes about because an excessive amount of inactive data has piled up in the operational database and will get "caught" on the first execution. There is a backlog of stuff ready to be moved. Some estimates run as high as 70 percent of the operational database will get moved on the initial extractor execution. This result needs to be estimated and managed for execution time, temporary space requirements, and disk storage space needed.

The stable volume is the volume that results after the extractor has been run a number of times and truly represents the average amount of data that "ripens" during the interval of time between extractor executions. This stable point may be reached immediately after the initial extractor execution, or it could take several executions to reach.

For example, if a database has 100,000 new transactions added to it per week, has a selection criterion of moving transaction data after 180 days, and has been accumulating data for four years, then:

- The initial run will find 17,800,000 transactions ready to move.
- The stable volume will be 100,000 transactions if run every week.
- The operational database will stabilize to 2,600,000 transactions.

This concept is illustrated in Figure 15.5.

The archive analyst should use STATISTICS to discover the volume expected on the initial execution. If the number is too high, a decision might be made to either change the selection criteria for a few weeks to grab less each time until you reach the stable point or to use the LIMIT execution parameter to control the amount of output processed on any single run. Using this approach will spread out the initial shock to the system.

The opposite effect might occur on the initial estimate. If the selection criteria call for data to be moved only after a period of time that is larger than the amount of time the application has been in production, the initial volume

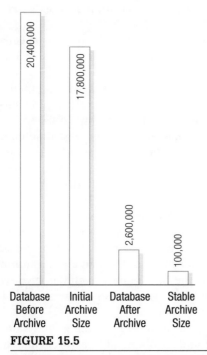

FIGURE 15.5

Example of initial versus stable volume estimates.

may be zero. It could take several weeks, months, or even years for anything to qualify. This also can be discovered through the STATISTICS function.

Another factor to consider is seasonality. If you have a database application where transaction volumes vary considerably by season, you are probably already cognizant of this fact and anticipate it in normal operations. However, be aware that the same volume impulse will show up in archive extraction but will lag by the period of time it takes to qualify records for movement to the archive. In the previous example, if the Christmas season experiences a threefold increase in transaction volume, the archive extractor will see a three-fold increase in volume in June.

The log can be used to monitor the volumes and times being experienced to help project needs for future executions and for the ever-growing archive data store capacity.

15.5.3 **Post-Extract Functions**

Every experienced database administrator knows that after you have deleted a bunch of data from a database, you probably need to reorganize the operational database and the indexes on them, generate image copies of the database files reorganized, and, based on the DBMS, run database STATISTICS and APPLICATION PLAN REBIND. This can add a lot of processing to the weekly archive extractor execution.

Clearly this should be done after the initial extractor execution up to the point of stable volumes. After that, the argument can be made that it is not necessary.

The argument goes that you have only deleted data and thereby created free space throughout the database files. Your application programs will not run more slowly if you do not reorganize. They might run faster for a while. However, you expect new data to be inserted over the next time interval (for example, the next week) that will use up the free space you just created. The volume coming in each period is expected to be about the same as the volume going out. If you simply leave the databases alone, the performance should stay about the same.

If you choose not to do reorganization after a run, it might be helpful to at least do an image copy. These can usually be run while online activity is going on. They will shorten any subsequent recovery operations considerably.

It is important that you never do a recovery to a point in time prior to the extractor run. If you do that, the data moved to the archive will reappear in the operational database and be in both places at the same time. You do not want this situation to occur.

Another important point to make is that executing utility functions to clean up after an extractor execution does not need to happen immediately after the extraction. The database can remain in online status and the functions executed at any time in the future.

SUMMARY

The extractor is a very complex component. There are lots of issues to consider, whether you are attempting to build one or are evaluating extractor components of vendor products.

A poorly designed extractor can be a disaster in production. The problems might not appear until after you have been using it for some time.

Vendor products have a mixed record of providing needed support. This is a new technology area and vendors are still learning the ropes. In the next chapter we'll explore the less complex but still important discard component.

CHAPTER

The Archive Discard Component

16

The next component to review is the discard component. This component will periodically read the archive data store to find business objects that have reached the end of their intended archive lives and need to be removed. The process removes them from the archive data store and records information about its actions. The steps in the process are shown in Figure 16.1.

This component is less complex and less critical than the extractor component. It is still important since no one wants to retain data longer than it's required. It is also important that the component not make mistakes and end up deleting data too early or too late. The discard component should not leave partial business objects in the archive.

16.1 DATA STRUCTURE CONSIDERATIONS

Discarding archived data is not as simple as discarding files for which their stipulated retention period has elapsed. The first topic to consider is the smallest unit of data that needs to be discarded. Within an archive data store there will likely be some data that needs to be discarded and other data that does not. The data that qualifies at any one point of time will not be conveniently packed together within the archive to facilitate easy removal. It will be spread out among other data. The discard process has to find the data that is ready and surgically remove it from within the archive data store.

16.1.1 Unit of Discard: The Business Object

The unit of discard is a single business object—nothing less and nothing more. This is the same definition that was used for extract and store. It makes no sense to discard only part of a business object.

This means that the discard process needs to identify those business objects that meet the discard policy criteria and then gather all the component parts

---

CHAPTER

The Archive Discard Component

16

The next component to review is the discard component. This component will periodically read the archive data store to find business objects that have reached the end of their intended archive lives and need to be removed. The process removes them from the archive data store and records information about its actions. The steps in the process are shown in Figure 16.1.

This component is less complex and less critical than the extractor component. It is still important since no one wants to retain data longer than it's required. It is also important that the component not make mistakes and end up deleting data too early or too late. The discard component should not leave partial business objects in the archive.

16.1 DATA STRUCTURE CONSIDERATIONS

Discarding archived data is not as simple as discarding files for which their stipulated retention period has elapsed. The first topic to consider is the smallest unit of data that needs to be discarded. Within an archive data store there will likely be some data that needs to be discarded and other data that does not. The data that qualifies at any one point of time will not be conveniently packed together within the archive to facilitate easy removal. It will be spread out among other data. The discard process has to find the data that is ready and surgically remove it from within the archive data store.

16.1.1 Unit of Discard: The Business Object

The unit of discard is a single business object—nothing less and nothing more. This is the same definition that was used for extract and store. It makes no sense to discard only part of a business object.

This means that the discard process needs to identify those business objects that meet the discard policy criteria and then gather all the component parts

215

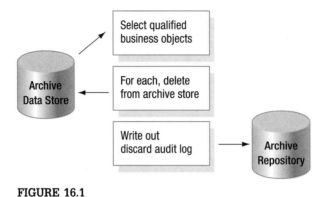

FIGURE 16.1

Functions of the discard component.

related to the objects found. It is the same process as extract except the policy is different and the source is the archive data store.

Business objects are hierarchical. They all have an archive root row with an identifier data element. They might consist of just that one row. This makes discard easy. More often they have related rows in other tables that are connected through data elements. These must be followed to find all the related rows.

Related rows come in two "flavors," as we described in Chapter 11. Those that are part of the business object need to be discarded along with the root row. However, those related rows that are reference rows could be connected to more than one business object. If so, they cannot be deleted until all business objects connected to them are discarded. Not understanding this is a common mistake that can leave retained business objects incomplete.

16.1.2 **Scope of Discard**

The purpose of discard is to eliminate the business object from your systems so that it cannot be discovered in any search. This means that removal from the archive must not be limited to the primary archive data store but also to any backup copies that are maintained as well.

Technically, all potential places where the data exists should be purged of the information, including data stores outside the archive. It is clearly not the archivist's responsibility to do this. The archivist should raise this concern as an issue during the archive application design phase so that every data store that has the potential of containing data beyond the archive discard period is identified and someone is assigned to remove the data at the time of discard from the archive. Most external stores will get rid of the data long before the archive discard date by virtue of natural processing. However, some might linger long after this point.

The IT organization can establish a procedure to find and destroy these other copies of data. One way that the archivist can help is to have the discard program produce an output list of the business object identifiers of all objects discarded from the archive. This list could then be used by others to find and destroy copies stored in other places.

16.1.3 **DBMS Data Store**

If the archive data store uses a standard DBMS such as DB2 LUW, discard is done by issuing DELETE SQL statements. Sometimes the CASCADE DELETE function will handle subordinate table rows for you.

Getting rid of backup copies is easy. Simply create a new image copy set for backup purposes after all the deletes have occurred. After this is done, all prior backups can be thrown away. This means that *all* copies of the discarded objects are no longer in existence. You don't have to search through and remove specific rows from the backup files.

The deleted data still remains on the DBMS log files. However, after you have created new image copy backups, those log files can safely be deleted as well.

This logic is contrary to what most database administrators would recommend. They typically keep image copy files and log files around for 30–60 days beyond their usefulness. However, when discard is considered, this leaves the data in an exposed state for that much longer. The sequence for doing a complete discard is shown in Figure 16.2.

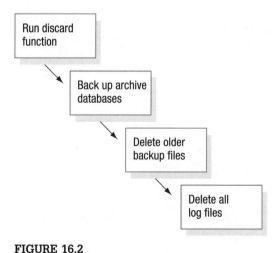

FIGURE 16.2

DBMS archive data store discard sequence.

16.1.4 **File Data Store**

If the archive data store is a collection of files such as UNLOAD, XML, or CUSTOM ARCHIVE units, the discard process is different. Each file could contain some business objects that are ready to be discarded along with some that are not ready. Some files contain only data that is not ready; and some contain data that is *all* ready. Any specific business object should reside entirely within only one file.

The archive discard process must look inside files and find specific business objects that qualify and remove them from the files without removing data that is not ready.

The best way to process against these data stores is to identify files that have the potential for having data that qualifies for discard within them, find any business objects that qualify, and then build a new replacement file that contains only the business objects that failed to qualify. You are leaving out the ones you want to discard. Then you replace the file in the data store with the new, shorter file.

To handle backups, you delete all backup files for which a replacement has been built and then write new backup copies of the replacement files. If all the data for a file is eliminated, the file itself can be removed; there's no need to write an empty replacement file. This process is shown in Figure 16.3.

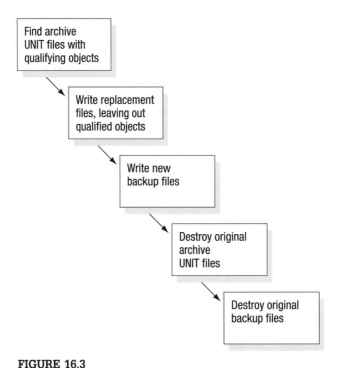

FIGURE 16.3

File data store discard sequence.

Storage subsystems   When you use a file-based approach, the data might be stored in a storage subsystem such as one of the many popular SAN devices. These devices handle many storage management functions for you; however, the discard process requires some careful consideration when you're using them.

First, do not set file-level retention dates for any files. You cannot predict in advance when any specific file will become ready to be disposed of. Retention dates translate to two things: (1) they prevent destruction of the file prior to the date specified, and (2) they automatically destroy the file when that date is reached. Neither of these actions is desirable for archived database data.

The data in a file can reach discard status prior to other data in the same file. The entire file can be placed on a legal hold requiring that it be kept longer than the intended destruction date.

When you use storage subsystems, leave the retention date alone; set it to "indefinite" and then manage the file deletes explicitly through the discard process.

WORM devices   A WORM device is often heralded as the only way to store archive data. These are write-once/read-multiple-times devices that prevent changing the data while it exists—a nice characteristic to have for archive data. They generally have removable media units where the unit of retention and destruction is the media itself.

WORM devices are not appropriate when you're using a DBMS data store for the archive. A DBMS cannot tolerate not being able to update data pages. However, WORM devices may be applicable and useful for file-level archiving data store structures.

WORM devices can be real or virtual. A real device actually does write to media that cannot be changed. These should never be used for file-level database archiving. They require that all data in all files be discard ready before the media can be physically destroyed. If the logic described earlier is used, the entire contents of the media would have to be replaced on a new media unit to achieve the same result. This is unreasonable.

Virtual WORM devices are implemented on standard disk storage devices. The front-end storage subsystem software will disallow any attempts to update a file. However, they generally have an API that allows destruction of a single file at any time. This is sufficient to implement the scheme described earlier. These devices are very much worth considering for use.

16.2 **IMPLEMENTATION FORM**

The discard function does not lend itself to multiple phases or steps. It is not complex.

It can either be a specific application program written for a single archive application or it can be a generic program that processes using a discard policy statement and metadata definitions. A locally written program would normally be a specific application program; a vendor package would normally include a generic solution.

For simple data structure applications, it might be possible to write the entire discard program as a script using SQL statements and file-level commands. This would be a rare opportunity.

16.3 INTEGRITY CONSIDERATIONS

Concerns about disruption of other operations are generally not present for discard. It is changing the archive data store that should have very little activity against it. You can generally always find time periods when the discard process can have exclusive control of the data stores.

16.3.1 Exclusive Locks

For archive stores in DBMSs, the unit of work for discard can be reasonably wide. It should always be on the boundary between business objects. A vertical strategy that handles all parts of a single business object at one time is the only logical way to process.

Having a lock strategy that keeps the unit of work to one that covers the entire execution is not reasonable. Although it would work and locking out users would normally not be a concern, interruptions could roll back a large amount of work, requiring you to start over from the beginning. It is wiser to have a *commit* strategy that does some number of business units within each unit of work. For example, a number of 10 business objects would be reasonable.

For file-based archive data stores, the unit of work should be set to a single storage file. All work against a file should be done and then the replacement file and appropriate backups committed to storage. Setting an exclusive lock on the file during processing might make sense, although it would not be harmful to allow readers of the file while it is being processed. The file switch function should wait if there are any read access processes still alive.

16.3.2 Interruptions

Interruption handling is not nearly as complex or critical for the discard component as it is for the extractor component. For DBMS data stores, the DBMS will roll back any partial work not committed.

For file-based archive data stores, the original file is still in place, and the replacement file being created will need to be discarded. The implied commit is on the boundary that occurred between the current file being processed and the previous one that was committed.

Out-of-space conditions should generally not occur; the only place where this makes sense is for a DBMS rollback log. Even there it would be unusual for it to not have enough space. If it does run out of space, discard processing might have to be broken into parts.

16.3.3 **Restart/Startover**

Restart after an interruption is generally quite easy. For a DBMS implementation, an interruption basically sets a completion boundary at the prior commit point. A STARTOVER would act like a new execution. It will not find business objects previously discarded and would merely apply the criteria to what remains in the archive database to find ones that were not committed. No specific RESTART or STARTOVER is needed.

For file-level data stores, there could be a need to handle operations that were in-flight at the time of the interruption. If in the middle of a file that has a replacement file partially built but not committed, the replacement file needs to be discarded. If in the middle of switching files, you have to know where it is. If the replacement file has not yet been committed, treat it as though in the middle: discard it. If it has been committed but the backups were not deleted nor the original primary and backup files not yet deleted, these actions must be completed. It is okay to simply go ahead and write/delete files as though on the boundary between commit of the primary and the other actions. If some of them have already completed, you will get either NOT FOUND or ALREADY EXISTS return codes. Just ignore these and you will be okay.

To handle these conditions you will need a log that records progress through execution. If this is a discard program output file, it can be read on RESTART and a determination made of what to do to fix things. Otherwise, you will need to look at the log and issue file commands to take comparable actions.

16.3.4 **Forensic Delete**

Some requirements call for deleting archive data with sufficient severity to prevent data forensic software from finding it.

If the archive data store is a DBMS, this might or might not be available as a feature. If it is, request it. If it's not, you are out of luck.

If the archive data store is a collection of files, supporting this is more complex. All storage subsystem implementations offer forensic delete as a file option. If they do, make sure you use it. If you are storing the files on a file system, it could be an option for the file system; if it is, use it.

If you are storing the files on a file system that does not offer this as an option, you are probably out of luck. If you write zeros or patterns to the file, there is no guarantee that the file system will write back to the same blocks.

If this is a hard requirement, the only reasonable way to handle it is through a storage subsystem or file system that offers this as a standard option.

16.4 OPERATIONAL CONSIDERATIONS

Other considerations for designing or evaluating a discard software program are included here.

16.4.1 Discard Policy Considerations

The discard policy is stated as selection criteria against data elements that are stored in the business objects in the archive. Since the archive data structure will generally always be relational, it would make sense for it to be an SQL statement. It simply needs to be executed against the archive data.

The archive policy would not normally be stated in terms of the length of time since an object was put into the archive. This means that individual archive storage units would not be treated as discard units; selected business objects within them would be.

The archive discard policy must be checked to ensure that it applies to all data in the archive. This might seem unnecessary; however, metadata changes between units of data in the archive could cause a policy to qualify on data elements that are in some of the archive units and not in others. This oversight could cause older data to never qualify for discard since it does not contain the data element used for qualification. Some method should be used to ensure that *all* the storage units have *all* the data elements that are referenced in the policy.

It is possible for an implementation to use external data sources to qualify business objects for discard. This would be unusual, but if it were true, the discard program would expect an external file or table to be input that contains the unique object identifiers for those objects that qualify. Generation of this list would be left up to a program or process that is external to the discard program.

An example of where this might be used is an implementation that says, "Discard every business object where the time since the object was created is greater than 10 years *unless* the object identifier is on a list of objects that are the subject of open lawsuits." This exclusion list is kept in a relational database outside the archive. To accomplish this, the discard program is run once to generate only a qualifying list. A secondary program is then run to exclude identifiers from the list by using the external table. The final list is then processed against the archive using the archive discard program to remove data.

If the discard program is handcrafted for this specific application, this could all be done in one program. You are not likely to find a vendor program that extends support this far.

16.4.2 Execution Options

Some execution options might be useful for the discard program. Some of the options described for the extractor component do not make sense here—for example, STATISTICS or STOP AFTER X TIME.

The LIST ONLY option would execute the policy qualification and produce an external list of business object identifiers that meet the discard criteria. It would not discard anything. It could be used in the scenario described earlier where a data source outside the archive needs to be checked for discard selection qualification.

The STOP AFTER *n* objects option limits the amount of work performed in a single execution. The purpose is to limit the amount of temporary space needed for a single execution. This would normally apply only to DBMS data stores where there is a concern about the size of the rollback log; but it could also be useful in conjunction with the next option.

The SIMULATION option would execute discard policy and output entire business objects to an external destination—for example, an XML file. No actual discarding of data takes place. SIMULATION is used to test the discard policy by allowing the archive analyst to visually check qualifying business objects to ensure that they are, in fact, what you intend to discard.

You would use SIMULATION along with the STOP AFTER *n* objects option to limit the amount of data you need to examine to be comfortable with the policy.

16.4.3 HOLD CHECK **Function**

For some applications there might be a need to place a HOLD on discarding data from the archive for a period of time. No archive discard executions are allowed during this period. It might be that a lawsuit mandates a HOLD. It could be that the business chooses to do a HOLD for other reasons.

A simple way of doing this is to simply not run the discard program. However, this invites the risk of inadvertent execution causing a violation of the intent of the HOLD and potential negative consequences to the corporation.

A better solution is for the archive repository to have a place to record HOLD requests. The archive discard program could then always check this place at the beginning of execution to ensure that the application data about to be processed is not the subject of a HOLD.

Another way of accomplishing this task is to change the policy statement at the time of the HOLD to qualify nothing. For example, set it to SELECT WHERE CREATE DATE > CURRENT_DATE. This will never be true for anything in the archive.

It is easier to have an external HOLD CHECK function than it is to change the discard policy. This way you know what the policy would be if there was no HOLD and you would not have to change it back when the HOLD is removed. Also, if the execution option of SIMULATION is available, you can always use the discard policy criteria to count the amount of data that is being backed up because of the HOLD.

16.4.4 **Performance**

Performance should not be an overriding concern for this component, since it is operating only on the archive. The archive is not supposed to have much activity going on against it. However, if the archive is very large and the discard program is not efficient, it might take an exorbitant amount of time to execute. This should be avoided if possible.

The selection criteria in the discard policy will almost always be keyed off a date data element that sets the start time for measuring the retention length. This is not normally a data element you would index. This means that the basic method of finding qualifying business objects is through scanning the entire archive.

If you are using a DBMS to store the archive data, you might consider partitioning on this date field. Setting partitions one month or one year apart will greatly facilitate discard. It would also minimize the amount of data to image copy and reorganize after a discard execution. Doing a full index on the field is probably not necessary and would create an enormous index.

If data files are used for storing archive data, it is wise to maintain a list somewhere outside the archive files that records, for each file, the earliest and latest dates for that data element present in business objects stored in each file. This way the discard program can determine which files to open and examine for qualifying data without opening all files.

These techniques will greatly enhance performance of the discard function. Further enhancement is generally not needed.

16.4.5 **Execution Authority**

The discard function is a critically important function to control. It is the program that actually deletes data forever. The authority to execute the program must be limited to only one person or a small number of people. Building an archive database that presents updates but allows discards leaves a small window for mischief. If you need to use the discard function, the only way to cope with this security hole is through administration control of the discard function execution authority and maintenance of an audit trail on discard activity.

Since the data to be eliminated is determined by the selection criteria in the discard policy, it is wise to make these independent access authorities. The individual authorized to set the policy should not be given authority to execute the discard program. The individual authorized to execute the discard program should not be permitted to change the discard policy.

16.4.6 **Capacity Issues**

Any disk storage capacity needed to store the archive should have been resolved long before execution of the discard program. It is freeing space up, not consuming more. The execution of the program consumes some space during execution in temporary places such as DBMS log files or replacement archive files, though these would not normally be unnecessarily large and will go away either during the discard process or shortly thereafter.

Elapsed execution time is a function of the amount of data that has to be examined and the amount of data that is deleted. Using techniques described earlier in this chapter will help reduce this considerably.

Amount of data discarded on one execution Discard volumes have a different dynamic than extract volumes because they are not as easy to predict.

It is not unusual for the discard policy to be looking for business objects older than any object in the repository. If you have a 10-year retention requirement and the operational application was put in place four years ago, the discard program will not find anything for six years. Knowing this can save a lot of executions.

If you choose to just not execute because of this factor, you could inadvertently forget to begin execution six years later and end up failing to discard data that should be discarded. It would be helpful to have a different program that you run on the archive that ages all business objects and produces an age/count chart from it. The discard policy date could be added to make this an interesting chart. This could be run periodically, possibly once a year, and stored in the repository. Such a report helps in anticipating when to start executing the discard program.

The opposite dynamic is also possible. The data in operations can include large amounts of data that were already past the discard date when they were initially archived. This will result in a larger-than-expected volume of discarded business objects on the first discard execution. However, it will be considerably smaller than the initial volume received from extract since that blast of data not only includes all those objects but many more that belong in the archive but are not old enough to discard.

Discard should reach a stable volume either after the first execution (if older data is present in the archive) or later (if no data is ready for discard when archiving begins). It should remain fairly stable from then on, with the typical seasonal variations.

16.5 **AUDIT TRAIL**

Careful records need to be kept to demonstrate that record destruction is based on sound policy and executed on a regular basis. Full evidence of discard program execution should be maintained in the archive repository forever.

16.5.1 **Execution Log**

The discard program should produce an execution log that shows:

- The user ID executing the function
- The date/time of execution

- The duration of execution
- The policy statement used
- The number of business objects discarded
- The number of files replaced (for file data storage)
- Any interruption and/or restart actions

These logs should be maintained in the archive repository. Again, it would be nice if these were generated as XML documents.

16.5.2 **Identification of Deleted Business Objects**

You obviously do not want to record the data you discarded. That would defeat the purpose of the discard function. However, it might be useful, or required, to keep a list of the object identifiers of objects deleted. If this is required, it should be kept in a safe place (possibly in a file in the archive).

16.5.3 **Audit Trail**

A separate audit trail should be maintained for the archive application. It should show all executions as well as the log information. An auditor should be able to look in one place to see the entire discard history. It should flag whenever the discard policy changes as well as when the executing user ID changes.

The archive loophole You can do everything described in this book to protect the data in the archive from mischievous update or delete. You can store in storage subsystems that prohibit updates. You can store on virtual WORM devices. However, there always exists the one loophole where these barriers can be walked around: DISCARD.

The loophole is that a mischievous person with discard authority can change the policy statement to look for records based on something other than legitimate selection criteria such as a specific account number, execute discard, and then change the policy back. This loophole exists as long as the archive analyst wants discards to occur.

To guard against this loophole you need an audit trail; one that flags changes helps most. Ideally the audit trail would be stored in the archive itself. If the archive store is file based, the audit trail for each specific file should be kept in that file. As the file gets replaced because of discarded data, the replacement process adds a new chunk of audit trail to it. The crafty evildoer cannot stop the audit information from being stored.

The audit What good is an audit trail if it is not audited? The archive administrator should schedule periodic audits of archiving activity for all important applications.

SUMMARY

Like the extractor component, the discard component is an important, although less complex, component of the archiving software package. You cannot settle for a process that does not satisfy all your requirements.

After reading this chapter, you should have enough information to design your own discard software or to use it as a checklist in evaluating vendor software for completeness. In the next chapter our focus will shift to ways to access data stored in the archive.

The Archive Access Component

Unlike the extractor and discard components, the archive access component is not a single piece of software. Instead it's a collection of services that allow those who need data from the archive to use it in a way that they require.

To review, the goals of the database archive relevant to accessing data are as follows:

- Become independent of the systems and applications that created the data
- Provide sufficient access support to satisfy all future needs directly from the archive
- Guarantee that the data you see on access is the same as it was in the operational systems
- Provide sufficient explanation of the data to ensure complete understanding
- Provide access in a reasonable amount of time
- Protect the data from unauthorized access

It takes a rich set of services to accomplish these goals. Figure 17.1 shows an array of services that you should expect to be available to accomplish them.

17.1 DIRECT PROGRAMMING ACCESS

A basic capability that should always be available is the capability to write application programs that can directly access the database archive. If this capability is available, any application program, including those of the current application, can be written or modified to read archive data. For example, if a specific application needs to look in the operational database for an account record and, if it's not found, look in the archive, it is possible to do so. Programs can look at both or only at data in the archive.

For example, if the archive data is accessible through a JDBC SQL driver, this is ideal. You only need to designate the JDBC driver in the archive software as a data source and off you go.

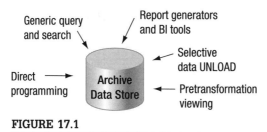

FIGURE 17.1

Database archive access services.

For this to work, the data needs to be stored in a relational structure with appropriate data types and a JDBC driver written (or modified) to read the data structures of the archive.

It is best if the user develops specific programs that run only on the archive and that run on the operating systems that have access to the archive data. This way the programs can survive over time without a dependence on original application programs. This library of programs can be expanded after the archive is in operation.

Metadata breaks   One of the problems of using typical SQL programming is that you need the capability to process a statement across archive data units that span a metadata break. This is a rare function that you cannot depend on being there. To get around this you need to have statements that are sensitive to differences across archive units and issue multiple statements where appropriate. An access component that automatically handles this task for you is ideal.

Duplicates   In processing a large swath of archived data, it is possible to get duplicate rows where none are expected. This can happen for a variety of reasons. To guard against this, always assume that business object identifiers will not be unique, and always process on a cursor.

Data storage issues   Database archives contain data that is most easily processed through traditional database programming services. If the data is stored in a database representation, it is relatively easy to access through programs. If it is not in a database representation, programs that access the data will be difficult if not impossible to construct. For example, storing data in UNLOAD format or XML format will have this problem.

The way the data is divided into storage units and how these units are positioned in the archive could also be a problem. If data is bunched into files and shoved off to inexpensive offline media, it might have to be copied to a different device before it can be processed by a JDBC driver. Even if this is automatic, it might take a long time to execute and cause the application program to time out before it completes.

17.2 ACCESS THROUGH GENERIC QUERY AND SEARCH TOOLS

You do not want to write programs every time you access data. It is helpful to have at your disposal generic search tools. If the data can be processed through a JDBC interface, pointing any one of dozens of freeware query tools to the JDBC interface should work. This capability is worth its weight in gold.

It is also beneficial to have a simpler search capability along the line of a Google-style search. This capability is less likely to be available but is often requested so that SQL-illiterate individuals, or SQL literate individuals who just want to save time, are able to directly search the archive data. This requirement is becoming more and more common for all databases, not just archive data stores. It comes up in connection with archive data since application programs to do that for you are less likely to exist.

A simple Google search does not make a lot of sense against structured data. For example, looking for all occurrences of the number 9 across all data elements stored in all table rows makes no sense. The result has no context. Structured data is all about context.

However, a more query-by-example solution tailored to the hierarchical data structure of a specific business object could be implemented to have the same effect as a Google-like search within the context of the structure. This is a capability that will emerge in the next few years. The demand for this solution is increasing because more and more people who neither know SQL nor want to depend on someone who does are demanding access to structured data. The archive function is an ideal function to cause this capability to emerge.

17.3 ACCESS THROUGH REPORT GENERATORS AND BI TOOLS

Another benefit of a JDBC SQL interface is that it enables a number of report generators such as Crystal Reports, Cognos, or Business Objects. These tools run automatically through standard JDBC interfaces. Most IT departments already have licenses for some, if not all, of them. Most users of the archive will already be familiar with at least one of them.

Most of the access requirements from the archive will be different from the report-generation outputs of the originating application. Access to the archive is always an exception situation, not a preplanned and repetitive function. For that reason you need to be able to fashion an output from the archive that fits the needs of a specific request.

You do not want to have to write programs to get output if you don't have to. You also don't want to have to work with an unknown report-generation facility.

17.4 **SELECTIVE DATA UNLOAD**

Another important function to have available is the ability to extract a chunk of data from the archive and load it into another database. Although you normally want to access data directly from the archive, there are times when you need to copy it out of the archive.

One example is when you plan to do considerable analysis over the data and the volume of data is somewhat large. Executing a large number of analytic routines over the archive data store will result in disappointing performance. It is better to copy the data you need, load it into a more responsive DBMS, and work with it there.

Another example is where you want to isolate the data from the archive for a specific purpose. If the enterprise is involved in a lawsuit that requires access to selected data, it is generally wiser to select the data from the archive and store it as a group of data somewhere else. That way the data for the lawsuit remains constant and under control of people managing the litigation. Figure 17.2 shows the basic process of generating an UNLOAD from the archive.

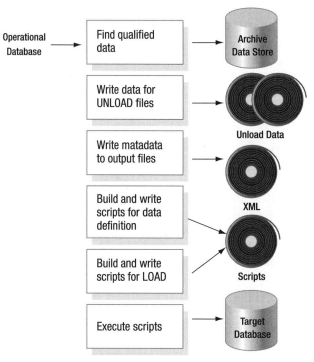

FIGURE 17.2

Data archive UNLOAD preprocess.

The ultimate target database for the data does not need to be the operational database it came from nor even the same type of DBMS. It should not matter what the target is as long as it has the capability of handling the data being delivered through the UNLOAD.

17.4.1 The UNLOAD Selection Criteria

It generally makes sense to unload only complete business objects, although there could be occasions when something less than complete business objects are desired. The selection criteria should qualify business objects for being included in the output through appropriate predicates. It should also stipulate what rows of what tables to include.

This can be done in a single step through a big JOIN SQL statement. However, the output would be reflected in a single UNLOAD file with each record containing data from all the rows. It would not be normalized. You would have to split this apart later through LOAD logic or a user-written program.

A better solution is to unload one table at a time. The selection criteria is used to produce a list of object identifiers that qualify. Then a separate select is done for each table containing required output with matching logic against this list. Sound familiar? It is the same logic as that used by the extractor component to extract business objects from the original operational database.

If you proceed in this fashion, you end up with one UNLOAD file per table. This is much easier to use subsequently to load into your temporary database.

17.4.2 The UNLOAD Package

The goal of this process is to produce a package of files. Some are UNLOAD files, some are explanatory files, and some are LOAD script files.

UNLOAD data files Individual data elements might need to be transformed from their representation in the archive to their required representation in the UNLOAD file. The format required in the UNLOAD file should be determined by the target DBMS into which the data is destined to be loaded. This is generally not a problem except for data types of DATE, TIME, FLOAT, or BINARY, which might require some manipulation to get to the target correctly. Whatever tool you use for UNLOAD should be able to make the transformations as needed based on the archive data format structure and the target format structure.

A growing number of databases include Large Object (LOB) data elements. Any UNLOAD facility should be able to handle LOBs. The support should be sensitive to the format of the data in the LOB. It should also be able to understand how the data needs to be positioned outside the archive to work as input on the subsequent load.

Data formats The format of data in the UNLOAD file needs to be compatible with the requirements of the LOAD program on the receiving end. Normally this would be an industry-standard comma-delimited character file. This works as LOAD input almost everywhere. However, it might be more appropriate to use a fixed format file structure or a proprietary structure required by the target DBMS. It also might make sense in some cases to unload the data into one or more XML files. It all depends on where you are going to put the data.

Metadata   The user should have the option of outputting the metadata that goes with the UNLOAD files. The metadata could be output as an XML file or as a report.

If the data has metadata breaks across data storage units, it might be necessary to create multiple metadata versions and be able to correlate them to UNLOAD files that were also created for specific archive storage units with common metadata.

For use in legal proceedings, having the full metadata available will be helpful if not required.

This function should be available on an optional basis. It should not be considered satisfied through the Data Definition Language (DDL) scripts described next. DDL scripts do not contain full metadata descriptions.

Data Definition Language scripts   The UNLOAD function should be able to create files for use in creating the appropriate table definitions in the target database. This includes CREATE TABLE, CREATE INDEX, and CREATE FOREIGN KEY functions. Whatever indexes are used in the archive should be included.

The function should be sensitive to the target DBMS type. It should produce DDL in the dialect of the target DBMS.

This function should also be optional. The tables could already exist at the target. However, if they do exist at the target, generating this file might be helpful in checking the target to ensure that it matches the UNLOAD file. In this case the DDL file is used as a report and should not be expected to be executed.

Load scripts   The UNLOAD function should be able to produce scripts for executing the LOAD function. It would order the table load steps in the proper order to ensure that referential constraints are handled properly. It would specify the relationship between the data elements in the UNLOAD file and the columns in the target tables.

UNLOAD log   The final package output is an inventory of all the files created with size information. It should also include the date and time created and the user ID executing the UNLOAD function.

17.5 **ACCESSING ORIGINAL DATA**

The data in the archive might have been transformed from the original source data to make it available for general access through standard tools. It all depends on how it was stored in the original operational database.

If transformations were performed on either object structure or data elements, it might be necessary to provide an archive viewer with a version of the data as it existed in the original data source. This could be a requirement for an audit or for a lawsuit to determine whether data is being faithfully transformed without data loss.

The archive system should provide this capability in much the same way it provides direct access or UNLOAD functions. The data provided might not be directly understandable since it might be encoded in a form that cannot be displayed through standard tools. If this is the case, hexadecimal display capabilities should also be provided.

All this must be anticipated at the archive application design level. For it to work, the pretransformation form of the data needs to be kept in the archive as well as the metadata that describes the way it looked in the operational database. Tools need to be put in place to extract and display the data from the archive. If any of these are not provided for, the capability will not be available later when it is needed. This can cause a serious problem for highly sensitive data sources.

Returning data to its original data source   Users often believe that they need the capability of returning data from the archive to the original data source. This is generally not a requirement if the data is truly inactive and if generic access routines are sufficient to work with it in the archive.

Backward paths are never a good idea. They assume that source systems, DBMS types, and application programs are still around and at the same version levels. They also assume that the metadata of the systems to which the data is intended to be returned matches the metadata in the archive. None of these conditions can be depended on to be true. They might be true for some of the data for some of the time. It is always necessary for the archive system to provide all access requirements. If it does, there is no need to provide a return path.

Nonetheless, many owners of applications feel that they need the comfort of knowing that the backward path exists. If this is true, some of the time (actually most of the time) use of the UNLOAD facility is sufficient to accomplish this task. You are, in effect, inserting new data into the operational system that just happens to come from the archive. Again, this works only if the original operational database is still around and has not changed data definitions.

In cases where the original operational database is something more complex, such as IMS or ADABAS, returning the data can be more complex. In these cases access to the original data before transformation of either data elements or data structure might be required. The archive facility could provide an UNLOAD of the original data segments or records in their pretransformation format. The user could then write an application program to insert the data into the operational database. In some cases it will not return exactly as it originally existed. For example, in IMS it would not be able to get siblings within a subordinate segment type exactly in the same original sequence and properly interspersed with segments that were there prior to the reinsertions.

If there is any chance this function might be required, it must be factored into the original archive application design.

17.6 **METADATA SERVICES**

Often, users of the archive will need access to metadata stored in the archive. This might be required to plan a data access. There will probably be no other source of this information.

The archive support must include the ability to view, extract, or create a report of the metadata for any part of the data stored in the archive. It should also include the ability to view variations of metadata for an application as the application moved through changes over time.

This information will be invaluable in formulating SQL statements, search arguments, or report specifications. Without it, the data may very well become unusable, even though it is all there.

Metadata updates   The metadata should be able to be updated with additional information after it's initially stored by allowing additional descriptions or comments to be attached to the metadata at any time after the initial storage.

The purpose of this is that often, a user of the data sometime in the future might have difficulty working with the metadata due to its incompleteness. They might have to spend considerable time and effort unraveling some aspect of the metadata to accomplish the required access task. It might be very helpful to someone trying to access the same data in the future to be able to read what that previous visitor learned.

17.7 **OTHER ACCESS CONSIDERATIONS**

Some other access issues need to be addressed concerning constructing an access capability around a database archive application. These considerations include access authority, auditing, performance, and data volumes.

17.7.1 **Access Authorities**

Data in the archive needs to be protected as well or better than it is protected in the operational environment.

Handling of access authorities for data in the archive needs to be done based solely on archive needs. Just because a person has DBA authority, UPDATE authority, or READ authority on the original operational database does not automatically give that person rights to access data in the archive.

The role of an archive reader should be separate from the role of the archive analyst. Of course, the archive analyst has archive read authority. However, there could be a number of people who only need authority to read data from the archive and nothing more.

That someone needs data from the archive is not, in and of itself, reason to give out read access authority to someone. If their need is very narrow, someone with access authority can be assigned to get the data for them in the form of a report or UNLOAD package. The person performing the access function should ensure that they fully understand the data the requestor is allowed or not allowed to see. They should get no more data than they have a need for.

Individuals unfamiliar with the access tools should not be given access authority. They can easily make mistakes that will result in getting wrong information. They can do no harm to the archive itself; they can only misrepresent what the archive is telling them. It makes more sense for trained personnel to handle requests for people who require information.

If a program is written that someone could use to search and view information from an archive, people who have a need should be restricted to using the program, not having full read authority.

17.7.2 Access Auditing

Depending on the importance of the data, access activities should be recorded in an audit trail. This includes all access activities: program access; access through generic search, query, and reporting tools; and UNLOAD actions. The audit trail should include the time and date, the user ID performing the access, the source of the access request, the statement that describes the selectivity of the request (usually the SQL statement); the result in terms of success or failure; and the number of rows of data returned.

It should not be necessary to record the identifiers of the actual data returned, since the data is not going to change. The statement used to fetch data can simply be executed again to determine what was returned unless a discard was run subsequently, in which case the result may differ.

If access is performed for a third party, there should be some way of recording that fact. An audit log should detail who that third party is, why the access was needed, and a correlation into the access audit trail. The audit trail should be reviewed periodically to ensure that only legitimate access attempts are being made.

17.7.3 Performance

Access of data in the archive can be very slow. This is because there is a lot of data, the data might not be on immediately accessible devices, and special processing might be needed to resolve metadata breaks. Users of archive data must be patient in waiting for results.

The archive system should not be susceptible to automatic application time-outs for excessive processing. Excessive processing will be the norm, not the exception.

Having said this, the design of the archive for an application should do as much as possible to enhance the performance of access. The use of internal indexes, external indexes, and scoping variables to limit the amount of data scanned to find an answer set must be part of every design. There should be no requirement to replatform the data into another database to make access possible. Most of the access requests should be possible directly from the archive data store.

17.7.4 **Data Volumes**

One area of concern is the volume of data that may be returned for a single request. The user might not be expecting large volumes, but the database archive could quickly rise to unprecedented volumes.

When attempting to do unplanned access requests, it's a good idea to probe the archive first using a query that returns a COUNT instead of actual data sought. Then, based on the output size, a more appropriate access strategy can be fashioned.

Not only can the output be a problem due to data volumes; the execution time may also be prohibitively long. Even if you are expecting only a small amount of output, the query might have to look at an extremely large amount of archived data to find it. This could be required by the nature of the request, or it could be that the request itself is poorly formed.

The user should monitor the execution of queries to ensure that they do not run endlessly. If a runaway query is found, it might be wise to stop it and find another approach. Unlike operational systems where runaway queries are thrown off the system, the archive should tolerate them if there is no other way to get the output. After all, these queries should not be disturbing other users.

If the archive is huge, it might be wise to break the request into multiple requests, each of which has selection criteria that will limit the amount of archive data examined in each execution. This approach also gives you confirmation that the query is working properly at the intervals between executions.

SUMMARY

When considering the archive access component, you should assume that the original application programs, databases, and systems that created the data are no longer available to process and view the data stored in the database archive. The access routines are critical to success. This requires that the data be stored in an accessible form, that the metadata be accessible, and that the user has easy-to-use tools for access.

If the data cannot be accessed, it is not an archive. If it cannot be understood, it is not an archive.

It would seem that a standard relational database is preferred for storing the archive data because it would already provide most of the outlined requirements. Still, relational databases do not handle some of the critical items such as metadata break processing. The arguments against a relational DBMS for the archive data store outlined in other chapters outweigh the value they provide in ease of access. It is better to have a more suitable data storage structure that also provides the services described in this chapter.

XML is a hard choice to make for storing archive data. Searching becomes difficult to impossible because of data volumes. Developing outputs for each request also is a nontrivial effort.

You must ensure that whatever archiving software you choose to use or build has the capabilities others will need in the future to effectively access the data. It is critical for you to test these capabilities before committing to a specific database archiving solution.

Now that we have examined the critical software components of an archive solution, we'll move on to the tasks involved in providing administrative support for the archiving activities.

PART
Administration of the Database Archive

5

We're now ready to cover some administrative functions that need to be a part of any database archive application. The common mindset is that you design an archiving application, implement it as a series of repetitive job executions, and then simply turn it loose. This mindset is far from reality. The archive requires continuous attention. It is a live application unto itself that requires time and effort to keep it vital and operational.

IT departments are used to constant change: change in application requirements, system configurations, technology, and people. All these factors will affect the operational database environment from which the archived data comes, so it only stands to reason that the archive itself must be responsive to these same changes.

The last chapter includes a few examples of using the database archive for data from sources other than the operational database. Some of this activity involves archiving data that is not the official corporate version of important data but is nonetheless data you want to keep. Once an archiving practice is put into place, it will become natural for people to want to use it for other purposes.

Ongoing Auditing and Testing | **18**

You've seen the terms *auditing* and *testing* in many of the prior chapters in connection with designing and implementing a database archiving application. So why do they emerge again under the topic of archive administration?

The answer is that a properly managed archiving practice maintains constant diligence over the archive to ensure that it continues to satisfy all requirements after it is implemented. It is a continuous, not a one-time, process.

Auditing and testing are different types of activities. *Auditing* is collecting information about operations and reviewing that information to ensure that everything is happening as it should. *Testing* is an action to try out a specific aspect of the archive implementation outside the normal activity.

The archive contains important data. It would not be in the archive if it were not important. By now you should know that archive data is different from operational data. Operational data is used every day by people with intimate knowledge of the data and the tools to access it. If there is anything wrong with the data or the processes that create, update, or use the operational data, it becomes evident very quickly. Any IT helpdesk knows that problems are noticed and reported almost instantly.

Archive data, on the other hand, can sit for long periods of time, even years, without being called on to satisfy some special need. People involved in building the archive mechanisms and defining the application structures for it have much more knowledge of the data than people will have years later. If there is a problem in executing the archiving functions or if the archive data is damaged or lost in some way, it could be a long time before it gets noticed. If the metadata is insufficient for explaining the data or if the access tools are inadequate for getting to the data, again, it could be years before that becomes apparent.

It might be too late to recognize and fix the problem. Unfortunately, recognition will most likely result from a need that is urgent and for which time is important in resolving any problems. You don't want this to happen. You want to find problems long before they block a legitimate need.

When the archiving application is initially designed, take into consideration the types of auditing and testing activities that will be done in the future. If provisions are not made at the onset, it might not be possible to take some of the actions described in this chapter.

18.1 RESPONSIBILITY FOR ONGOING AUDITING AND TESTING

Each database archiving application has an owner: the archive administrator for the application. In some cases the administrator will also be the archive analyst. In other cases it will be someone else.

One of the archive administrator's responsibilities is to ensure that regular audit and test activities get scheduled, executed, reviewed, and documented. Other individuals could be needed to complete these activities. It is the administrator's responsibility to identify who they are and get them to spend the time needed to diligently execute their role.

It might be that the enterprise considers archived data important enough to have someone look over the shoulder of the archive administrator. For example, an IT compliance officer might require the archive administrator to periodically defend the practices used to operate and manage the archive. This individual could also require periodic reports designed to demonstrate that proper actions are being taken.

18.2 AUDITING ACTIVITIES

A comprehensive discussion of auditing activities is beyond the scope of this book, but it is important to cover some basic auditing possibilities that pertain specifically to the archiving function.

The archive administrator could become involved in audits conducted by others that have to do with a higher-level need. For example, the IT CIO office might routinely audit IT best practices to ensure that the IT organization is doing the best that it can. The database archiving practice might be a part of that audit. The archive function could get involved in a data quality audit or a disaster recovery audit that involves the entire application, not just the archive portion.

The point is that archived data is not managed outside IT. It remains a vital part of the responsibility of the IT function to manage archive data as it would manage any other operational data.

18.2.1 Access Auditing

Access auditing has two parts: (1) looking at who has authority to access archive data and (2) looking at who has accessed archive data. In short, access auditing refers to who can do it and who did do it.

Access authority audit For this audit you need to produce a list of everyone who has the potential of accessing the data or files that make up the archive data store and the archive repository. This list should include those who have authority either through a direct or indirect grant.

Direct grant authorities were probably made by the archive administrator. They may have been made by an administrator in the past who no longer is the administrator.

Indirect grant authorities are those that someone has because they were granted authority on the objects used to store the archive data. For example, a database administrator or a storage administrator often possess indirect grant authorities necessitated by the very nature of their jobs. These individuals are frequently referred to as *privileged users*. It's easy to overlook this group of people because the archive administrator did not specifically give them authorities.

The level of activity that each person has must be recorded along with the each name. Some of the possible authorities are:

- Administrator authority over the archive application
- Archive analyst authority
- Execution authority for extractor
- Execution authority for discard
- Read access authority of the archive data store
- Read access authority of the archive repository
- File access authority for DELETE to archive data store physical files
- Database administration authority for the archive repository

Some of these authorities come about because of the type of data store structure you use. If you use a DBMS to store the archive data then you will have more authorities than if you have a file based or custom archive DBMS data store.

The purpose of the audit is not to just produce a list. It is to review the list and determine whether the entries are appropriate. Things to look for are:

- People authorized but who have left the company
- People authorized but who have changed jobs and are not entitled anymore
- People with stronger authorities than required to do their job
- Missing people: those who should have authority but don't

One aspect to examine is whether authorities exist for people to get to the repository or data if a primary person is not available. If the archive administrator gets run over by a truck, does that mean that no one can jump in and assume the role? The audit should be critical of any authority level that belongs to only one person.

Access audit The audit of who did access the archive is designed to serve another purpose. It looks at access audit trails to determine if people are using the archive appropriately and also whether they are getting what they need from it.

Just because a person has authorization based on a real need does not mean that that person is using that authority specifically for that need. For example, someone might require read access to the archive because they need to look up past payments if requested by a customer. Read authority allows them to do much more than this. You are expecting to see requests for data on a single account for a bracketed period of time. If you see instead that a user is doing UNLOAD actions for thousands of records at a time, an alert needs to be raised. The granted READ authority was not intended for that type of access.

Gathering the information might be difficult if the archive system does not provide for an access audit trail to be updated for all access activity. If it does not, the auditor might have to resort to interviewing people who have access authority and ask them if they used it and how. Having access tools that leave behind a log of actions taken is the only way to catch inappropriate use.

The primary questions to answer are:

- Who is using the archive?
- Who is not? Should their authority be revoked?
- Are uses reasonable for the person with the authority level?
- How often do users use the archive?
- How old is data that is being accessed?
- What is the volume of data returned on average? Most? Least?
- What tools are users using to access the archive?
- What performance is being observed?
- Is performance adequate for users' needs?

Some of these questions are aimed at looking at *appropriate uses* and determining that archive access tools are adequate. Users should be questioned as to whether they can get what they want, whether the tools could be improved, and whether they have difficulty in formulating requests.

The frequency of access can lead to a conclusion that data is being archived too early (high frequency) or too late (low frequency). This can lead to a change in the extract policy.

Performance should be checked to see how long access requests take to run. Sometimes the users accept poor performance and don't complain. If access is infrequent, they might not feel it worth complaining about. However, as the administrator, you need to know if the access run times are getting longer as the archive gets larger. Will run times reach a critical point and eventually cause all requests to run too long?

This audit could turn up some cases of misuse of the archive. It also could uncover opportunities for improving the level of service being provided to legitimate users with legitimate requests.

18.2.2 **Extract Auditing**

This audit is done by examining the execution logs of the extractor program. You don't want to do this every time it is run, but rather you should look through the logs once a year or so.

Things to look for in the audit are:

- Are extract jobs running as expected?
- Are volumes extracted per run increasing?
- Are volumes lower than expected?
- Are elapsed times to execute increasing?
- Are job execution interruptions happening too frequently?
- Are data error rates on transformation happening too frequently?

The normal tendency is to let these jobs run and not monitor them. Problems can begin to appear and go unnoticed until they explode into a more serious problem. Without auditing, as long as a process executes in its window of time available, no one cares. If the times increase to the point where they run over and cause operational problems, a crisis is created. Auditing will see the trend toward longer execution times or growing resource consumption and be able to predict when this crossover will occur.

Extract auditing should lead to tuning the extract process where it is needed.

18.2.3 **Discard Auditing**

Discard auditing is very similar to extract auditing. You are looking at execution logs. You don't do this every time it is run but periodically instead.

The things you are looking for are:

- Are discard jobs being run?
- Are the volumes of business objects discarded reasonable?
- Are unexpected discard jobs being run?
- Are the selection criteria being used consistently across runs?

The issue of unexpected runs or consistency of discard selection criteria is targeting inappropriate use of the discard function. If someone wants to exploit the discard vulnerability described earlier, it should show up on the audit. It might be too late to recover the data but not too late to catch the fraudster.

18.2.4 **Policy Auditing**

Auditing policies should be completed to ensure that they are still valid. Extract auditing will try to find the correct balance between archiving too early and archiving too late. Discard auditing will ensure that the discard policy is being executed as planned. Policy auditing looks at the two policies outside the context of job executions.

The extract policy has to do with the availability of the data to operational staff. The way to do this audit is to show the policy to operational users of the operational database and asking them if this is still an acceptable policy.

The discard policy audit is similar. Periodically check to ensure that the rules for when to discard data have not changed and remain consistent with the policy being used. This audit is much more important than the extract policy. If the law changes the rules on the length of required data retention, you could be in violation of the law if it is not implemented. You might be keeping data too long or discarding too early.

18.3 TESTING ACTIVITIES

The testing described here does not involve testing the programs or the implementation of an application. That is done during the development part of the archiving application and again whenever either the software or the archive application design changes. The testing described in this section is used to ensure that the support is adequate for future users to find, access, and understand the archive data they need.

18.3.1 Testing Access

The administrator should ensure that the archive data is always accessible through the toolkit being made available to the users. Of course, data should be tested at the initiation of an application; however, testing should not stop there.

One reason to continue testing periodically is that the archive data stores can grow to large size and adversely affect the ability to find or retrieve data. This would not show up at the beginning. There might be no one stressing the tools against large volumes. However, when the big request arrives, you need to be prepared.

Another issue that will not show up until later is the problem of handling metadata breaks in the archive data streams. Initially there will be none—then one, then two, and then before you know it, a whole bunch. The ability to search and retrieve in the presence of multiple metadata breaks should be checked periodically. Each metadata break could present a different challenge.

There could be new versions of tools that have been used in the past to access the archive. These new versions need to be exercised to ensure that they work with the archive. They are not likely to be tested unless the administrator forces a test.

These tests would ideally be executed by someone from the user community. This not only achieves the purpose of the test but also updates the user's knowledge of the toolset. Users can be given access authority for archived data and not use it for years. Get them involved early.

Continuous regression testing   It is possible, and beneficial, to create a regression test of archive access that runs on a regular basis—say, once a week. This test could be automated through one of any number of automated test tools. It could exercise the most common tool or tools. This would help in ensuring that there are no issues blocking access that pop up without anyone noticing.

18.3.2 **Testing Metadata Clarity**

Another important problem is caused by changing users of the archive data. The initial set of users will probably be more familiar with the data and the application than those that show up later. The archive will probably contain many data stores for retired applications—applications no longer in use. As time goes on, the knowledge base dwindles.

The purpose of the metadata clarity test is to take a user who has not been working with the application and have them attempt to access data using the metadata within the archive. For important data stores, this type of test should be done at least once a year.

The people used in the test should either be newly authorized people or people from outside the authorized set who have job functions that could require working with the data in the future.

The goal is to expose them to the metadata and some reports of data from the archive. They then can provide feedback on whether they understand the meaning of data values or not. They can comment on the adequacy of the metadata. The point is that adequate metadata is a slippery slope. In the beginning users have more external knowledge of the data and can tolerate less complete metadata. As time goes on the user group has less external familiarity with the data and are less tolerant of metadata that falls short.

Any opportunities to improve the metadata that comes out of this test should be addressed either through updating the formal metadata definitions held in the archive or in documenting them somewhere else that will be available to future users.

18.3.3 **e-Discovery Readiness Test**

Since a primary use of the archive is to satisfy lawsuit discovery requests, it only makes sense to focus a test on the ability of the archive data and access routines to accomplish this task. Much of the data in the archive has the potential of playing a role in major litigation whose outcome could have profound impacts on the enterprise. This is comparable to a disaster recovery readiness test.

The method of achieving this goal is to have the inside legal department select a team that normally handles discovery requests. Have them conjure up a test that might reflect a data request that is similar to one that would be expected for a real lawsuit.

The team would then interact with the archive administrator by going through all the steps to search for and retrieve data from the archive. This should include delivering some of the data in an UNLOAD and loading it into a database on a legal department server. They would also retrieve the metadata and attempt to make sense of it.

Since e-discovery requests often need to gather data from both the operational database and the archive database, this should also be included in preparedness testing. It should show how to integrate the two sources of data. This process can have its own set of problems.

Most of the time the legal department would not access the archive for e-discovery requests. They would formulate a request and deliver it to the archive administrator for the application who would either do the actions himself or designate someone else to do them. The test would include the ability of the legal staff to communicate their needs effectively to the person who ultimately does the data extraction.

The legal department could then critique the process and make suggestions for making it more effective. Factors such as difficulty in understanding the data, difficulty in using the tools, and time to deliver would all be examined and critiqued.

18.4 **FREQUENCY OF AUDITS AND TESTS**

Planning for audit and test activity should be done in advance and a schedule should be created. The important point is not the frequency of execution but that they occur regularly. Some will be needed only on an annual basis, others quarterly, and still others more frequently.

Anyone auditing the archive administration function will look for thoroughness and regularity.

SUMMARY

Auditing and testing on a regular schedule will ensure that the archive application is sound and ready to be used when needed.

The archive can be running along very quietly for long periods of time with no one paying attention to it. In this situation there it a high risk of something going wrong and remaining unaddressed until a crisis occurs.

The functions outlined in this chapter are comparable to conducting fire drills, city-wide drills on major attacks, or other disasters. Being prepared for the unexpected is the goal of a successful database archivist.

Managing the Archive Over Time

The archive administrator is responsible for the protection of the data. This could involve either direct involvement by performing the functions defined in this chapter or indirect involvement through database administrators or storage administrators. If indirect, the archive administrator is responsible for creating and maintaining a protection plan and ensuring that the other administrators follow it.

The archive administrator needs to have a schedule of actions that must be taken periodically. When these actions are performed, a record should be recorded in an audit trail. If a problem occurs that causes data to be lost, the administrator will be called on to demonstrate that reasonable actions were planned and taken to prevent it.

The protection of the data might be subject to audits by others in the company to ensure that the archived data is maintained properly. If so, the archive administrator needs to shape the plan of action around those audits as much as possible.

19.1 MANAGING THE ARCHIVE DATABASE

The archive data store must be maintained in a manner that maximizes its durability over time. This is the primary goal. The issues that are involved in ongoing administration of the archive are:

- Protection from media rot
- Protection from data loss
- Recovery
- Disaster recovery

DBMS archive data store   If the archive is stored in a standard DBMS, it will have a database administrator assigned. This would not normally be the archive administrator. The administration of the data would be accomplished through the functions of the DBMS.

Media rot, or the loss of data through media deterioration, is normally not considered a problem with DBMS storage. The DBMS would require front-line disk storage. Specific locations on disk are visited frequently through normal DBMS activity and thus a read error would normally be detected early in the rotting process. DBMS systems have recovery procedures to prevent read errors from causing data loss.

The DBMS can be placed on a server machine dedicated to archiving. It can sit in a rack for years where its media would be subject to deterioration. To judge that this is occurring, the database administrator should be monitoring the frequency of recoveries due to read errors to determine whether the media on the server or the server itself needs to be replaced. This would normally be expected of a database administrator.

Other forms of data loss are generally not a problem. Losing a file, inadvertent overwriting of data, and other actions that can cause data loss are generally protected through normal database administrator actions by setting file protections to allow only DBMS access and then depend on the capabilities of the DBMS for protection.

Recovery procedures for a DBMS are standard fare. All database administrators know how to prepare for and execute them. It is important to give the archive the maximum protection. Most DBMSs have options that allow for dual image copies and recovery logs. This should always be used for archive data. The same protections that are given to the operational systems should be given to the archive.

Disaster recovery requires some work. Most IT departments have a disaster recovery plan for the important databases. They either use offsite real-time replication or, as a minimum, keep copies of image copy and recovery log datasets offsite. The disaster recovery implementations for the archive should be at least as strong as those of the operational databases the data comes from. Real-time replication should not be necessary for the archive data store.

One problem to look out for is that often the archive data store will be on a different DBMS type than the operational database. The recovery and disaster recovery capabilities may be different. If this is the case, the archive administrator might need to design implementations that provide an equivalent level of support. This might not be possible with the support provided. If so, you might have to consider changing the DBMS type for the archive. Do not accept a lesser level of safety for the archive than what is used for the operational database.

File archive-level data store   If you store the archive in a collection of files such as XML, UNLOAD, or custom archive files, it's a challenge to manage the physical aspect of the data to be comparable to the operational database environment from which the data comes.

It is preferable to use a storage management solution such as a SAN device to keep the files. These and similar systems offer many of the necessary functions. The functions you need include the ability to:

- Automatically create multiple backup copies of each file
- Distribute the backup files across multiple geographic locations
- Create file signatures to enable detection of unwanted changes

- Prevent updates
- Read files periodically to check the signatures and detect read errors
- Recover from failures by reconstituting files internally or fetching and copying a backup copy
- Delete files with forensic cleanliness
- Delete backup copies when a primary copy is deleted

All these functions are available from commercial storage management systems.

The archive administrator's responsibility is to ensure that the correct storage options are being used for the archive data files. The administrator should also monitor all reports from the storage system in regard to errors found, recoveries performed, and capacity concerns.

Normally IT will have a storage management group that provides for the care and feeding of the storage system. The archive administrator would work through this group to ensure that the proper options are used and that everything runs smoothly. They should become partners in managing the files.

Managing files locally If you choose to manage a file-based archive data store yourself, be forewarned that the job becomes very hard. Files will be placed in folders on disk drives that are either embedded in the archive server machine or accessed as a network-mounted drive. In administering this system, you must achieve the same level of control as you would if you were using a storage system. All the functions are needed.

Procedures must be put in place to create file signatures, make backup copies, place backups on drives to achieve geographical dispersion, periodically read files, and perform recoveries when needed. This is all possible but entails a great deal of work.

In addition to all that, managing your own storage for files requires monitoring capacity on the drives, since archive data can consume all the space on a drive before you become aware of it. When drives fill up, new drives need to be acquired and procedures modified to use them. Be sure to check any vendor products to determine their level of support of these functions.

Recovery testing The administrator should develop and execute periodic tests to ensure that the recovery and disaster recovery procedures are working and that people know how to invoke them. It is always a risk that these procedures will be put into place and then forgotten. Years later, when they are needed, there is a mad scramble to figure out how they are supposed to work.

19.2 MANAGING THE ARCHIVE REPOSITORY

A separate but equally important administrative chore is to care for the archive repository. Loss of the repository could be catastrophic, depending on how tightly aligned it is to the archive data stores.

How important is the repository?   The first step is to determine how dependent the archive data store is on the archive repository. Can the archive data store survive loss of the archive repository and be capable of delivering all the needed functions without the repository?

To answer the question, you need to divide the repository into parts. The major divisions of data within the repository are:

- Archive application design
- Archive data store inventories
- Execution logs and audit trail files

Clearly the archive data store inventories are the most critical part. Not having them makes the archive disappear to any intended user. There must be a way to protect or to recapture that part of the repository in case of a catastrophic failure.

The archive application design documentation is the next most critical component. It could be reconstructed from scratch if it's lost. A critical factor here is whether the stored archive data depends on this documentation for metadata definitions for access. Ideally it does not. Hopefully the documentation is stored in the archive data store along with the data. If it is only stored in the archive repository, it rises to the level of importance of the archive inventory.

The logs and audit trail files are probably less important. If they are lost, the archive can still be accessed and understood. You would lose the ability to demonstrate the steps taken to manage the archive and to defend your practices under attack by a lawsuit or investigation. If that is important to you, logs and audit trails should be managed as though they are critical information as well.

Managing the repository data   The main storage component of the archive repository is usually a DBMS application. It is stored in a relational database on a server. This should be managed as strongly as the operational database the archive data comes from. It's the same rule as for the archive data store. It requires a database administration function.

This rule is easily violated by oversight. Most people do not regard the application as being as important as the data. This attitude possibly results from years of not protecting and regarding metadata as important as the data it describes. That has been a mistake of the past. Don't repeat that mistake with your archive.

The archive repository might also have a second component where some of the information is stored outside the DBMS used as the primary repository store. It can be stored in files in a server drive folder or folders. It can be stored in the repositories of other products such as data-modeling tools. You are probably not going to want to put it in a formal storage system, which makes access less responsive.

Protecting these files requires special procedures and administration. Depending on the nightly server backups is a bad idea. This could work for some of the files, but others require more protection. Having procedures to make copies in other locations when the file is first created is a possible practice.

It would be better if the files, at least those files you consider critical to protect, be stored in the repository DBMS as BLOB columns on identifying rows. If this is done, the DBMS backup, recovery, and disaster recovery procedures would take care of the problem.

Another option to consider is to periodically archive data from the repository tables into a separate database archiving application. This protects everything equally.

19.3 USING HOSTED SOLUTIONS

Many organizations are outsourcing data storage to third-party companies. Some of the companies offer disk storage space and nothing more. Others offer storage system facilities or archiving services in addition to storage.

The primary motivations for using outsourced facilities instead of in-house facilities are:

- Lower cost
- Better deals with hardware providers
  - More favorable locations for electricity prices
  - Expertise in managing storage systems
- Quick start

If you are starting a practice, using outsourced facilities could mitigate the need to find floor space in data centers, shop for and buy new servers and disk storage devices, and hire additional personnel to manage the new stuff. Paying someone else gets you off to a fast start.

There are three levels from which you can choose to house the archive software and hardware. These are shown in Figure 19.1.

In the first model, you do it all yourself. Setting up a practice becomes a large planning chore involving several people.

The second model pushes the physical storage to a third party. All the software runs in your shop on your machines, but the storage is written to and accessed over IP links. You would probably not push the archive repository to the hosted site. The amount of data in it would not warrant the risk of having it offsite.

The third model pushes the software to the third party as well. This is a software-as-a-service configuration. In this model the archive repository would be at the site of the software: the hosted site.

The archive administrator will evaluate the benefits and risks of using outsourced services considering the tradeoff between short-term benefits and long-term cost.

The risk factor should be considered carefully. Outsourcing will require you to develop a requirements list to which the outsourcer must adhere to be selected. You should not compromise on any aspect of the requirements for

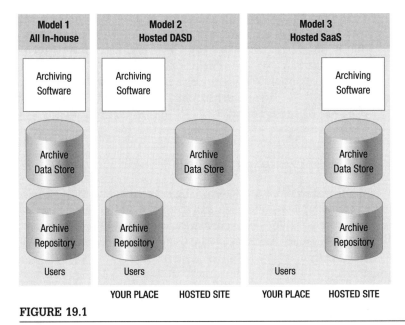

FIGURE 19.1

Three models of hosting archived solutions.

managing archive data. It should not matter where the data is managed, only how it is managed.

The administrator should also audit the outsourcer frequently to ensure that they continue to deliver on their promises. Without having them in your own house, you could become complacent in ensuring that everything happens as expected. Do not make this careless mistake.

19.4 MANAGING ARCHIVE USERS

Managing users is another primary job of the archive administrator that requires continuous attention.

Recognize that the database archive is an extension of the operational database where the data originates; managing users must be addressed in a manner that equals or exceeds the requirements for managing the source operational database. That said, there are some clear differences worth discussing.

19.4.1 User Management Functions

The functions of user administration for a database archive are no different from managing users for any database.

You first define *roles*. What functions can people take in regard to the data? For a database archive the standard roles are:

- Archive application administrator
- Archive analyst
- Archive reader

The administrator role might break out archive data store administration and archive repository database administration as separate roles. It depends on whether the administrator will delegate these roles or not.

The archive analyst role can also break out a separate role of archive application design, execution of extract jobs, and execution of discard jobs.

After roles are created, security *groups* need to be defined. This is a major issue for the operational database but should not be for the database archive since there should not be a large number of individuals involved. One general rule is that if the number of individuals expected to share a function is small, don't create groups. The only aspect of archive activity for an application that could warrant a group is archive readers. For some archive applications this group will be needed, but for others the list will be small enough to do without a group definition.

The next function is to *grant authority* to people and programs against these roles. Establish a procedure for doing this with appropriate review and approvals.

Along with granting authority comes the inverse: *revoking authority*. This function is the most commonly neglected function in security management. The reason is that when a revoke is warranted, the person for whom the revoke is targeted is not motivated to ask for it. If they want grant authority given to them, they will be knocking down your door to get it.

You will need a procedure to tell you when to revoke authorities. The procedure should include a request form with review and signatures that would be filled out by another department when a person no longer needs authority. In addition, the procedure should include a monitoring mechanism for personnel changes—people leaving the enterprise or changing jobs. If any names cross-reference, you can make a check to see if those people's authorities should be revoked. A final procedure is to review the authorization list on a periodic basis and requalify people. This is the access authorization audit.

There should not be a large number of people on the authorization list, so it should not take a great deal of effort to maintain control of authorizations.

19.4.2 Different Group of Users

Even though the archive for an application is an extension of the operational database, the group of people who should be authorized to read the archive is not the same group of people who need access to the operational database. This is because a group of people are needed to execute business transactions that create and update business objects in the operational database. Once a business object has become inactive and is no longer subject to updates, this group of people has no further interest in it. This is a large group of individuals.

The group that has a continued need to access business objects after they have become inactive is a smaller group. Anyone asking for authorization to data in the archive should be scrutinized thoroughly to ensure that they have a need that continues beyond the operational and reference phases of the data life.

There is another group of individuals who have access rights to the operational database for the purpose of extracting data for business intelligence analysis. They might also ask for access to the archive. Before it is granted, the archive administrator needs to ensure that they truly need archived data. Most of the time they want data that is more recent than the policy for extraction would find ready for moving to the archive. If they need data that goes into the archive, consideration might be given to changing the extract policy to keep data in the operational database longer.

One-time users   There will be individuals who need data from the archive for a special project, possibly for extracting data to be used in defense against a lawsuit. They do not have a longtime need, only a one-time need or access rights for a short period of time. These people should be handled by granting them authority and, at the outset, setting a time when the grant will be revoked.

Sometimes a better way to handle this is to not give them authority but have someone else that does have authority do the access requests for them.

The application expert   It is a good idea to have someone designated for the application as the application subject matter expert who handles all requests for nonrecurring needs. This person would be known as the go-to expert for getting data from the archive. This could be a role assumed by the archive analyst for the application.

Having someone like this who is always available will ensure that knowledge of the data structures is preserved over time. Another benefit is that this person would be an SQL expert and would not make mistakes in formulating requests. Allowing those who are unfamiliar with the application, unfamiliar with the application structures, and weak on SQL skills will ultimately lead to people getting the wrong data and making wrong interpretations from it.

When this practice is followed, it is important for the specialist to keep records of who asked for what data when and what extract criteria was used. The administrator should approve all requests made of the specialist.

19.4.3 **Permissions for Using the Archive Data Store**

The form and location of the archive will dictate how authorizations are manifested in operating system, file, or database permissions. Clearly the archive data store will be in a different form and in a different place from the operational database.

This could make it difficult to provide a comparable level of security and access control. If the operational database is on an IBM mainframe that has world-class protection mechanisms and the archive is stored on a network server with less than world-class protections, this will take some work. The archive administrator must work through this issue with the security and storage administrators to get the level of access control protection needed.

If the archive data store is implemented using a commercial DBMS, at least one person has authority to change the data. In some systems this person is referred to as a "sysadm" who has "superuser" authority. This authority is implicitly granted to the superuser, which can cause the authenticity of the archive data to be brought into question.

19.4.4 **Permissions for Using the Archive Repository**

Granting access to use the archive data store should not automatically roll over to having permissions against the archive repository. Most readers of archive data will not need access to the repository.

The question of authorization depends on what you expect the person to do. If he or she needs access to metadata information or change log information, that person must look at the repository. Each authorization given to the repository needs to be evaluated based on need.

This is another case where having an expert who can work with the repository and perform functions for clients is a plus. When that person uses this authority on others' behalf, the expert should be qualified to determine the level of authorization those people would have if they did it themselves. Too often using a surrogate to access data leads to requests being honored that would not be granted if the requestor had to get explicit access authorization.

SUMMARY

The data in the archive is critically important. Too often the attitude is that the archive is easy to slough off; "it has been put away," or "not to worry." The right attitude is that the archive is an extension of the operational database. It is a choice to put data in the archive. If not in the archive, it would still be in the operational database. Storing in the archive does not change the requirements for data protection. Data in the archive requires the same level of data protection as that required for the operational databases it comes from.

The archive repository is equally important. Without it the archive is either worthless or severely crippled. It should be protected at the same level as the archive data store.

The archive administrator needs to be continuously managing user access. The users of the archive will be different people from those who use the operational database. There will be some small overlap. The uses they make of the archive data will be different from what they do with the operational database.

The archive administrator needs to be diligent it taking care of this part of the business, which is one of the most important aspects of the archive administrator's job.

Nonoperational Sources of Data

Thus far we have had a thorough discussion of database archiving revolving around saving data from operational databases. The data represents the official corporate version of the business objects. It is the place where anyone wanting a legally authentic version of your data would look.

We'll close this book by discussing some special cases of operational data sources and other data sources that are nonoperational and the way archive mechanisms can be considered and used. This is not an exhaustive list. There will probably be many more examples in which unusual applications will find use of the database archiving system.

20.1 RETIRED APPLICATIONS

Moving data from a retired application to a database archive is a common motivator. It fits the model of database archiving in that the data is the official version of the data. A retired application is one that is no longer in use. It has been replaced by another function and in the process the data has been left behind. It is possible the data did not easily map to the data structures of the new application. The data must still be retained for a long period of time. The originating application programs, DBMS, and systems continue to be retained in case the data needs to be accessed again. Sometimes these are referred to as "sunset" applications.

The business case for archiving retired applications is easy. The cost of maintenance of the required systems and software that might be used to access the data is a drag on the IT budget. It also requires that people on staff be available to work with the applications, DBMS, and systems. Sometimes this is the last remaining application on a legacy system, causing a large impediment to ridding the IT operations of the legacy environment.

Archiving the data and dropping support of the old environment can free up a lot of money in an IT budget. It is a good justification for building a database archiving application. It is also a lower-risk first application choice.

One-time extraction   One nice thing about retired applications is that extraction is a one-time event. New data is not coming into the operational database, providing many advantages for the archiving process. The process can proceed without pressure to complete quickly. It does not require special operational windows within which to execute and there is no concern about disruption of operational activity.

Special challenges   Retired applications are often found on systems that are not active, either. The operating system and DBMS could very likely be down-level—very down-level. This can present a special problem for working with database archiving software.

If the DBMS of the data is not one that the extractor can read, a two-stage process can be used. It is not uncommon for the data to be stored in an older legacy DBMS that is not supported by the database archiving software you are using. If it was an active operational application, this would present a problem. However, as a retired application it is possible, and preferable, to restage the data to another DBMS system from which the archive extraction will be performed. This process is illustrated in Figure 20.1. This strategy can also be used to solve a down-level operating system problem.

Retired applications are also more likely than active applications to have poor-quality metadata. They are also more likely to have poorly designed and almost unworkable data structures. The older the data, the more likely that the data structures contain workarounds and programmer tricks to avoid expanding segment sizes. This leads to a liberal use of REDEFINE structures, data element overloading, and complex data-encoding schemes. Working through these problems and getting a good transformation design could take some effort.

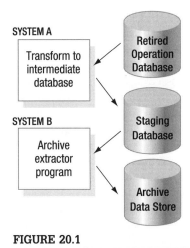

FIGURE 20.1

Intermediate staging of data for extraction.

Accessing the data   After the project is complete, the data will be in an independent archive stream. It will be separate from any archive stream created for the replacement application.

It is easy to forget that the stream is there. Users accessing the archive years later could overlook the archive stream and not get data they need.

Access against the retired application archive stream will have to be separate from access to the newer archive stream. The access logic will probably not work on both. This rises to a level beyond that manageable through metadata break resolution logic. You need to get one output for the retired application archive stream and another from the replacement application archive stream.

The archive stream created will test the 100 percent rule of all access requirements being satisfied from the archive. The originating application will be gone as soon as archiving is complete. It saves money. There is no possibility of reverting to originating systems to look at data. This means that thorough access testing must be done before you can declare victory.

20.2 DATA FROM MERGERS AND ACQUISITIONS

When two organizations merge, they usually have parallel applications for their most important business processes. It does not matter whether the organizations are companies or divisions within a single company. Either organization might or might not have been archiving data from databases.

Neither enterprise is archiving   If neither enterprise has been archiving data, the best response is to wait until the decision is made on whether the operational systems will be combined into one or kept separate. If kept separate, the case for database archiving is the same as though the systems had never merged. If they are to be combined, the data from both could end up in one of the two operational applications, or one could be used going forward and the other one retired. The case is made for database archiving the data in the retired application.

If they are combined and the data from one is merged into the data from the other, the business case for database archiving needs to be applied to the merged database. It is very likely that the process of combining will create a new single operational database that is overloaded with data—a perfect candidate for archiving. The best strategy is to let the merge take place before archiving is considered.

One is archiving, one is not archiving   In this case you deal with one existing database archive. The easiest way to deal with this is to end the archive data stream of the application that is being archived and start a new stream after the two operational applications are merged.

If the application being archived is chosen as the one to be merged into, data archiving can continue after the data merge. It will most likely result in a surge of data on the first extract.

Most of the time, the process of merging applications causes some change to the data structures at the time of merge. These changes can be minor or significant. If they are significant, it might be wiser to not move all the data to one system but to treat one or both systems as retired applications and the new modified system as a new application.

Both enterprises are archiving   If both enterprises have been doing database archiving for the application, there are larger problems to deal with.

One strategy is to treat all archived data as complete and end the archive data streams. After the two operational systems have been combined, archiving against a new, single archive data stream will commence.

If the two archiving systems are different, it might be advantageous to replatform the archived data from one application using the new system. This avoids the problem of maintaining and working with multiple database archiving solutions. The exercise of replatforming can be treated as a retired application. There is no urgency in accomplishing this goal.

20.3 e-DISCOVERY APPLICATIONS

When a lawsuit hits an enterprise, the enterprise is obligated to freeze data that might be requested in connection with the litigation. The suit goes to the internal legal department. They notify IT that a hold needs to be placed on data. They define the data in terms of the lawsuit, not in IT terms. For example, it could involve all transactions for account number X for the last five years, or all transactions involving stocks XXX and XXY between April 2002 and January 2006.

The IT department must prohibit updates and deletes against the data and stand by to provide data that might be requested. The legal department might want a hold on more data than required, just in case they might need it later.

Once the plaintiff lawyers figure out what they want, they provide a discovery request for data. This might or might not involve database data. At this point the request will usually be more specific about which data to hold.

If database data is involved, the IT department carves out the requested data and places a hold on it for the duration of the litigation. The requested data is delivered to the internal legal department for analysis and disposition.

Discovery holds and the database archive   If the application in question has a database archiving implementation on it, the archive might contain some of the data. The request could span the operational database and the archive data store.

You do not want to hold the operational database, nor do you want to stop discard activity against the archive, but you still want to satisfy the letter of the law. The goal is to select the data in question and isolate it from both the operational database and the archive data store.

Use the archive for the hold   The database archive is the ideal location to place a copy of the data that corresponds to the e-discovery request. It has all the protections to ensure that the data will be safe for the duration of the litigation.

Figure 20.2 shows the concept of using the archive for the e-discovery hold. Data is extracted from the operational database and placed in a special archive application created for the lawsuit. Note that the extraction process is the same as the extraction process for normal archive activity. The policy is different; it reflects the lawsuit selection criteria.

Additional data is selected from the archive data store using the same policy. This is also put into the same lawsuit archive application as the data from the operational database.

All of the data is UNLOADED in one step from the lawsuit archive application and delivered to the legal department. They can then load it into their own systems for use in analysis and delivery to the external law firm.

Metadata   This approach also delivers enriched metadata to the legal department. This should be the most thorough and accurate metadata available; it will aid the legal staff in interpreting what they see.

Use of the lawsuit application archive   The legal department can access the archive built for the lawsuit the same way as any other archive data store.

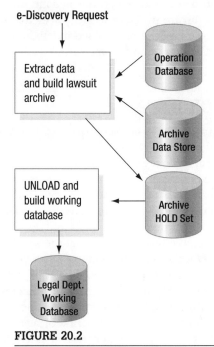

FIGURE 20.2

Example e-discovery process.

They can search, query, report, and do analysis directly on the archive. They would probably prefer to use their own systems, but the archive is always available if they want it.

Giving them read access on the lawsuit archiving application keeps them from asking for read authority on the operational database or the application archive data store. This keeps them from seeing data that is not relevant to the litigation.

The special archive you created can be used to satisfy the hold requirement, freeing up the operational database and the archive data store for normal operations.

If you do not archive data for the application, you need to extract all the required data from the operational database. You need to structure this for delivery into a relational form. You also need to gather and enrich the metadata. This is the same process as used for normal archive application design. If you have an archiving practice, you can take the same step to create the lawsuit application archive from only the operational database. Remember, the steps are the same. The archive provides all the necessary process and protections.

If this process is adopted, all lawsuits involving database data will go to the archivist who will prepare the e-discovery deliverable.

After the lawsuit is completed, the legal department will advise the archivist when the special archive can be deleted. When this is done, all the data is discarded at once. Simply run a discard program with a policy that catches everything. If desired, the entire contents can be retained indefinitely in the archive data store. It will not get in the way of anything else.

20.4 **BUSINESS INTELLIGENCE DATA**

Sometimes people want to archive data assembled to perform business intelligence analytics. This is not operational data. It has been extracted from operational systems, cleansed, summarized, and integrated with data from other sources.

The data warehouse is the biggest example of this, although it is not the only example. Targeted analytic databases that are either drawn from the data warehouse or built directly from operational databases are more often the target of this requirement.

The motivation for archiving the data might be that the sources want to free up disk space for more analytical data. For example, if a set of sales data is assembled representing a three-month period worth of transactions and then reassembled three months later with more current data, sometimes there is a desire to save the previous three-month set. In essence, the sources want a group of sets that each represent a three-month period of business data.

Sometimes the motivation goes further. Enterprises might want to save the analytic underpinnings of important business decisions. In this sense, it is pure archiving.

In archiving analytic data, it is important to tag the data with a version identifier. If the data is all intermixed in a single archive application, it might be hard to separate out later. If the archive data store is a DBMS, this is more difficult. Either you store each time period's data in a separate set of archive tables or you add a time-period identifier to every row. Selecting the data later could be slow, since these applications store a lot of data. If you are using a file-based archive data store, isolating the data from each period is easier. Retrieval is also more efficient.

Is the data warehouse a data archive? The question often comes up of whether the data warehouse can serve as the data archive or the source of data for the archive. The answer is no. The data warehouse has two problems.

One problem is that it does not represent the data exactly as it occurred in the operational database. It has been cleansed, summarized, and integrated. It cannot serve as a reliable authentic version of the data.

If it did include all detailed transactions as they occurred in the operational database, the second problem comes into play. This is that the data warehouse update is a delayed process. The data takes several days (or weeks) to get to the warehouse and be stored so it can be used. If it is the source of data for the database archive, there would always be a period of time when the data is nowhere—not in the operational database, not in the archive. This is unacceptable.

Data warehouse extraction and updating and database archive extraction and loading must always remain separate processes. They serve different purposes.

Access impacts   If there emerges a need to go back to an old version of the data, it can be very slow to attempt to execute analytic routines directly on the archive. It is much better to use the archive UNLOAD feature to move the version of the needed data back to an analytic server before attempting to mash the data again.

Removing data from the operational database   If data is extracted from the data warehouse instead of the operational databases, a problem remains on deleting data from the operational database. If this process is not coordinated with extraction from the data warehouse, data will exist in the operational database and in the archive data store at the same time.

20.5 LOGS, AUDIT TRAILS, AND OTHER MISCELLANEOUS STUFF

There is also a desire to store operational information in the database archive. This includes things such as activity logs showing execution activity, audit trails, SMF records (a mainframe file containing system event information), SYSOUT files, and electronic form of reports. Historically it's always been difficult to maintain a consistent retention policy for these things.

If you do attempt to store these in a database archive, you need to create a database form of these objects first. This means creating a row in a table that has columns describing the object and an LOB column containing the actual content. The columns would contain things such as date created, object type, user ID running the job, completion codes, and errors conditions.

This is not the first application you want to attack for a new database archiving project. Get a lot of practice on normal database applications first.

SUMMARY

After a database archiving practice is established, people will want to use it for other things besides normal database archiving activities. You can expect requests to archive data from retired applications, handle merger and acquisition archiving consolidation, keep e-discovery data stores, save business intelligence data, and more. As you can see from the discussions in this book, the database archive is an excellent solution for some of these other uses.

Final Thoughts

The information in this book represents my view of the current state of thinking on this topic. I have done my best to think through all that I have seen in this space.

Database archiving is a new topic for data management. The vendors are new, IT departments are new, and the data archivists are tackling their first applications. The field is far from mature. Much is left to be learned from these early experiences. It could be that some of the lessons will not surface for years, since we have no experience in dealing with old data. The data archived today will take some years to grow old enough to expose some of the flaws in current thinking.

I doubt that the requirements for database archiving will change. Certainly the laws will not get softer. Enforcement of the existing laws will only become more strict. If anything, having a smooth-running, efficient practice might encourage enterprises to keep data longer. It could also increase the types of data enterprises choose to keep in an archiving platform. I predict that all medium-size to large IT departments will have an established database archiving practice within just a few years, and the practice will grow, not diminish, as time goes on.

I would hope that the emergence of yet another data management function will encourage universities to commit more classroom time to the overall data management area. These topics involve enough complexity and academic content to justify a degree devoted to data management.

It will be interesting to compare the contents of this book with the state of the art for database archiving five years from now. I expect that this book will need considerable updating by then.

Generic Archiving Checklist

1. Define motivations for archiving
   - Legal requirements
     - ☐ Multiple overlapping laws
     - ☐ Laws from multiple countries
   - Business policy
   - Object value
   - Historical significance
   - Scientific significance

2. Identify objects to keep in the archive
   - Official versions
   - Criteria for what's *in*, what's *not*
   - Who decides?

3. Determine when to move objects to the archive
   - Consequences of moving too early
     - ☐ Excessive access from archive
   - Consequences of moving too late
     - ☐ Loss due to exposure in nonarchive
   - How precise should timing be?
   - Special considerations for selected objects

4. Determine how long to keep objects in the archive
   - Consequences of keeping longer than necessary
   - Classification
     - ☐ Indefinite
     - ☐ Start plus time
     - ☐ Event plus time
   - Define start time
   - Set criteria for when to discard

5. Determine how to discard objects from the archive
   - Does it need to be destroyed?
   - Does it have residual value?
     - Can it be sold?
   - Do you need to record facts about objects discarded?

6. Determine who needs access to archive objects
   - Direct access
   - Surrogate access
   - Can archive objects be copied?
   - Can they remove objects from the archive and return them later?
   - Is assistance required to find things in the archive?

7. Determine the form of objects in the archive
   - Originals or copies
   - Preservation required to keep objects
     - Altering objects
     - Protective coatings
     - Data transformation
     - Special places
   - Will periodic restoration be needed?
   - Are backups required?
   - Does it require separate explanations?
     - Context information
     - Metadata
     - Indexes

8. Determine where to house the archive
   - Establish cost of losing archive objects
   - Determine what to protect against
     - Theft
     - Damage
     - Corruption/alteration
     - War
     - Fire
     - Flood
     - Tornadoes
     - Earthquakes
     - Tsunamis
     - Erosion
     - Loss of meaning
     - Loss of authenticity
     - Loss from organizational change
   - Is it possible to keep multiple copies?
     - Keep metadata in duplicate also
     - Multiple geographic locations possible

9. Determine requirements for making archive objects accessible
   - Special building
   - Equipment
     - ☐ Computer terminals
     - ☐ Copiers
     - ☐ Printers
     - ☐ Microfiche readers
   - Is special security required?
     - ☐ Entry/exit
     - ☐ Continuous monitoring

10. Determine operational processes needed to move objects into and out of the archive
    - For identifying objects ready to move
    - For removing from operational environment
    - For preparing for long-term storage
    - For putting into the archive
    - For making objects available for access
    - For identifying objects ready for discard
    - For discarding objects

11. Determine administrative processes needed to manage an archive
    - Security of individuals working with the archive
    - Security of individuals accessing the archive
    - Keeping activity logs
    - Keeping inventories of objects in archive
    - Conducting audits of archive design
    - Conducting audits of archive operations

12. Determine change processes needed
    - Changes in mandates
    - Changes in object definitions
    - Changes in policies
    - Changes in personnel
    - Changes in organization

Goals of a Database Archiving System

A robust database archiving system should have the ability to:

- Keep data for a very long period of time
- Support a very large volume of data
- Provide independence from operational application programs
- Allow independence from operational database systems
- Provide independence from operational computing systems
- Encapsulate sufficient metadata to explain data content
- Introduce minimal disruption of operational systems when performing extracts
- Implement a policy-based extraction criteria based on data values in the database
- Maintain full integrity in the extract process at all times
- Use a policy-based discard criteria based on data values in the archive
- Completely discard data from the archive
- Satisfy all data use requirements directly from the archive
- Retain the ability to display the original storage format
- Manage changes to data structures and metadata
- Protect from data loss
- Protect from data update
- Protect from unauthorized access
- Protect authenticity of data
- Keep audit trails of all activity

Job Description of a
Database Archive Analyst

C

The database archive analyst is the key player in implementing a database archiving practice. This is a new position to almost all IT departments. If you do a job search for "database archivist" on Monster.com or through other headhunting sources, you will get zip. There are only a few people who have established this skill set. You need to employ someone who can quickly learn the concepts of database archiving and lead your early implementation efforts.

The following example job description lists the primary duties and skills that are most helpful for someone to possess when venturing into this area.

POSITION

Database Archive Analyst
Reports to IT Director of Data Management Services

JOB RESPONSIBILITIES

The database archive analyst will work with IT database professionals and with application groups to identify opportunities for archiving data from operational databases. Types of databases that are expected to be sources of data are DB2, IMS, ORACLE, DB2 LUW, SQL Server, Sybase, and possibly other relational databases on distributed systems. Archiving may also be required from nonrelational legacy database sources such as ADABAS, IDMS, or M204.

The archive analyst will assist in preparing the business case for potential applications. The analyst will define the appropriate requirements and archiving strategy for each application.

After an application is approved for implementation, the archive analyst will identify operational data sources that will be used for acquiring data for the archive and associated metadata that describes the data. The archive analyst will analyze the data and metadata to determine its accuracy and completeness. Metadata will be enhanced to overcome shortcomings.

The analyst will design data structures that will be extracted for archiving and their archive representation. Policies for when to extract data and when to discard data from the archive will be developed. A storage policy will be created that considers long-term retention requirements, data loss protection, and cost.

The analyst will be responsible for the proper scheduling and execution of database archiving tasks. The analyst will also provide assistance to users in developing access to information in the archive. This will include finding the relevant archive structures, interpreting the metadata, and possibly formulating access queries.

REQUIRED QUALIFICATIONS

The analyst must be experienced in relational database concepts, data modeling using ER diagrams, and the SQL query language. Experience in working with metadata is also required.

The analyst must have operational experience in setting up and executing processes on multiple system types, including mainframes, Unix servers, Linux servers, and Windows servers.

The analyst should possess good project management skills.

A degree in computer science is a must.

OTHER HELPFUL QUALIFICATIONS AND CHARACTERISTICS

Working experience in one or more of the following job types is a plus:

- Database administrator for major DBMS applications
- Data architect, data designer
- Data warehouse designer
- Metadata management
- Data quality analyst
- Data steward

Knowledge of metadata repositories, ER diagramming, enterprise data modeling, and other related topics is also helpful.

Work experience that involves collaboration with multiple people across multiple departments is a strong plus. The analyst should work well with other people.

The analyst should possess strong analytical skills and be well organized.

The analyst must be a quick learner.

Glossary

archive   (*n*) A collection of like objects that are maintained in a special place different from their place of origin for the purpose of long-term preservation for future use. (*v*) the act of removing objects from their normal environment and placing them in an archive.

archive access component   A component of a database archive solution that provides tools necessary for authorized users to obtain data they need from a database archive.

archive administrator   An individual assigned to ensure that a database archive satisfies all requirements and is properly managed and maintained.

archive analyst   An individual who designs database archiving applications.

archive data store   The physical place where data is stored in a database archive. This may be a commercial product, a DBMS, a collection of XML files, a collection of database unload files, or a custom archive DBMS.

archive phase   The period of time in the life cycle of a data object when it is not expected to be updated, participate in another transaction, or be referenced for business reporting purposes but still needs to be retained due to requirements set by the enterprise or by outside regulatory agencies.

archive root   The table row or segment that defines a single business object. It is the anchor for connecting through database links to other data elements needed to fully describe a single business object.

archive storage unit   The smallest unit of storage of database archiving data. This may hold the data for multiple business objects. For a DBMS archive data store, it can include all the archived data for the application. For other archive data stores, it typically contains all the data resulting from one execution of the archive extractor program.

archive stream   A sequence of archive storage units for a single application and a single business object that share a database structure that has identical or similar metadata. The storage units in the stream are created from successive executions of the archive extractor program.

archivist   A person who performs the tasks of archiving.

create phase   The period of the data life cycle of a data object when it is first created and appears in an operational database. This period is normally very short.

custom archive DBMS   A database management system designed exclusively to optimize functions to the requirements of a database archive that will store lots (and lots) of data for a very (very) long time.

data archiving The process and art of archiving any data. This broad category covers many subcategories such as database archiving, file archiving, document archiving, email archiving, and even physical paper-document archiving.

data authenticity The recognition that a data collection is the official version of the data and that it is accurate and has not been maliciously modified.

data object The collection of data that describes a single business transaction or entity; for example, a single stock trade, a loan application, or an employee.

database archive application The archiving design and activities related to archiving database data for a single business area; for example, HR, deposits and withdrawals, auto production, etc.

database archiving The act of removing selected business objects that have a low expectation of being used from operational databases and storing them in an archive data store for the remainder of their required retention period, from which they can be accessed if needed.

database metadata The complete set of descriptions of the data stored in a database. The description describes the purpose, meaning, encoding, and storage structure of each element of data for an application.

discard The process of removing objects from an archive.

discard component The software used to remove business objects from a database archive.

discard phase The period of the life cycle of a data object when it is no longer expected to be used and it has no requirement to be retained. The data object can be destroyed without harm to the enterprise.

discard policy The part of a database archiving design that specifies the rules for determining when a business object needs to be removed from the archive data store. In addition to specifying the criteria for removal, it specifies the degree to which removal is required to prevent forensic software from subsequently discovering it. It also specifies any records that need to be maintained to record discard activities.

enterprise For purposes of this book, any organization that is large enough to have a formal IT department and databases that require consideration of database archiving. This includes commercial corporations, government agencies, large educational institutions, and large nonprofit organizations.

extract component The software component of a database archiving solution that is used to identify data in operational databases that qualifies for movement to the database archive, extracts the data, formats it for storage, stores it in the database archive data store, and deletes or marks it as archived in the operational database.

extract policy The criteria that is used to determine whether a business object residing in an operational database is eligible to be moved to its database archive.

e-discovery The process of extracting electronic data records and providing them as requested by a legal requirement as part of litigation. For database data this covers the data of qualifying business objects and all associated metadata.

inactive data Data in an enterprise database that has no expected uses but that must be retained for legal or business reasons and that may be accessed if a need arises.

legal hold The preventing of any updates or deletes to data identified in an e-discovery request until the litigation causing the hold is resolved.

metadata   Descriptive information about any object.

metadata break   For database data, a point in time that identifies a change in the metadata for a database. All data created prior to the metadata break has one definition; data created after the break has another definition.

object link   A link connecting data across tables or segments where both parts of the data are exclusively part of the definition of a single business object.

operational database   A database in which data is initially created and/or is expected to be updated or to be used in creating or updating other business objects in the same or a different operational database.

operational phase   The phase of the life cycle for a data object when it is first created and during which it is expected to be updated or to participate in transactions that will update or create other data objects.

operational replicate database   An operational database in which the data comes from a different operational database but which retains all the characteristics of an operational database. It is expected to participate in new database transactions that will either update data objects in it or create new data objects.

physical database archiving   Database archiving applications for which the extraction from operational databases is done from the physical tables or stored segments of the operational database.

reference database   An operational database containing data that will no longer be updated but that is expected to be used for queries, searches, reports, and analysis. The data has too much expected read activity to be eligible for movement to an archive. A reference database normally has a data structure that mirrors the operational database that initially created and updated the data.

reference link   A link connecting data across tables or segments where one part of the link defines a single business object and the other part provides additional explanation of some data element in the business object. For example, a loan application may link to a customer master record to provide the loan applicant's name and address information. The connection between these two data structures is a reference link.

reference phase   The phase of the life cycle for a data object in which it is not expected to be updated or to participate in other transactions that create or update data but during which it is expected to be referenced for query, search, reporting, or analysis.

retention period   The period of time that a business object is required to be retained. The starting time for retention is when the object is officially recognized by the policy as having been created. The end time is determined by adding the retention period to the start time. A retention period may be specified as "indefinite."

retired application   An application that is no longer operational but that created data that must continue to be maintained; also referred to as a *sunset application*.

storage policy   The portion of a database archiving application design that defines the rules that need to be followed in storing data for the long term and that will provide adequate protection and security of the archived data.

sunset application   An application that is no longer operational but that created data that must continue to be maintained; also referred to as a *retired application*.

virtual database archiving   Database archiving applications in which the data is extracted from the operational databases through an application programming interface instead of by directly accessing the tables or storage segments of the physical DBMS.

References

1.0 Software Companies in Space
NEON Enterprise Software (TITAN Archive)
Princeton Softech (recently acquired by IBM)
HP (Outer Bay)
Applimation
Solix
EMC

2.0 Analyst Coverage
All the key analyst firms cover database archiving:
Gartner: Carolyn DiCenzo, John Base, Debra Logan
Forrester: Noel Yuhanna
IDC: Carl Olafson
Enterprise Strategy Group: Brian Babineau

3.0 Organizations and Conferences Where Database Archiving Is Covered
American Records Management Association (ARMA)
AIIM: Mostly focused on enterprise content management (ECM) but has started paying attention to data retention because of e-discovery
DAMA: Both international and regional user group meetings/conferences
IBM IOD Conference: Not a primary focus, but database archiving vendors are present and there is some interest from a portion of the attendees
Data Protection Summit: Data archiving is a topic that is covered in these conferences
Sedona Conference Institute: A think tank organization made up of lawyers and subject matter experts; they publish opinion papers on e-discovery and records retention and also have conferences
Gartner Compliance and Risk Management Summit: Gartner has a few conferences throughout the year that include the topic of data archiving; the Compliance and Risk Management summit, Data Center Conference
Oracle: Regional and international user group meetings
DB2: Regional DB2 user group meetings

4.0 Articles
www.informationweek.com/management/showArticle.jhtml?
  articleID=204301244&pgno=1&queryText=

Articles by Craig Mullins on database archiving:

"The Impact of Data Volume on Operational Databases," *Database Trends and Applications*, October 2007.

"Financial Institutions' Sensitive Data Requires Careful Archiving," *Houston Business Journal*, August 3–9, 2007.

"Database Archiving for Long-Term Data Retention," *IT Compliance Magazine*, Spring 2007.

"Database Archiving for Long-Term Data Retention," zJournal, December/January 2007.

5.0 Presentations

DFW IMS UG, Feb. 21, 2007: The Impact of Regulatory Compliance on DBA.

LAARUG, March 1, 2007: Managing Data for Long Retention Periods.

DAMA Symposium, March 7, 2007: Using TITAN Archive . . . Data Retention.

CODUG Columbus, March 28, 2007: Managing Data for Long Retention Periods.

SIRDUG Charlotte, April 13, 2007: Managing Data for Long Retention Periods.

DB2 Symposium, Bonn, April 25, 2007: Managing Data for Long Retention Periods.

IDUG San Jose, May 7, 2007: The Impact of Regulatory Compliance on DBA.

DAMA NYC, May 17, 2007: The Impact of Regulatory Compliance on Data Mgmt.

TBRUG, June 8, 2007: Managing Data for Long Retention Periods.

Houston DB2 UG, July 17, 2007: Managing Data for Long Retention Periods.

SHARE San Diego, Aug. 15, 2007: The Impact of Regulatory Compliance on DBA.

SFDUG San Francisco, Sept. 13, 2007: Managing Data for Long Retention Periods.

BMO Toronto, Oct. 2, 2007: Managing Data for Long Retention Periods.

BMO Toronto, Oct. 2, 2007: The Impact of Regulatory Compliance on DBA.

IBM IOD Las Vegas, Oct. 16, 2007: Managing Data for Long Retention Periods.

IDUG Athens, Greece, Nov. 5, 2007: Managing Data for Long Retention Periods.

PDUG Pittsburgh, Dec. 5, 2007: The Impact of Regulatory Compliance on DBA.

RICDUG Richmond, Dec. 12, 2007: The Impact of Regulatory Compliance on DBA.

6.0 White Papers

http://www.neonesoft.com/doc/wp/TAR_wp.pdf

http://www.neonesoft.com/doc/wp/ESTGA_wp.pdf

http://www.applimation.com

Index